INDIVIDUALS

by the same author

*

INTRODUCTION TO LOGICAL THEORY

THE BOUNDS OF SENSE
An Essay on Kant's *Critique of Pure Reason*

LOGICO-LINGUISTIC PAPERS

'FREEDOM AND RESENTMENT' AND
OTHER ESSAYS

SUBJECT AND
PREDICATE IN LOGIC AND GRAMMAR

SKEPTICISM AND NATURALISM
SOME VARIETIES

P. F. STRAWSON

INDIVIDUALS

An Essay in Descriptive Metaphysics

METHUEN
LONDON and NEW YORK

First published in 1959
Reprinted three times
Reprinted 1971

First published as a University Paperback 1964
Reprinted seven times
Reprinted 1987

Published in the USA by
Methuen & Co.
in association with Methuen, Inc.
29 West 35th Street, New York, NY 10001

© 1959 P. F. Strawson

Printed in Great Britain by
J. W. Arrowsmith Ltd, Bristol

ISBN 0 416 68310 x

PREFACE

This book is based on lectures which were originally given in Oxford University in 1954–5 and were later used as material for a seminar in Duke University, N. Carolina in 1955–6. I am grateful for the help I received in discussion from my colleagues at Duke; and I wish also to acknowledge my great indebtedness to Miss Ruby Meager, Professor H. L. A. Hart and Professor Gilbert Ryle, all of whom read a part or the whole of the book in manuscript and gave me much helpful and friendly advice, which I have generally tried to follow.

Much of Chapter 3 is a revised and expanded version of an article which appeared in Vol. II of the *Minnesota Studies in the Philosophy of Science*, edited by Herbert Feigl, Michael Scriven and Grover Maxwell and published by the University of Minnesota Press in 1958. Parts of Chapters 5 and 6 are taken, with substantial modifications, from papers which appeared in the *Proceedings of the Aristotelian Society* for 1953–4 and 1957. I have to thank the editors and publishers of these volumes for permission to make use of this matter again.

P. F. S.

CONTENTS

Contents

Contents

7

Contents

8

INTRODUCTION

Metaphysics has been often revisionary, and less often descriptive. Descriptive metaphysics is content to describe the actual structure of our thought about the world, revisionary metaphysics is concerned to produce a better structure. The productions of revisionary metaphysics remain permanently interesting, and not only as key episodes in the history of thought. Because of their articulation, and the intensity of their partial vision, the best of them are both intrinsically admirable and of enduring philosophical utility. But this last merit can be ascribed to them only because there is another kind of metaphysics which needs no justification at all beyond that of inquiry in general. Revisionary metaphysics is at the service of descriptive metaphysics. Perhaps no actual metaphysician has ever been, both in intention and effect, wholly the one thing or the other. But we can distinguish broadly: Descartes, Leibniz, Berkeley are revisionary, Aristotle and Kant descriptive. Hume, the ironist of philosophy, is more difficult to place. He appears now under one aspect, now under another.

The idea of descriptive metaphysics is liable to be met with scepticism. How should it differ from what is called philosophical, or logical, or conceptual analysis? It does not differ in kind of intention, but only in scope and generality. Aiming to lay bare the most general features of our conceptual structure, it can take far less for granted than a more limited and partial conceptual inquiry. Hence, also, a certain difference in method. Up to a point, the reliance upon a close examination of the actual use of words is the best, and indeed the only sure, way in philosophy. But the discriminations we can make, and the connexions we can establish,

9

in this way, are not general enough and not far-reaching enough to meet the full metaphysical demand for understanding. For when we ask how we use this or that expression, our answers, however revealing at a certain level, are apt to assume, and not to expose, those general elements of structure which the metaphysician wants revealed. The structure he seeks does not readily display itself on the surface of language, but lies submerged. He must abandon his only sure guide when the guide cannot take him as far as he wishes to go.

The idea of a descriptive metaphysics might be assailed from another direction. For it might be held that metaphysics was essentially an instrument of conceptual change, a means of furthering or registering new directions or styles of thought. Certainly concepts do change, and not only, though mainly, on the specialist periphery; and even specialist changes react on ordinary thinking. Certainly, too, metaphysics has been largely concerned with such changes, in both the suggested ways. But it would be a great blunder to think of metaphysics only in this historical style. For there is a massive central core of human thinking which has no history—or none recorded in histories of thought; there are categories and concepts which, in their most fundamental character, change not at all. Obviously these are not the specialities of the most refined thinking. They are the commonplaces of the least refined thinking; and are yet the indispensable core of the conceptual equipment of the most sophisticated human beings. It is with these, their interconnexions, and the structure that they form, that a descriptive metaphysics will be primarily concerned.

Metaphysics has a long and distinguished history, and it is consequently unlikely that there are any new truths to be discovered in descriptive metaphysics. But this does not mean that the task of descriptive metaphysics has been, or can be, done once for all. It has constantly to be done over again. If there are no new truths to be discovered, there are old truths to be rediscovered. For though the central subject-matter of descriptive metaphysics does not change, the critical and analytical idiom of philosophy changes constantly. Permanent relationships are described in an impermanent idiom, which reflects both the age's climate of thought and the individual philosopher's personal style of thinking. No philosopher understands his predecessors until he has re-thought their thought in his own contemporary terms; and it is characteristic of the very greatest philosophers, like Kant and Aristotle, that they, more than any others, repay this effort of re-thinking.

This book is, in part, and in a modest way, an essay in descriptive metaphysics. Only in a modest way—for though some of the themes discussed are sufficiently general, the discussion is undertaken from a certain limited viewpoint and is by no means comprehensive; and only in part—for some of the logical and linguistic classifications around which discussion turns in the second part may well be of relatively local and temporary significance. On my method of treatment of these classifications I may make now one general comment. It is often admitted, in the analytical treatment of some fairly specific concept, that the wish to understand is less likely to be served by the search for a single strict statement of the necessary and sufficient conditions of its application than by seeing its applications—in Wittgenstein's simile—as forming a family, the members of which may, perhaps, be grouped around a central paradigm case and linked with the latter by various direct or indirect links of logical connexion and analogy. This principle of tolerance in understanding can, I think, be as usefully invoked in the attempt to understand general logical and grammatical structures as in that analysis of specific concepts which is undertaken in, say, the philosophy of perception or the philosophy of mind.

It seemed to me natural to divide the book into two parts. The first part aims at establishing the central position which material bodies and persons occupy among particulars in general. It shows that, in our conceptual scheme as it is, particulars of these two categories are the basic or fundamental particulars, that the concepts of other types of particular must be seen as secondary in relation to the concepts of these. In the second part of the book the aim is to establish and explain the connexion between the idea of a particular in general and that of an object of reference or logical subject. The link between these two notions and, with it, the explanation of the status of the particular as the paradigm logical subject is found in a certain idea of 'completeness' which is expounded in the first half of the second chapter of this part. This is the crucial passage of the second part of the book. The two parts of the book are not, however, independent of each other. Theses of the first part are at many points presupposed, and at some points extended and further explained, by arguments of the second part. I doubt if it is possible for us fully to understand the main topics of either part without consideration of the main topics of the other.

PART ONE

PARTICULARS

BODIES

I. THE IDENTIFICATION OF PARTICULARS

[1] We think of the world as containing particular things some
of which are independent of ourselves; we think of the world's
history as made up of particular episodes in which we may or may
not have a part; and we think of these particular things and events
as included in the topics of our common discourse, as things about
which we can talk to each other. These are remarks about the way
we think of the world, about our conceptual scheme. A more
recognizably philosophical, though no clearer, way of expressing
them would be to say that our ontology comprises objective
particulars. It may comprise much else besides.

Part of my aim is to exhibit some general and structural features
of the conceptual scheme in terms of which we think about particular things. I shall speak, to begin with, of the identification of
particulars. I shall not, at the moment, try to give a general explanation of my use of the word 'identify' and associated words,
nor of my use of the word 'particular'. This latter word certainly
has a familiar core, or central area, of philosophical use, even if
the outer boundaries of its application are vague. So all I need say
for the moment is that my use of it is in no way eccentric. For instance, in mine, as in most familiar philosophical uses, historical
occurrences, material objects, people and their shadows are all
particulars; whereas qualities and properties, numbers and species
are not. As for the words 'identify', 'identification', &c., these I
shall use in a number of different, but closely connected, ways and
I shall try to explain each of these uses as I introduce it.

The application of the phrase 'identification of particulars'
which I shall first be concerned with is this. Very often, when two

people are talking, one of them, the speaker, refers to or mentions some particular or other. Very often, the other, the hearer, knows what, or which, particular the speaker is talking about; but sometimes he does not. I shall express this alternative by saying that the hearer either is, or is not, able to *identify* the particular referred to by the speaker. Among the kinds of expressions which we, as speakers, use to make references to particulars are some of which a standard function is, in the circumstances of their use, to enable a hearer to identify the particular which is being referred to. Expressions of these kinds include some proper names, some pronouns, some descriptive phrases beginning with the definite article, and expressions compounded of these. When a speaker uses such an expression to refer to a particular, I shall say that he makes an *identifying reference* to a particular. It does not follow, of course, from the fact that a speaker, on a given occasion, makes an identifying reference to a particular, that his hearer does in fact identify that particular.   I may mention someone to you by name, and you may not know who it is. But when a speaker makes an identifying reference to a particular, and his hearer does, on the strength of it, identify the particular referred to, then, I shall say, the speaker not only makes an identifying reference to, but also *identifies*, that particular. So we have a hearer's sense, and a speaker's sense, of 'identify'.

It is not merely a happy accident that we are often able, as speakers and hearers, to identify the particulars which enter into our discourse. That it should be possible to identify particulars of a given type seems a necessary condition of the inclusion of that type in our ontology. For what could we mean by claiming to acknowledge the existence of a class of particular things and to talk to each other about members of this class, if we qualified the claim by adding that it was in principle impossible for any one of us to make any other of us understand which member, or members, of this class he was at any time talking about? The qualification would seem to stultify the claim. This reflexion may lead to another. It often enough happens that the identification of a particular of one kind is made to depend on the identification of another particular of another kind. Thus a speaker may, in referring to a certain particular, speak of it as *the* thing of a certain general kind which uniquely stands in a certain specified relation to another particular. He may, for example, refer to a house as 'the house that Jack built' or to a man as 'the assassin of Abraham Lincoln'. In such cases, the hearer's identification of the first particular depends on his identification of the second. He knows what particular is referred to by the identifying phrase as a whole because he knows what particular is referred to by a part of it. The fact that the identification of one particular often depends in this way on the identification of another is not very significant in itself. But it suggests the possibility that the identifiability of particulars of some sorts may be in some *general* way dependent on the identifiability of particulars of other sorts. If this were so, the fact would have some significance for an inquiry into the general structure of the conceptual scheme in terms of which we think about particulars. Suppose, for instance, it should turn out that there is a type of particulars, β, such that particulars of type β cannot be identified without reference to particulars of another type, a, whereas particulars of type a can be identified without reference to particulars of type β. Then it would be a general characteristic of our scheme, that the ability to talk about β-particulars at all was dependent on the ability to talk about a-particulars, but not vice versa. This fact could reasonably be expressed by saying that in our scheme a-particulars were ontologically prior to β-particulars, or were more fundamental or more basic than they. It seems, perhaps, unlikely that dependence, in respect of member-identifiability, of one type of particulars on another, should take the direct and simple form I have just suggested, unlikely, that is, that it should be generally impossible to make identifying references to particulars of the relatively dependent type without mentioning particulars of the relatively independent type. But there may be other and less direct ways in which the identifiability of one type of particular is dependent on that of another.

[2] What are the tests for hearer's identification? When shall we say that a hearer knows what particular is being referred to by a

speaker? Consider first the following case. A speaker tells a story which he claims to be factual. It begins: 'A man and a boy were standing by a fountain', and it continues: 'The man had a drink'. Shall we say that the hearer knows which or what particular is being referred to by the subject-expression in the second sentence? We might say so. For, of a certain range of two particulars, the words 'the man' serve to distinguish the one being referred to, by means of a description which applies only to him. But though this is, in a weak sense, a case of identification, I shall call it only a *story-relative*, or, for short, a *relative* identification. For it is identification only relative to a range of particulars (a range of two members) which is itself identified only as the range of particulars being talked about by the speaker. That is to say, the hearer, hearing the second sentence, knows *which* particular creature is being referred to *of the two particular creatures being talked about by the speaker*; but he does not, without this qualification, know what particular creature is being referred to. The identification is within a certain story told by a certain speaker. It is identification within his story; but not identification within history.

We need a requirement stringent enough to eliminate relative identification. The hearer, in the example, is able to place the particular referred to within the picture painted by the speaker. This means that in a sense he can place the particular in his own general picture of the world. For he can place the speaker, and hence the speaker's picture, in that general picture of his own. But he cannot place the figures, without the frame, of the speaker's picture in his own general picture of the world. For this reason the full requirement for hearer's identification is not satisfied.

A sufficient, but not necessary, condition of the full requirement's being satisfied is—to state it loosely at first—that the hearer can pick out by sight or hearing or touch, or can otherwise sensibly discriminate, the particular being referred to, knowing that it is that particular. This condition I shall slightly liberalize to cover certain cases where one cannot at the very moment of reference sensibly discriminate the particular being referred to— owing, for example, to its having ceased or disappeared—but could do so a moment before. Such cases will be among those in which 'that' is a more appropriate demonstrative than 'this'; as when one says 'That car was going very fast', or 'That noise was deafening'. In general, then, this sufficient condition is satisfied only in the case of particulars which one can perceive now, or at least could perceive a moment ago. It is obvious that there are many cases of identification falling under this condition. An expression is used which, given the setting and accompaniments of its use, can properly, or at least naturally, be taken, as then used, to apply only to a certain single member of the range of particulars which the hearer is able, or a moment before was able, sensibly to discriminate, and to nothing outside that range. Cases of this kind are the cases, *par excellence*, for the use of demonstratives, whether helped out by descriptive words or not; though, of course, the use of demonstratives is not confined to cases of this kind, and expressions of other kinds may also be used in these cases. I shall say, when this first condition for identification is satisfied, that the hearer is able *directly to locate* the particular referred to. We may also speak of these cases as cases of the *demonstrative identification* of particulars.

It is obvious that not all cases of identification of particulars are cases of demonstrative identification in the sense which I have just given to this phrase. In this fact lies the ground of an old worry, which is both practically and theoretically baseless. The reasons for its practical and its theoretical baselessness are in the end the same. The nature of this worry and the reasons for its baselessness must now be made plain.

Demonstrative identification of a particular is not always an easy matter. The scene may be blurred, its elements confused. Different sections of the scene may be very like each other, and so may the items to be discriminated; and it is easy to make mistakes in applying such descriptions as 'the twelfth man from the left in the fifteenth row from the top'. Nevertheless one thing at least is clear in demonstrative identification: viz. the identity of the range of particulars, of the sector of the universe, within which the identification is to be made. It is just the entire scene, the entire range of particulars now sensibly present. (It may be said that its *limits* may be different for speaker and hearer. I leave the reader to solve any problems raised by this fact.) There can be no question as to *which scene* we are talking about, though there may be question enough as to which part of it, which element in which part of it, and so on. These are questions which we have the linguistic means of settling.

But now consider the cases where demonstrative identification, in the sense I have given to this phrase, is not possible, because the particular to be identified is not within the range of those sensibly present. What linguistic means of identification have we available? We can use descriptions or names or both. But it is no good using a name for a particular unless one knows who or what is referred to by the use of the name. A name is worthless without a backing of descriptions which can be produced on demand to explain its application. So, it may seem, in the non-demonstrative identification of particulars, we depend ultimately on description in general terms alone. Now one may be very well informed about a particular sector of the universe. One may know beyond any doubt that there is only one particular thing or person in that sector which answers to a certain general description. But this, it might be argued, does not guarantee that the description applies uniquely. For there might be another particular, answering to the same description, in another sector of the universe. Even if one enlarges the description so that it incorporates a description of the salient features of the sector of the universe concerned, one still lacks a guarantee that the description individuates. For the other sector might reproduce these features too. However much one adds to the description of the sector one knows about—its internal detail and its external relations—this possibility of massive reduplication remains open. No extension of one's knowledge of the world can eliminate this possibility. So, however extensive the speaker's knowledge and however extensive the hearer's, neither can know that the former's identifying description in fact applies uniquely.

To this argument it may be replied that it is not necessary to know that the identifying description applies uniquely. All that is necessary, in order for identification to be secured, is that the hearer should come to know, on the strength of the speaker's words, what, or which, particular the speaker is in fact referring to. Now for a speaker to use the words of a description with a certain reference, and for a hearer to understand them as making a certain reference—whether or not the intended reference and the understood reference are in fact the same—it is at least required that each should know of *a* particular which the description fits. (Or the hearer may at that instant learn, from the speaker's words, of such a particular.) But each may know of only one such particular; and each may have conclusive reason to suppose that the other knows of only one such particular, and that the particular the other knows of is the same as the particular he himself knows of. Or, even if this condition is not satisfied in full, each may still have conclusive reasons for thinking that the particular which one is *referring to* is the same as the particular which the other *takes* him to be referring to.

This reply is adequate to show the practical baselessness of doubts about the possibility of non-demonstrative identification, where such doubts have their ground in the foregoing argument. But the reply concedes too much and explains too little. It does not explain the possibility of our having the conclusive reasons we may have. It yields no clues to the general structure of our thinking about identification. It is better, if we can, to meet the argument on its own theoretical terms; for by doing so we may learn something of that general structure.

To meet the argument on its own terms, it is sufficient to show how the situation of non-demonstrative identification may be linked with the situation of demonstrative identification. The argument supposes that where the particular to be identified cannot be directly located, its identification must rest ultimately on description in purely general terms. But this supposition is false. For even though the particular in question cannot itself be demonstratively identified, it may be identified by a description which relates it uniquely to another particular which can be demonstratively identified. The question, what sector of the universe it occupies, may be answered by relating that sector uniquely to the sector which speaker and hearer themselves currently occupy. Whatever the possibilities of massive reduplication in the universe, these possibilities create, from the point of view of identification, no theoretical difficulties which cannot theoretically be overcome in this way.

Now we can see why the previous reply conceded too much. It conceded, in the face of the argument from the possibility of reduplication, that, where non-demonstrative identification was in question, we could never be sure that an identifying description in fact applied uniquely; and then claimed that this did not matter, in view of other things we could be sure of. The reply did not say exactly what these other things might be. But now, in seeing what they might be, we see also that the argument from the possibility of reduplication has no force at all to show that we cannot be sure that an identifying description in fact applies uniquely. For non-demonstrative identification may rest securely upon demonstrative identification. All identifying description of particulars may include, ultimately, a demonstrative element.

The solution raises a further question. Is it plausible to suppose —unless indeed we are to fall back on relative identification—that of every particular we may refer to there is some description uniquely relating it to the participants in, or the immediate setting of, the conversation in which the reference is made? The particulars we refer to are so very diverse. Can we plausibly claim that there is a single system of relations in which each has a place, and which includes whatever particulars are directly locatable? To this question the reply, very general at first, may run as follows. For all particulars in space and time, it is not only plausible to claim, it is necessary to admit, that there is just such a system: the system of spatial and temporal relations, in which every particular is uniquely related to every other. The universe might be repetitive in various ways. But this fact is no obstacle in principle to supplying descriptions of the kind required. For by demonstrative identification we can determine a common reference point and common axes of spatial direction; and with these at our disposal we have also the theoretical possibility of a description of every other particular in space and time as uniquely related to our reference point. Perhaps not all particulars are in both time *and* space. But it is at least plausible to assume that every particular which is not, is uniquely related in some other way to one which is.

[3] This is a theoretical solution to a theoretical problem. We do not in fact regard ourselves as faced with the possibility of massive reduplications of patterns of things and events. Nevertheless, the fact that the theoretical solution is available, is a very important fact about our conceptual scheme. It shows something of the structure of that scheme; and it has a connexion with our practical requirements in identification.

The connexion may not be obvious. It seems that the general requirements of hearer-identification could be regarded as fulfilled if the hearer knew that the particular being referred to was identical with some particular about which he knew some individuating fact, or facts, other than the fact that it was the particular being referred to. To know an individuating fact about a particular is to know that such-and-such a thing is true of that particular and of no other particular whatever. One who could make all his knowledge articulate would satisfy this condition for particular-identification only if he could give a description which applied uniquely to the particular in question and could nontautologically add that the particular to which this description applied was the same as the particular being currently referred to; but we need not insist that the ability to make one's knowledge articulate in just this way is a condition of really knowing who, or what, a speaker is referring to. This, then, is the general condition for hearer-identification in the non-demonstrative case; and it is obvious that, if a genuine reference is being made, the speaker, too, must satisfy a similar condition. To rule out merely 'story-relative' identification, we must add a further requirement: viz. that the known individuating fact must not be such that its statement essentially involves identifying the particular in question by reference to someone's discourse about it, or about any other particular by reference to which it is identified.

Now how are these conditions satisfied in practice? We may note, to begin with, that they would be amply satisfied by anyone who could give such descriptions as would alleviate the theoretical anxieties discussed in section [2]. The conditions just laid down are formally less exacting than those anxieties: whatever would allay the latter in a particular case would also meet the former. But we can conclude nothing decisive from this; it was admitted that those anxieties were, in practice, unreal. So the connexion between our theoretical solution and the satisfaction of our practical requirements is still not obvious.

It might seem, indeed, remote. Surely we do not know, or need to know, of every particular we refer to or understand another's reference to, an individuating fact which relates it uniquely to the present situation of reference, to objects or people which figure in that situation? But we must consider whether this suggestion is really as absurd as it sounds. Of course we do not often, in practice, *explicitly* relate the particulars of which we speak to ourselves or to other items in the present situation of reference. But this fact may show no more than a justified confidence that there is no need for such explicit indications; since the circumstances of a conversation, the participants' knowledge of each other's background, are in general such that a lot may be taken for granted. Again we may sometimes be content with 'story-relative' identifications, not caring for anything more, not wishing, at least at the moment, to fit the spoken-of particulars directly into the framework of our knowledge of the world and its history.

Yet it cannot be denied that each of us is, at any moment, in possession of such a framework—a unified framework of knowledge of particulars, in which we ourselves and, usually, our immediate surroundings have their place, and of which each element is uniquely related to every other and hence to ourselves and our surroundings. It cannot be denied that this framework of knowledge supplies a uniquely efficient means of adding identified particulars to our stock. This framework we use for this purpose: not just occasionally and adventitiously, but always and essentially. It is a necessary truth that any new particular of which we learn is somehow identifyingly connected with the framework, even if only through the occasion and method of our learning of it. Even when the identification is 'story-relative', the connexion with the framework remains, through the identity of the story-teller. When we become sophisticated, we systematize the framework with calendars, maps, co-ordinate systems; but the use of such systems turns, fundamentally, on our knowing our own place in them; though a man can lose his place, and have to be told it. Such systems, developed or embryonic, help us to escape from story-relative identification to full identification. Of course, nothing in what I say has the consequence that a man is unable to identify a particular unless he can give precise spatio-temporal locations for it. This is by no means required. Any fact uniquely relating the particular to other, identified elements in the framework will serve as an individuating fact. A description, itself in no way locating, may be known to individuate *within* a very extensive spatio-temporal range of particulars; all that is then required is that that range should itself be located in the framework at large.

But why, it may be asked, accord any pre-eminence to *spatio-temporal* relations to a common point of reference? Are there not other kinds of relation enough which will serve the same purpose? All that is formally required is a kind of relation such that, given an already identified object, O, it is possible for us to know that there is, in fact, only one thing answering to a certain description which is related by that relation to O. Does not almost any relation which one thing may have to another thing satisfy this not very exacting requirement? Indeed, some relations carry a guarantee that there is only one such thing. Thus, though we may indeed know, perhaps by being told, that there is in fact only one bridge across a certain stretch of river, we know without being told that there cannot be more than one man who is a certain man's paternal grandfather.

To this it may be replied that the system of spatio-temporal relations has a peculiar comprehensiveness and pervasiveness, which qualify it uniquely to serve as the framework within which we can organize our individuating thought about particulars. Every particular either has its place in this system, or is of a kind the members of which cannot in general be identified except by reference to particulars of other kinds which have their place in it; and every particular which has its place in the system has a unique place there. There is no other system of relations between particulars of which all this is true. Indeed any antithesis between this and other systems of relations between particulars would be a false antithesis. Though we may freely depend on heterogeneous relations in framing identifying descriptions, the system of spatio-temporal relations remains the groundwork of these additions; most other relations between particulars incorporate spatio-temporal elements, involve or are symbolized by spatio-temporal transactions, the relative movements of bodies.

A general doubt may remain. The formal conditions of identification are satisfied if an individuating fact is known about the particular concerned. But why should such an individuating fact be such as to relate the particular concerned in any way to other items in that unified framework of knowledge of particulars of which each of us has a part in his possession? Descriptions can be framed which begin with phrases like 'the only . . .' or 'the first . . .' and thus proclaim, as it were, the uniqueness of their application. Let us call them 'logically individuating descriptions'. No doubt, in general, logically individuating descriptions will also incorporate proper names of persons, or place-names, or dates, and thereby relate the particulars they apply to to other items in the unified framework of knowledge of particulars; or, if they contain none of these, they will in general incorporate demonstrative indications, or will rely in some way on the setting of their use to assist in determining their reference. But we can also frame logically individuating descriptions which are altogether free from such features. Let us call these 'pure individuating descriptions'. 'The first boy in the class' is not a pure individuating description, for it depends on the context of its use to determine its application. 'The first dog to be born in England in the nineteenth century' is not a pure individuating description, for it contains a date and a place-name. But 'the first dog to be born at sea' is a pure individuating description; so is 'the only dog to be born at sea which subsequently saved a monarch's life'. Besides pure individuating descriptions we may recognize a class of quasi-pure individuating descriptions, which depend on the setting of their utterance to determine their application only in the sense that their application is restricted to what existed before or exists at the same time as the moment of utterance. They are like pure individuating descriptions with the addition of the words 'so far'. An example of a quasi-pure individuating description would be 'the tallest man who ever lived'. Now surely, it might be said, we can sometimes know that a pure or quasi-pure individuating description has application; and granted that such a phrase has application, its acceptance by both hearer and speaker is sufficient to guarantee that each understands by it one and the same particular. Our individuating thought about particulars need not, therefore, involve incorporating them in the single unified framework of knowledge of particulars.

But one who makes this objection is himself in the position of remote and impractical theorist. There are many replies to him. Suppose a speaker and a hearer claimed to have identified a certain particular by agreement on a pure or quasi-pure individuating description; and suppose they accompanied the claim with the remark that they knew nothing else whatever about the particular in question. That is to say, they were quite unable to locate the particular concerned within any definite spatio-temporal region of the common framework, however extensive, or to connect it in any definite way with any item which they could so locate; they were quite unable even to relate it to any occasion of discourse which they could connect with some item in the common spatio-temporal framework. They could not, for example, say that either of them had been authoritatively told of it. In general, they disclaimed any ability to connect the particular of which they claimed to speak with their general unified framework of knowledge of particulars, and disclaimed any ability to recognize any such connexion, if it were to be suggested to them, as one which they had been aware of, but had forgotten. There would appear to be an element of frivolity in any such claim, so accompanied. In the first place, we should be inclined to infer, from the accompanying *dis*claimer, that the speaker and hearer had in fact no grounds, except those of general probability, for thinking that the pure individuating description had application at all. A pure individuating description, like any other logically individuating description, may fail of application not only when there are no candidates for the title, but also when there are two or more candidates with equally good and hence mutually destructive claims and no candidate with a better claim. Thus the description, 'the first dog to be born at sea', would fail of application not only if no dog was born at sea, but if the first two dogs to be born at sea were born simultaneously. We may indeed increase the improbability of the second kind of application-failure by adding to the detail of the description; but we thereby increase at the same time the probability of the first kind of application-failure. The only safe way, in general, to elaborate the description sufficiently to eliminate the one risk, without increasing the other, would be to draw on our actual knowledge of stretches of the world and its history; but in so far as we do this, we can no longer sincerely claim to be unable to connect our description at any point with items belonging to the unified framework of our knowledge of particulars. This first reply, then, is tantamount to disputing that it is possible to know an individuating fact about a particular unless something is known about the relations of that particular to identified items in the spatio-temporal framework. It might be possible, with sufficient ingenuity, to produce cases which would circumvent this objection. But other objections would then arise. Even if it were possible to satisfy the formal conditions of particular-identification in a way which left the particular completely detached and cut off, as it were, from the general unified framework of knowledge of particulars, the achievement would be a peculiarly useless one. *So long as our knowledge of it retained this completely detached character*, the particular would have no part to play in our general scheme of knowledge; we could for example, learn nothing new about it except by learning new general truths. I do not think we need pursue the question any further; for it is obvious enough that the possibility envisaged, if it is one, plays no significant part in our general scheme of knowledge of particular things.

We may agree, then, that we build up our single picture of the world, of particular things and events, untroubled by possibilities of massive reduplications, content, sometimes, with the roughest locations of the situations and objects we speak of, allowing agreed proper names to bear, without further explanation, an immense individuating load. This we do quite rationally, confident in a certain community of experience and sources of instruction. Yet it is a single picture which we build, a unified structure, in which we ourselves have a place, and in which every element is thought of as directly or indirectly related to every other; and the framework of the structure, the common, unifying system of relations is spatio-temporal. By means of identifying references, we fit other people's reports and stories, along with our own, into the single story about empirical reality; and this fitting together, this connexion, rests ultimately on relating the particulars which figure in the stories in the single spatio-temporal system which we ourselves occupy.

We might now ask whether it is inevitable, or necessary, that any scheme which provides for particulars capable of being the subject-matter of discourse in a common language—or at least any such scheme as we can envisage—should be a scheme of the kind I have just described. Certainly it does not seem to be a contingent matter about empirical reality that it forms a single spatio-temporal system. Suppose someone told of a thing of a certain kind, and of certain things that had happened to it; and, when asked where that thing had been, and when the events he recounted had occurred, said, not that he did not know, but that they did not belong at all to our spatio-temporal system, that they did not take place at any distance from here or at any distance of time from now. Then we should say, and take him to be saying, that the events in question had not *really* occurred, that the thing in question did not *really* exist. In saying this, we should show how we operate with the concept of reality. But this is not to say that our concept might not have been different, had the nature of our experience been fundamentally different. Later I shall explore some ways in which it might have been different; and there are others which I shall not explore. We are dealing here with something that conditions our whole way of talking and thinking, and it is for this reason that we feel it to be non-contingent. But this fact need not prevent us from undertaking a deeper analysis of the concept of a particular, and considering, though at no small risk of absurdity, quite different possibilities.

For the time being I shall leave aside such possibilities, and raise, instead, questions about our own conceptual scheme. There are questions enough to be raised. But it is worth first re-emphasizing the illusoriness of certain difficulties. There is, for example, the belief which we made our starting-point, the belief that however elaborate a description we produce of a network of spatially and temporally related things and incidents, we can never be sure of producing an individuating description of a single particular item, for we can never rule out the possibility of another exactly similar network. To experience this theoretical anxiety is, as we have seen, to overlook the fact that we, the speakers, the users of the dating and placing systems, have our own place in that system and know that place; that we ourselves, therefore, and our own immediate environment, provide a point of reference which individuates the network and hence helps to individuate the particulars located in the network. A different, but not un-related, error is made by those who, very well aware that *here-and-now* provides a point of reference, yet suppose that 'here' and 'now' and 'this' and all such utterance-centred words refer to something private and personal to each individual user of them. They see how for each person at any moment there is on this basis a single spatio-temporal network; but see also that, on this basis, there are as many networks, as many worlds, as there are persons. Such philosophers deprive themselves of a public point of reference by making the point of reference private. They are unable to admit that we are in the system because they think that the system is within us; or, rather, that each has his own system within him. This is not to say that the schemes they construct may not help us to understand our own. But it is with our own that we are con-cerned. So we shall not give up the platitude that 'here' and 'now' and 'this' and 'I' and 'you' are words of our common language, which each can use to indicate, or help to indicate, to another, who is with him, what he is talking about.

2. REIDENTIFICATION

[4] We operate with the scheme of a single, unified spatio-temporal system. The system is unified in this sense. Of things of which it makes sense to inquire about the spatial position, we think it always significant not only to ask how any two such things are spatially related at any one time, the same for each, but also to inquire about the spatial relations of any one thing at any moment of its history to any other thing at any moment of its history, when the moments may be different. Thus we say: A is now in just the place where B was a thousand years ago. We have, then, the idea of a system of elements every one of which can be both spatially and temporally related to every other.

Let us consider, first, some conditions, and then some consequences, of our possession and use of this scheme. One of the conditions of our use of this scheme is that we should be able to identify particulars in a sense, or application, of the word 'identify' different from that which I have so far considered. If a man in my presence, refers to a copy of a book which he has in his hand, I may, in the application of the word we have so far considered, identify the particular he is referring to: it is the book in his hand. But in another application of the word I may fail to identify that particular. I may think I have never seen it before, when it is in fact my own copy. I fail to identify it as, say, the copy I bought yesterday.

Now if we are to operate the scheme of a single unified spatio-temporal system or framework of particulars, it is essential that we should be able sometimes to identify particulars in the way I have just illustrated. More generally, we must have criteria or methods of identifying a particular encountered on one occasion, or described in respect of one occasion, as *the same individual* as a particular encountered on another occasion, or described in respect of another occasion. For the sake of terminological clarity we may, when necessary, distinguish between referential, or speaker–hearer, identification on the one hand, and reidentification on the other. It is not surprising that it should be natural to use the word 'identify' in both connexions. In both kinds of case, identifying involves thinking that something is *the same*:

that the particular copy I see in the speaker's hand is the same particular as that to which he is referring; that the copy in his hand is the same particular as the copy I bought yesterday.

Why are criteria of reidentification necessary to our operating the scheme of a single unified spatio-temporal framework for referential identification? The necessity may be brought out in the following way. It is not the only way. Evidently we can sometimes referentially identify a member of the spatio-temporal framework by giving, or being given, its position relative to others. No less evidently we cannot make the identification of every element in the system in this way relative to that of other elements. An immediate answer is that we have no need to, because we can identify some elements by direct location. But this answer, by itself, is insufficient. For we do not use a different scheme, a different framework, on each occasion. It is the essence of the matter that we use the same framework on different occasions. We must not only identify some elements in a non-relative way, we must identify them as just the elements they are of a single continuously usable system of elements. For the occasions of reference themselves have different places in the single system of reference. We cannot attach one occasion to another unless, from occasion to occasion, we can reidentify elements common to different occasions.

Our methods, or criteria, of reidentification must allow for such facts as these: that the field of our observation is limited; that we go to sleep; that we move. That is to say, they must allow for the facts that we cannot at any moment observe the whole of the spatial framework we use, that there is no part of it that we can observe continuously, and that we ourselves do not occupy a fixed position within it. These facts have, among other consequences, this one: that there can be no question of continuous and comprehensive attention to the preservation or change of spatial boundaries and the preservation or continuous change of spatial relations on the part of things mostly undergoing no, or only gradual, qualitative change. Perhaps some philosophers of a Hume-like turn of mind have felt that only by this impossible method could we be sure of the continued identity of physical things; that in its absence identity was something feigned or illusory or at best doubtful. The conclusion, like all philosophically sceptical conclusions, is necessarily avoidable. But the fact from which it has seemed to follow is important. Whatever our account may be, it must allow for discontinuities and limits of observation. So it must lean heavily on what we may for the moment call 'qualitative recurrences'—that is to say, on the fact of repeated observational encounters with the same patterns or arrangements of objects—where, for the moment, we allow to this phrase 'same patterns or arrangements of objects' all the ambiguity, as between qualitative and numerical (or particular) identity, that it confusingly, but also helpfully, has. But now it might seem that if we do in fact lean thus heavily on such recurrences, then *either* we are driven to scepticism about particular-identity *or* the whole distinction between qualitative and numerical identity comes into question, except when it applies to what falls within the field of an uninterrupted stretch of observation. What I mean by the whole distinction coming into question is something like this. When we say 'the same' of what does fall within the field of an uninterrupted stretch of observation, we can clearly distinguish between the cases where we mean to speak of qualitative identity and the cases where we mean to speak of numerical identity.

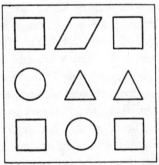

If, for instance, we say:

   The figure in the top-left-hand corner of this diagram is the same as the figure which has a parallellogram to the right of it and a circle beneath it, we use 'the same' to speak of numerical identity; whereas if we say:

> The figure in the top-left-hand corner of the diagram is the same as the figure in the bottom-right-hand corner of the diagram,

we have a simple case of using 'the same' to speak of qualitative identity. Where we say 'the same' of what is not continuously observed, *we think* we can as clearly make just this same distinction. But can we? Since spatio-temporally continuous existence is, by hypothesis, observed *neither* in the case where we are inclined to speak of qualitative identity *nor* in the case where we are inclined to speak of numerical identity, by what right do we suppose that there is a fundamental difference between these cases, or that there is just *the* difference in question? There *are* differences, certainly; but they are just differences in the ways in which observation-situations or scenes resemble and differ from one another; or in the ways in which certain features of observation-situations or scenes resemble one another and differ from one another. To take a Hume-like position, we might say: these differences suggest to us an unobserved continuity in one set of cases and its absence in another set, make us perhaps *imagine* this; and thus we are led to confuse these differences with the difference between numerical and qualitative identity. But really all we have, in the case of non-continuous observation, is different *kinds* of qualitative identity. If we ever mean more than this in talking of identity, in cases of non-continuous observation, then we cannot be sure of identity; if we can be sure of identity, then we cannot mean more than this.

But now we see we are just in one of the characteristic situations of philosophical scepticism: which allows us the alternatives of meaning something different from what we do mean, or of being for ever unsure; because the standard for being sure while meaning what we do mean is set self-contradictorily high, viz. having *continuous* observation where we have non-continuous observation. So the complaint that you cannot be sure reduces to the tautology that you do not continuously observe what you do not continuously observe.

But the point can be better put another way. There is no doubt that we have the idea of a single spatio-temporal system of material things; the idea of every material thing at any time being spatially related, in various ways at various times, to every other at every time. There is no doubt at all that this *is* our conceptual scheme. Now I say that a *condition* of our having this conceptual scheme is the unquestioning acceptance of particular-identity in at least some cases of non-continuous observation. Let us suppose for a moment that we were *never* willing to ascribe particular-identity in such cases. Then we should, as it were, have the idea of a new, a different, spatial system for each new continuous stretch of observation. (Most of the common concepts of material things that we have would not exist; for the continuous stretches of observation that do occur are not long enough or comprehensive enough to allow of any use for them.) Each new system would be wholly independent of every other. There would be no question of *doubt* about the identity of an item in one system with an item in another. For such a doubt makes sense only if the two systems are not independent, if they are parts, in some way related, of a single system which includes them both. But the condition of having such a system is precisely the condition that there should be satisfiable and commonly satisfied criteria for the identity of at least some items in one sub-system with some items in the other. This gives us a more profound characterization of the sceptic's position. He pretends to accept a conceptual scheme, but at the same time quietly rejects one of the conditions of its employment. Thus his doubts are unreal, not simply because they are logically irresoluble doubts, but because they amount to the rejection of the whole conceptual scheme within which alone such doubts make sense. So, naturally enough, the alternative to doubt which he offers us is the suggestion that we do not really, or should not really, have the conceptual scheme that we do have; that we do not really, or should not really, mean what we think we mean, what we do mean. But this alternative is absurd. For the whole process of reasoning only starts because the scheme is as it is; and we cannot change it even if we would. Finally, we may, if we choose, see the sceptic as offering for contemplation the sketch of an alternative scheme; and this is to see him as a revisionary metaphysician with whom we do not wish to quarrel, but whom we do not need to follow.

There are a hundred complications about the idea of a stretch of continuous observation, about what would count as such a stretch. To go into these fully we should have to consider many facts and questions: ranging from questions about the special position of our own bodies, and about the relations between sight and touch, to simple facts like the fact that we cannot look in all directions at once. But I am not now concerned with these complications, though to some of these questions—e.g. that of the special position of one's own body—I shall have to return later.

[5] There is, however, one complication of a quite different kind which I must mention now. The description which I gave of the condition of our having the scheme we do have—the scheme of a single spatio-temporal system of physical things—is in a certain respect incomplete. It is not enough that we should be able to say 'the same thing'; we must also be able to say 'the same place'. For suppose I encounter a thing x at a time t and reidentify x at a later time t'. Then, it appears, the fact that I know the spatial relations which an object y stood to x at t, and the spatial relations in which an object z stands to x at t' does not mean that I know anything at all about the spatial relations between y and z. Yet if we are to operate the scheme of a single spatio-temporal framework there must be an answerable question of the form: What are the spatial relations between y at t and z at t'?; or, more perspicuously: What, in relation to the spatial position of z at t', was the spatial position of y at t? And if I cannot answer this question on the strength of knowing the spatial relations of y at t and of z at t' to one and the same thing, namely x, how can I answer it at all? To be able to answer such questions, I must be able to reidentify not only things, but places.

Yet this is a misleading way to bring out the incompleteness of the account I gave. For the reidentification of places is not something quite different from, and independent of, the reidentification of things. There is, rather, a complex and intricate interplay between the two. For on the one hand places are defined only by the relations of things; and, on the other, one of the requirements for the identity of a material thing is that its existence, as well as being continuous in time, should be continuous in space. That is to say, for many kinds of thing, it counts against saying that a thing, x, at one place at one time is the same as a thing, y, at another place at another time, if we think there is not some continuous set of places between these two places such that x was at each successive member of this set of places at successive times between these two times and y was at the same member of the set of places at the same time.

So the identification and distinction of places turn on the identification and distinction of things; and the identification and distinction of things turn, in part, on the identification and distinction of places. There is no mystery about this mutual dependence. To exhibit its detail is simply to describe the criteria by which we criticize, amend and extend our ascription of identity to things and places. I shall not try to exhibit its detail in full. I shall just describe one side of this dependence. If we encounter a set of things which we are prepared to call the same as a previously encountered set, and if the relative spatial positions of these things are unchanged, then, *so long as we confine our remarks within the limits of that set of things*, we say that each member of the set is in the same place as it was before. If some, but not all, members of such a set have changed their relative positions, then we may say of some that they are in different places and of some that they are in the same place. Of *which* we shall say *which*, depends on our selection of certain members of the set as constituting a dominant framework for the set as a whole. This selection need in no way depend, though it may depend, on our surreptitiously thinking outside the limits of the set. On the whole, we shall select those elements of the set, if any, which can be thought of as containing or supporting the remainder, or on which the set can be thought of as centred. We do not change these criteria, but merely enlarge their application, when we consider the place of the set itself, or of things in it, in relation to other things or sets of things. It is easy to see how, consequently, we can construct antinomies, if we choose, by varying the frame of reference in which we ask of one thing the question: Is it in the same place? My hat is in the same place as it was; for it is still on the back seat of the car. But it is in a different place; for the car has travelled from London to Manchester. But these antinomies should perplex no one. They certainly do not count against the principle that we employ the scheme of a single unified spatio-temporal system for the things we talk about. They show merely how, in different contexts of discussion, we may narrow or broaden the range of our talk. The grip of the principle on our discourse about particulars is never abandoned; but it is not so tight as to inhibit shifts in the frames of reference of our spatial talk.

3. BASIC PARTICULARS

[6] We can make it clear to each other what or which particular things our discourse is about because we can fit together each other's reports and stories into a single picture of the world; and the framework of that picture is a unitary spatio-temporal framework, of one temporal and three spatial dimensions. Hence, as things are, particular-identification in general rests ultimately on the possibility of locating the particular things we speak of in a single unified spatio-temporal system. Many qualifications are covered by the word 'ultimately'. We can, for example, be arguing about the same man, though we disagree about his dates. We can speak of the same thing, though we disagree about its position in space at different times. But such disagreements are possible only in a context of larger, if looser, agreement about the relations of these entities to others about which we do not disagree.

The question I want now to ask is one already foreshadowed. Given the general character of the conceptual scheme I have described, is there any one distinguishable class or category of particulars which must be basic from the point of view of particular-identification? This question resolves itself into two. First, is there a class or category of particulars such that, as things are, it would not be possible to make all the identifying references which we do make to particulars of other classes, unless we made identifying references to particulars of that class, whereas it would be possible to make all the identifying references we do make to particulars of that class without making identifying reference to particulars of other classes? Second, can we argue to an affirmative answer to this question from the general character of the conceptual scheme I have described?

It seems that we can construct an argument from the premise that identification rests ultimately on location in a unitary spatio-temporal framework of four dimensions, to the conclusion that a certain class of particulars is basic in the sense I have explained. For that framework is not something extraneous to the objects in reality of which we speak. If we ask what constitutes the framework, we must look to those objects themselves, or some among them. But not every category of particular objects which we recognize is competent to constitute such a framework. The only objects which can constitute it are those which can confer upon it its own fundamental characteristics. That is to say, they must be three-dimensional objects with some endurance through time. They must also be accessible to such means of observation as we have; and, since those means are strictly limited in power, they must collectively have enough diversity, richness, stability and endurance to make possible and natural just that conception of a single unitary framework which we possess. Of the categories of objects which we recognize, only those satisfy these requirements which are, or possess, material bodies—in a broad sense of the expression. Material bodies constitute the framework. Hence, given a certain general feature of the conceptual scheme we possess, and given the character of the available major categories, things which are, or possess, material bodies must be the basic particulars.

I shall have more to say later about this qualifying phrase 'given the character of the available major categories'. But one point I shall mention now. We might regard it as a necessary condition of something being a material body, that it should tend to exhibit some felt resistance to touch; or, perhaps more generally, that it should possess some qualities of the tactual range. If we do, then this is a more stringent requirement than any that Descartes intended by 'extension' or Locke by 'solidity'; that is to say, it is a more stringent requirement than that of the three-dimensional occupation of space. For this latter requirement, which is what the argument seems to lead to, might be satisfied empirically, it seems, by purely visual occupiers-of-space. (It is in fact satisfied for the blind by purely tactual occupiers-of-space.) In practice, not many purely visual occupiers-of-space are to be found: some cases that might be suggested, such as ghosts, are altogether questionable; others, such as shafts of light or volumes of coloured gas, certainly do not satisfy the requirements of richness, endurance and stability. But in so far as they are to be found, we do hesitate to call them material bodies. So it appears that there exists the theoretical possibility that the requirements of the argument might be met by a category of entities which we should not call material bodies; though, as things are, these requirements are met only by what we are ready to call material bodies. The theoretical possibility, if it is one, seems of only moderate interest, and I shall refrain from exploring it. In any case we can satisfy ourselves formally, by introducing a weak sense of 'material body' for which the supposed purely visual three-dimensional objects are allowed to qualify; and then re-state the conclusion of the argument more simply as follows. Given a certain general feature of the conceptual scheme of particular-identification which we have, it follows that material bodies must be the basic particulars.

The form of this argument might possibly mislead. It is not that on the one hand we have a conceptual scheme which presents us with a certain problem of particular-identification; while on the other hand there exist material objects in sufficient richness and strength to make possible the solution of such problems. It is only because the solution is possible that the problem exists. So with all transcendental arguments.

[7] To rest any philosophical position on an argument so general and so vague would be undesirable. But there is no need to do so. We can inquire more directly and in greater detail whether there is reason to suppose that identification of particulars belonging to some categories is in fact dependent on identification

of particulars belonging to others, and whether there is any category of particulars which is basic in this respect.

I remarked earlier that speaker and hearer often identify one particular by reference to another; that is to say, that often an identifying reference to one particular, when supplemented, if necessary, from the linguistic context, contains a mention of another particular; and that a hearer's successful identification of the first may then depend on his successful identification of the second. The clearest possible case of general identifiability-dependence of one type of particular on another would be the case in which it was impossible to identify a particular of one type without this kind of dependence on the identification of a particular of the other type. Perhaps there are no pure cases of such direct identifiability-dependence. But there is at least one very important case which approximates to being of this kind. That is to say, there are two important general types or categories of particular, the identification of the members of one of which is, in almost this way, dependent on the identification of members of the other. The dependent type is the class of what might be called 'private particulars'—comprising the perhaps overlapping groups of sensations, mental events and, in one common acceptance of this term, sense-data. The type on which it is dependent is the class of persons. (Perhaps we should add 'or animals'; for perhaps we sometimes refer identifyingly to the particular experiences of animals. But this is a complication I shall neglect.) On other criteria than the present, private experiences have often been the most favoured candidates for the status of 'basic' particulars; on the present criteria, they are the most obviously inadmissible. The principles of individuation of such experiences essentially turn on the identities of the persons to whose histories they belong. A twinge of toothache or a private impression of red cannot in general be identified in our common language except as the twinge which such-and-such an identified person suffered or is suffering, the impression which such-and-such an identified person had or is having. Identifying references to 'private particulars' depend on identifying references to particulars of another type altogether, namely persons.

There might seem to be an obvious objection to this view. If someone is writhing on the ground and says. 'This (the) pain is terrible', has he not made an identifying reference to a private particular, viz. his sensation of pain, without mentioning or referring to the person who is suffering the pain, viz. himself? Certainly there need be no linguistic context, involving reference to another particular, with which the hearer need supplement the reference in order to identify the particular concerned. He identifies it straight away as the pain that the speaker is suffering. Similarly a doctor may apply a pressure to a patient and then ask: 'How severe was that pain?' and the patient will successfully identify the pain the doctor refers to as that which he, the hearer, has just suffered or is suffering. In these cases, however, it may fairly be said of the demonstrative phrases that they really do have the function which is sometimes mistakenly said to be always theirs. That is to say, they really do contain an implicit reference to a particular person; they really are a kind of shorthand for 'the pain I am suffering', in the first example, or 'the pain you have just suffered', in the second. If it is asked why a similar thing is not true of any identifying demonstrative phrase referring to a *public* object, e.g. why 'This tree' is not short for 'The tree you (I) can see over there', the answer is as follows. The demonstrative identifying phrase, 'This tree', used of a particular tree, may be spoken to anybody by anybody, in the appropriate surroundings, without change of identificatory force. No implicit reference to a particular *person* is essential to its identificatory force; all that is essential is that the surroundings and context are such that the reference is clearly to a particular *tree*. The implicit reference to a particular person is, however, essential to the identificatory force of demonstrative phrases referring to private experiences. This constitutes a sufficient reason for distinguishing the two types of case in the way I have suggested, and hence for maintaining that the apparent exception is not a real one.

Another way of putting the point, which may later have certain advantages, is as follows. We may admit, if we like, that an implicit reference to speaker and hearer is involved in *any* demonstrative identifying reference made in the presence of the object referred to; and then say that this implicit reference to persons, being absolutely general in such situations, is to be discounted in the context of the present discussion, so long as it is simply a consequence of the fact that the persons concerned are respectively speaker and hearer. Now the implicit reference to a person in the case we are concerned with—the case of a private experience —is not simply a consequence of this fact, but also of the fact that he is the person whose private experience we are referring to. That this is so may be seen clearly from the case in which A says to B, apropos the manifestly suffering C, in whose presence they are, 'The pain must be acute'. The implicit reference to C is here quite independent of his having the role of speaker or hearer; for he does not have either role.

Why then did I qualify my initial statement of the relation of identifiability-dependence between 'private' particulars and persons? I qualified it for the following reason. It would be possible for an experience to be identified as the one experience of a certain kind suffered in a certain identified place at a certain time; it would be possible for someone to be authoritatively told that such a description had application, and hence to identify the experience when it was referred to, without any independent knowledge of the identity of the sufferer of the experience. This, then, would be a case in which the most direct relation of identifiability-dependence between experiences and persons did not hold. The qualification which such a possibility necessitates, however, is not very important or far-reaching. For it could be known that such an identifying description had application only under certain conditions. It would be necessary, in order for the experience-description to be given currency, that someone or other, who gave it currency, should also have been able to give an independent identification of the sufferer of the experience. So even though, on a particular occasion of reference, the identification of a private experience need not be directly dependent on the identification of the person whose experience it was, it must still be indirectly so dependent.

With this qualification, which is in practice of small importance, we may say, then, that private particulars exhibit the most direct kind of identifiability-dependence on particulars of another type. In extreme contrast with the class of private experiences lies another, though less well-defined, class of particulars, which suffers equally obviously from identifiability-dependence. This is the class of particulars which might be called 'theoretical constructs'. Certain particles of physics might provide one set of examples. These are not in any sense private objects; but they are unobservable objects. We must regard it as in principle possible to make identifying references to such particulars, if not individually, at least in groups or collections; otherwise they forfeit their status as admitted particulars. Perhaps we do not often make such references in fact. These items play a role of their own in our intellectual economy, which it is not my concern to describe. But it is clear enough that in so far as we do make identifying references to particulars of this sort, we must ultimately identify them, or groups of them, by identifying reference to those grosser, observable bodies of which perhaps, like Locke, we think of them as the minute, unobservable constituents.

Particles of physics are one kind of example of particulars of this class. I mentioned them first, because, like private experiences, they exhibit the most direct kind of identifiability-dependence. There are many others which need exhibit no more than a general identifiability-dependence. I spoke of the class as ill-defined; and clearly it is, so far, no better defined than the extremely vague concept of observability. We speak of a particular political situation or economic depression. We may even speak of *observing* such phenomena. But it would be clearly vain to hope to find basic particulars among such items as these. The possession of the concepts under which such particulars fall all too evidently presupposes the possession of other concepts under which fall particulars of wholly different and far less sophisticated types. We could not, for example, have the concept of a strike or a lockout unless we had such concepts as those of men, tools and factories. From this there follows immediately a general identifiability-dependence of particulars of the more sophisticated, upon particulars of the less sophisticated, type. For we could not speak of, and hence, identify, particulars of the more sophisticated type unless we could speak of, and hence identify, particulars of the less sophisticated type. This does not mean that on any particular occasion of reference we must mediate an identifying reference to a particular of a more sophisticated type by an identifying reference to a particular of a less sophisticated type. We might refer quite directly, for example, to 'the present economic depression'.

If, then, there are any basic particulars in the sense I have indicated, it seems that the sense in which they must be observable is not merely this: that it should be correct to speak of observing them. It seems likely, rather, that they must be public objects of perception, particular objects of such kinds that different people can quite literally see or hear or feel by contact or taste or smell the same objects of these kinds. They must, it seems, be objects belonging to kinds such that objects of these kinds can be directly located by both hearer and speaker on some particular occasions of discourse. Nevertheless, I shall construe the limits of the class of the publicly observable fairly liberally. The more liberally these limits are construed, the less is my dependence on the argument from presupposition of concepts. It is desirable to reduce dependence on this argument as much as possible. Its application would be a matter of detail and dispute; and its explanatory power is small. We shall return later to consider further a more exact form of the argument.

Now it is evident that any item which can be directly located, can to that extent be identified without a mediating reference to any other particular at all, and hence without reference to any particular of a type or category other than its own. But, of course, it does not follow from this that the category to which such an item belongs is a category of basic particulars. For the range of actual particular items directly locatable on any particular occasion of discourse is severely restricted; and it may well be that the identifiability on a particular occasion of some items which lie outside that range is dependent on the identifiability of other items of different types or categories from theirs. The fact that an item falls within the general class of the publicly perceptible does not, therefore, preclude its belonging to some category which suffers from identifiability-dependence on some other category also falling within the general class of the publicly perceptible.

But how shall we divide publicly perceptible, or publicly observable, particulars into types or categories? Clearly there are many ways of doing so, adapted to different philosophical purposes. I shall be content with the roughest of divisions. I shall speak, for example, of *events* and *processes*, *states* and *conditions* on the one hand; and of *material bodies* or things possessing material bodies, on the other. I shall use these terms loosely: for example, a field or a river will count as material bodies or things possessing material bodies. In general, I shall not claim that my distinctions are very clear, or that they are precise or exhaustive. They may nevertheless serve my purpose. Another distinction, worth mentioning now, to which I shall later refer is that between, e.g. events and processes which, as named and conceived of by us, necessarily are *of*, or performed or undergone *by*, material bodies or things possessing material bodies, and events and processes not of this kind. Thus a death is necessarily the death of some creature. But that a flash or a bang occurred does not entail that anything flashed or banged. 'Let there be light' does not mean 'Let something shine'.

We have already seen that it is quite possible, in certain circumstances, to identify, e.g., events and processes without any dependence on identification of particulars of other types. For public events and processes may be directly locatable. Such expressions as 'That flash', uttered immediately after there has been a flash, 'That terrible noise', uttered while the noise continues, enable the hearer directly to locate the particular in question. They involve no reference to any other particular at all, except at most for the discountable implicit references to hearer and speaker which have already been discussed, and *a fortiori* no reference to particulars of other types. This is surely not the only case in which such a particular can be identified without reference to particulars of other types. Suppose, for example, all the flashes and bangs that occurred could be ordered in a single temporal series. Then, in principle, every member of the series could be identified without reference to anything that was not a member of the series: it could be identified, say, as the bang that immediately preceded the *n*th flash before the last. Now, on occasion, we *can* work with the idea of a partial sequence, or series, of a somewhat similar kind. We can work with it, for example, in the case of what I shall call a *directly locatable sequence*. This concept is to be understood as relative in its application to a time, and to a speaker–hearer pair. Thus a directly locatable sequence of bangs for a speaker–hearer pair at a certain time would be a series of bangs which was going on at that time, or had just ceased at that time, and all the members of which were audible to both members of the pair. So long as the range of reference was understood as restricted within the limits of the series, every member of the series could be identified, on the model indicated above, without reference to any particular of a type other than its own.

But of course not all flashes and bangs that may be identifyingly referred to are, on the occasion of the reference, members of a directly locatable sequence for those who refer to them. Nor is there any other kind of humanly constructible flash–bang sequence, with the two properties (1) that at least one member of such a sequence can always be identified directly, i.e. without reference to any other particular at all, and (2) that every reference to any other such particular can identify it solely by its position relative to that of other members of such a sequence. Perhaps this is merely a contingent limitation of the human condition. If so, it is a limitation which determines the nature of our identifying reference to flashes and bangs. In practice, when we wish to refer identifyingly to a particular phenomenon of this kind, and are not in the artificially favourable position of being able to do so by placing it in a directly locatable sequence, we do so by way of a reference, usually implicit in the linguistic context, to a particular of some quite different sort; for example, to a place at which it was audible or visible, or to a particular material object which was causally connected with it. In practice, that is to say, there are other dimensions of identification involved besides the simple one of temporal position within a single determinable series of roughly homogeneous particulars.

The point may be made clearer by considering one or two

moderately convincing instances of humanly constructible series of particular states or processes, such that there are no particulars of the kind concerned which are not members of this single series, and such that one member of the series can always be directly identified. The sequence of nights and days, considered simply as alternating periods of prolonged and general light or darkness, is one example, and the sequence of years, regarded simply as seasonal cycles, another. This must be understood with certain qualifications: for instance, we must ignore the confusing consequences of going round the world. With these reservations, we may say that since there are no nights and days, or seasonal cycles, which are not members of such a single series, any particular member can be identified as the *n*th before, or after, the present one. It is no accident that our dating system makes use of such convenient phenomena.

If we inquire about the underlying reasons for this difference between the two types of phenomena, a part, though only a part, of the answer is this. The members of the night–day sequence are relatively general, in the sense of generally discriminable, throughout the areas of space we are concerned with. (Here again certain obvious reservations are to be made.) But this is by no means true of the members of any hypothetical flash–bang sequence that we may dream of. The day that dawns in Scotland dawns in England too. But the bang made by an exploding tyre in London is not audible in Edinburgh.

Apart from such special, and dubious, cases as the night–day sequence, what I have said of the jejune example of flashes and bangs holds for other publicly observable events and processes, states and conditions. This, I think, is true, however liberally we construe the concept of a humanly constructible identification-series, of which the members are to be only particulars of these types, and of which at least one member is always to be identifiable without reference to any other particular at all. Thus we might, perhaps, allow a series of battles to constitute such a series for two generals now engaged in a particular war; a series of viva-voce examinations to constitute another for the examiners conducting them. Then any particular battle, or any particular viva-voce examination within the series, could be identified by means of its position in the series. Further, we must allow, in principle, for the construction of complex series, series of heterogeneous events or processes, in which identifying references would take such a form as 'The first ϕ before the last ψ before the second χ before the last'. But obviously this method of identifying events, processes or states, *while avoiding reference to particulars of other types than these*, suffers in general from severe practical limitations of the kind we have already encountered. Except in such special cases as that of a directly locatable sequence, there is no reason to suppose that any such series which any one person was able to *make use of* for identificatory purposes would be identical with any similar series which any other person was able to make use of for these purposes. It is useless to appeal to such a theoretical notion as that of the *complete* series of events of one specific kind, e.g. of deaths. For it is obvious that no one who wishes to refer to a particular death could know its position in that series. Again, this is perhaps a contingent matter; but one that radically conditions the nature of identifying reference.

It might appear that in concentrating on what could be seen as contingent limitations of human powers, I have neglected to use two powerful theoretical arguments against the general possibility of identifying events, processes, states and conditions by the method described, without reference to particulars of other types. The first argument is that this method of identifying events &c. provides no means of distinguishing *simultaneous* similar events in any given series; since they are always identified by their position in a temporal order only. But this is easily answered. For there is no logical reason why the relations exploited in the construction of such a series should be those of temporal order alone. For instance, we often say that one event was the cause of another; and clearly, of two simultaneous events of the same specific kind, one will indeed have causal antecedents and consequences which the other lacks. Nor does the fact that reference is restricted to, say, events and processes, preclude the use of spatial discriminations. If we consider again the favourable case of a directly locatable sequence, it may be perfectly possible to distinguish between simultaneous similar members of such a sequence by means of their spatial relations, without reference to particulars of other types. Imagine, for example, a series of moves in chess, which in fact constitute two distinct games played by two distinct pairs of players: but the moves in each game are identical and simultaneous. Nevertheless a watching speaker and hearer can distinguish between the two streams of moves as, say, the left-hand and the right-hand stream, and hence can refer identifyingly to the last move but one in the left-hand stream. The objection, therefore, is not decisive. But it is not without value. For it serves to emphasize once again the severe practical limitations of the method.

The other theoretical argument which I might seem to have neglected is this. It is true of a significant, perhaps of a preponderant, proportion of the kinds of events, processes, states or conditions for which we have names, that these events or processes are necessarily the actions or undergoings of things which are not themselves processes, states or events; that these states or conditions are necessarily states or conditions *of* things which are not themselves states, conditions, processes or events. It might be thought that from this fact alone it could be argued directly that the identification of most events, states or processes must proceed *via* the identification of those particulars of other types to the history of which they belonged; that e.g. where a particular event was of a kind such that all events of this kind necessarily happen to things of another type, then the identification of the particular event necessarily involved the identification of the particular thing to which it happened. Thus no particular death could be identifyingly referred to without an at least implicit identifying reference to the creature whose death it was; for all deaths are necessarily deaths of creatures. For someone directly to locate a death, he would have directly to locate the creature whose death it was. Thus 'This death', when used as a true demonstrative identifying reference, i.e. in the presence of the death concerned, would have the force of 'The death of this creature'.

This argument is unsatisfactory as it stands. For it is simply untrue that we cannot refer identifyingly to an observable event of a kind such that the occurrence of events of that kind entails the existence of particulars of a different type, without dependence upon an implicit identifying reference to some particular of that type. My identifying reference to a scream need in no way depend, for its identificatory force, on an implicit identifying reference to the screamer. The original argument errs in trying to infer from a conceptual dependence too direct a kind of identifiability-dependence of particulars.

The argument may, however, be replaced by one with a weaker conclusion. Suppose that βs are necessarily βs of αs (e.g. that births are necessarily births of animals). Then, though on a particular occasion I may identify a particular β without identifying the α it is of, yet it would not in general be possible to identify βs unless it were in general possible to identify αs. For we could not speak of βs as we do speak of them, or have the concept we do have of βs, unless we spoke of αs; and we could not speak of αs unless it were in principle possible to identify an α. So, in a general sense, βs show identifiability-dependence on αs.

But now the amended argument seems to prove too much. For if we say that having the concept we do have of a birth entails having the concept we do have of an animal, on the ground that *This is a birth* entails *There is some animal of which this is the birth*, we must, it seems, also say that having the concept we do have of an animal entails having the concept we do have of a birth; for *This is an animal* entails *There is some birth which is the birth of this animal*. Whence, by parity of reasoning, the argument shows a mutual identifiability-dependence between births and animals. And so the argument is useless to us. For we are interested only in non-symmetrical relations of dependence.

Nevertheless, I think the amended argument can be restated so as to avoid this consequence. For there is after all a certain asymmetry in the relations between the concept of an animal and the concept of a birth. It is true that *This is an animal* entails *There is some birth which is the birth of this*. But this entailment admits of the following paraphrase: *This is an animal* entails *This was born*. Now while it may seem reasonable to maintain that our concept of an animal would be different if we could not express the entailment in the second form, it also seems reasonable to deny that our concept of an animal would be different if we merely lacked a means of expressing the entailment in its first form. In other words, it can reasonably be maintained that in order to speak of animals with the sense which this word in fact has for us, we must find a place in our discourse for the concept *being born*; but there is no reason to conclude from the fact that we speak of animals with the sense this word has for us, that we must *also* find a place in our discourse for the idea of a certain range of particulars, viz. births. Whether we *also* do this or not is *irrelevant* to our having the concept of an animal that we do have. Here there is a real asymmetry. For there is no corresponding paraphrase of the entailment from *This is a birth* to *There is an animal of which this is the birth*. We can paraphrase one entailment so as to eliminate what logicians might call quantification over births; but we cannot paraphrase the other so as to eliminate quantification over animals. In other words, the admission into our discourse of the range of particulars, *births*, conceived of as we conceive of them, does require the admission into our discourse of the range of particulars, *animals*; but the admission into our discourse of the range of particulars, *animals*, conceived of as we conceive of them, does not require the admission into our discourse of the range of particulars, *births*.

As finally amended, the argument, I think, is sound. A large class of particular states and conditions, events and processes, are conceived of as necessarily states and conditions of, or as performed or suffered by, particulars of other types, notably things which are or have material bodies. The argument establishes a general and one-way identifiability-dependence of the former class of particulars on the latter, given just the concepts that we have. The reason why it is desirable to rest as little weight as possible upon the argument is that, though it is sound, it has, as I have already suggested, little or no explanatory power. The argument does not explain the existence of the general identifiability-dependence it establishes. It remains a question why particulars which figure in our conceptual scheme should exhibit the relation on which the argument draws, why we should conceive of the relevant particulars just in these ways.

Let us return, then, to those already noticed general limitations to which events, processes, states and conditions are subject as candidates for identification without reference to other types of thing. To summarize what I have said about these limitations. The minimum conditions of independent identifiability for a type of particulars were that its members should be neither private nor unobservable. Many kinds of state, process, event or condition satisfy these two conditions. In suitable circumstances such a particular can be directly located and thus identified without reference to any other particular at all. Even when not directly locatable, such a particular *may* be identified without any reference, explicit or implicit, to any particular which is not itself a state, process, event or condition, as the case may be. But the cases in which this intra-typical identification is possible are severely restricted. For they require that the parties to an identifying reference should be operating with one and the same type-homogeneous referential framework. And the fundamental limitations of states, processes, events and conditions, as independently identifiable particulars, is their failure to supply frameworks of this kind which are at all adequate to our referring needs. Still less can they supply, of themselves, a *single*, comprehensive and continuously usable framework of this kind. So we enormously extend the range of our possible identifying references to states, processes &c. by allowing them to be mediated by reference to places, persons and material things.

Now, in the respects just mentioned, material bodies appear to be much better candidates for the status of basic particulars than any we have so far considered. They supply both literally and figuratively, both in the short and in the long term, both widely and narrowly, our physical geography, the features we note on our maps. They include, that is to say, a sufficiency of relatively enduring objects (e.g. geographical features, buildings &c.) maintaining with each other relatively fixed or regularly changing spatial relations. Here 'sufficient' and 'relative' refer to our human situation and needs. When we were considering states, processes &c., we noted that there was no rich complexity of time-taking things which were generally discriminable and similarly related throughout the areas of space we are concerned with. But there is a rich complexity of space-taking things which are relatively enduring and similarly related throughout the tracts of time we are concerned with. Material bodies, in a broad sense of the word, secure to us one single common and continuously extendable framework of reference, any constituent of which can be identifyingly referred to without reference to any particular of any other type. This is the framework for spatial location in general. The detailed constitution of this framework changes; but without detriment to its unity. Knowledge of the detail of its composition varies from one person to another; but without detriment to its identity. Of course not all material bodies, or things which have them, are regarded as even transient parts of such a framework: many bodies are too much in movement, or too ephemeral, or both. One would not, so to speak, use them in giving spatial directions unless they were then and there observable. But that does not preclude their identification, when necessary, by reference, first, to each other, and ultimately, to constituent elements of the framework. If we take as a sufficient condition of type-homogeneity, for these purposes, the being or possessing a material body, we may venture to think that all things which satisfy this condition qualify as basic particulars. The fact that identification in general has a temporal as well as a spatial aspect is no objection. For material bodies, or things which have them, exhibit relations between themselves which have a temporal aspect. One thing replaces or begets another. Things pass through places.

It is not, then, only in special circumstances that material bodies, in the broad sense in which I am using the expression, may be identified without reference to particulars of types other than their own. For the fundamental condition of identification without dependence on alien types—viz. the forming of a comprehensive and sufficiently complex type-homogeneous framework of reference—is satisfied for the case of material bodies. On the other hand, it is, as we have seen, only in special circumstances that identification of particulars of other types may avoid any dependence on reference to things which are or possess material bodies. Material bodies, therefore, are basic to particular-identification.

The conclusion may be reinforced by giving the argument a different turn. I have argued that a fundamental condition of identifying reference without dependence on alien types is the possession of a common, comprehensive and sufficiently complex type-homogeneous framework of reference. I have claimed that this condition is satisfied in the case of material bodies, and not generally in other cases. But earlier, in the second part of this chapter, I asserted that a condition, in turn, of the possession of a single, continuously usable framework of. this kind, was the ability to *re*identify at least some elements of the framework in spite of discontinuities of observation: that is to say, one must be able to identify some particular things as *the same again* as those encountered on a previous occasion. Evidently the ability to do this entails the existence of general criteria or methods of re-identification for different kinds of particular. These considerations taken together suggest that, if material bodies are basic from the point of view of referential identification, they must also be basic from the point of view of reidentification. That is to say, the reidentification criteria for material bodies should not be found to turn on the identities of other particulars except such as themselves are or have material bodies, whereas the reidentification criteria for particulars of other categories should be found to turn in part on the identity of material bodies. This expectation is amply fulfilled. If, for example, we take any familiar process-name, such as 'thaw' or 'battle', we shall find it impossible to give a detailed account of means of identifying a particular process of the kind concerned as *the same again*, which do not involve any reference to some material bodies or other—either those which make up its setting, its surroundings, or the places through which it passes; or some causally connected with it in some way; or some which the process involves more directly, e.g. the body or bodies undergoing or taking part in it; or some in some other way connected with the identity of the process. If, on the other hand, we consider the identity through time of material bodies themselves, we shall indeed find that a fundamental requirement is that which we have already noted, viz. continuity of existence in space; and determining whether this requirement is fulfilled may turn on identifying places; but this, in its turn, rests upon the identification of bodies.

Both from the point of view, then, of distinguishing a particular non-demonstratively referred to from others of the same general kind, and from the point of view of identifying a particular encountered on one occasion, or described in respect of one occasion, with a particular encountered on another, or described in respect of another, we find that material bodies play a unique and fundamental role in particular-identification. This conclusion should be in no way surprising or unexpected, if we recall that our general framework of particular-reference is a unified spatio-temporal system of one temporal and three spatial dimensions, and reflect once more that, of the available major categories, that of material bodies is the only one competent to constitute such a framework. For this category alone supplies enduring occupiers of space possessing sufficiently stable relations to meet, and hence to create, the needs with which the use of such a framework confronts us.

Two objections may now be briefly mentioned.

First, it might be objected that the argument rests on a fundamental, but in fact dubious, opposition or contrast between material bodies and processes. After all, it may be said, the erosion of a cliff can last as long as the cliff, and maintain as constant a spatial relation to the erosion of the next cliff as the two cliffs do to each other. The growth and senescence of a man lasts as long as the man, and can also be said to have the same spatial relations at various times to other processes as he is said to have to other things: it goes on just where he is. With what justification is a fundamental distinction of category assumed between things and processes?—So some philosophers have reasoned, making their point by saying, for example, that 'Caesar' is the name of a series of events, a biography. In so reasoning, they may be said to draw attention to the possibility of our recognizing a category of objects which we do not in fact recognize: a category of four-dimensional objects, which might be called 'process-things', and of which each of the temporally successive parts is three-dimensional, is, as it were, the thing taken at successive stages of its history from the beginning to the end. But the way in which I have to describe these objects shows that they are not to be identified *either* with the processes which things undergo *or* with the things which undergo them. I remarked earlier that I was concerned to investigate the relations of identifiability-dependence between the available major categories, the categories we actually possess; and the category of process-things is one we neither have nor need. We do in fact distinguish between a thing and its history, or the phases of its history; we cannot appropriately speak of one in the ways appropriate to the other; and we do not speak of either in ways appropriate to the category of process-things. Granted the distinction we do draw, there is, as we have already seen, a general identifiability-dependence of processes which things undergo upon the things which undergo them, and not vice versa. This is partly, though not only, because, granted that distinction, it is the things themselves, and not the processes they undergo, which are the primary *occupiers* of space, the possessors not only of spatial position, but of spatial *dimensions*. If one tried to give the spatial dimensions of such a process, say a death or a battle, one could only trace the outline of the dying *man* or indicate the extent of the *ground* the battle was fought over.

A more tentative, yet more serious, objection might be advanced. We began by considering a certain type of speech-situation, that in which identifying references to particulars were made and understood. We were to consider the conditions of successful identification in this kind of situation. Yet it is far from obvious how the very general and theoretical considerations advanced in the course of these arguments bear upon or reflect our actual speech-procedures, and correspondingly far from obvious in what sense, if in any, it has really been established that material bodies and things possessing them enjoy a primacy from the point of view of identification.

This objection must, in a sense, be allowed to stand. It would be a task of enormous complexity to show exactly how these general considerations are related to our actual procedures in learning and speech. If we attempted it, we should lose the generality in the detail. But a point may be made in mitigation of the refusal to attempt it. Clearly we do not, in ordinary conversation, make explicit the referential frameworks we employ. We do indeed often use demonstratives in reference to things in our immediate surroundings. But when our talk transcends them, we do not elaborately relate the things we speak of to the things we see. The place of the explicit relational framework is taken in part by that linguistic device which has so often and so justly absorbed the attention of logicians—the proper name. Demonstratives or quasi-demonstratives apart, it is proper names which tend to be the resting-places of reference to particulars, the points on which the descriptive phrases pivot. Now, among particulars, the bearers *par excellence* of proper names are persons and places. It is a conceptual truth, as we have seen, that places are defined by the relations of material bodies; and it is also a conceptual truth, of which we shall see the significance more fully hereafter, that persons have material bodies.

2

SOUNDS

[1] Claiming a special status for one class or category of entities as opposed to others is very common in philosophy. It is the philosophical phenomenon of category-preference. I have been exhibiting category-preference in claiming that material bodies are, in a certain sense, basic in relation to other categories of particulars. But I should like to emphasize the point that there are certain ways in which category-preference may be exhibited, in which I am not exhibiting it. Suppose αs are the favoured type of entity. Then sometimes preference is manifested by the declaration that the word 'exist' has a primary sense or meaning, and that only αs exist in this sense, other things only in a secondary sense; sometimes by the declaration that only αs are real; and sometimes by the declaration that other things are reducible to αs, that to talk about other things is an abbreviated way of talking about αs. I want to emphasize that in saying that material bodies are basic among particulars, at least in our conceptual scheme as it is, I am not saying any of these things. The meaning given to the term 'basic' is strictly in terms of particular-identification. On the other hand, I believe that the facts I have tried to indicate may underlie and explain, if not justify, some of the more striking formulations, which I disavow, of the category-preference which I acknowledge. It seems to me also unobjectionable to use the expression, 'onto-logically prior', in such a way that the claim that material bodies are basic particulars in our conceptual scheme is equivalent to the claim that material bodies are ontologically prior, in that scheme, to other types of particular.

These things, I have maintained, are true of our conceptual scheme as it is. The next thing I want to consider is whether, and if so how, it could be otherwise. Could there exist a conceptual scheme which was like ours in that it provided for a system of objective and identifiable particulars, but was unlike ours in that material bodies were not the basic particulars of the system? When I say, 'Could there exist such a scheme?' I mean 'Can we make intelligible to ourselves the idea of such a scheme?'

I have spoken of two sides, or aspects, of identification. They might be called the distinguishing aspect and the reidentifying aspect. The second has not, in the preceding exposition, been at all closely tied to a speech-situation involving a speaker and a hearer. Reidentification may involve merely thinking of a particular encountered on one occasion, or thought of in respect of one occasion, as the same as a particular encountered on another, or thought of in respect of another. Now such thinking clearly involves distinguishing, in thought or observation, one particular from others. So the distinguishing aspect of identification is quite fundamental. But so far in the exposition the idea of distinguishing one particular from others has been closely tied to the situation in which a hearer identifies a particular as the one currently referred to by a speaker. This tie I want now to loosen, while preserving the conclusion that material bodies are, in our actual conceptual scheme, basic to our thinking about particular-identification. I may legitimately do so; for it is not to be supposed that the general structure of such thinking is different when we are concerned to communicate with each other in speech and when we are not. The assertion that material bodies are basic particulars in our actual conceptual scheme, then, is now to be understood as the assertion that, as things are, identifying *thought* about particulars other than material bodies rests in general on identifying *thought* about material bodies, but not vice versa; and the question I have just raised, viz. 'Could we conceive of a scheme providing for identifiable particulars in which material bodies were not basic?', must be understood in a correspondingly revised and more general sense. This loosening of the tie with actual speech-situations gives more freedom of manœuvre in the next stage of the inquiry, without prejudicing the possibility that the connexion may ultimately have to be tightened up again.

It gives more freedom of manœuvre in the following way. So long as 'identification' means 'speaker–hearer identification', any question about the general conditions of a scheme providing for identifiable particulars is a question about the general conditions of speaker–hearer identification of particulars. So it is a question which can only arise given that we at least have speakers and hearers communicating with each other. But we can, or at least it seems that we can, raise a similar question without any such prior assumption of speakers and hearers. For each of us can *think* identifyingly about particulars without talking about them. Now of course it may be that the ability to think identifyingly about particulars is logically dependent on the ability to talk identifyingly to others about particulars. But this, if so, is at least not obviously so. We do not want to prejudge the question whether it is so or not; and we may, without prejudging it, raise a more general question about the conditions of the possibility of identifying thought about particulars.

But how general do we want our question to be? I am going to impose one limit on its generality. In one's own identifying thought, and indeed in one's own identifying talk, about particulars, one can certainly recognize a certain distinction: viz. the distinction between those particular occurrences, processes, states or conditions which are experiences or states of consciousness of one's own, and those particulars which are not experiences or states of consciousness of one's own, or of anyone else's either, though they may be objects of such experiences. Thus, if a tree is struck by lightning, that is one kind of happening; and if I see the tree being struck by lightning, that is another kind of happening. The knife entering my flesh is one kind of event, and my feeling the pain is another. The limit I want to impose on my general question is this: that I intend it as a question about the conditions of the possibility of identifying thought about particulars distinguished by the thinker from himself and from his own experiences or states of mind, and regarded as actual or possible *objects* of those experiences. I shall henceforth use the phrase, 'objective particulars' as an abbreviation of the entire phrase, 'particulars distinguished by the thinker &c.'. Now it may be that this limit on my question is, in a sense, no limit at all; for it may be that there could be no such thing as identifying thought about particulars which did not involve this distinction. But this, too, is a question which I shall shelve. It is not necessary for me to answer it; and perhaps it cannot be answered.

I can, then, indicate the line of enquiry I have in mind by posing two questions, reminiscent in form and partly in content of Kantian questions: (1) What are the most general statable conditions of knowledge of objective particulars? (2) Do these most general conditions involve the requirement that material bodies should be the basic particulars, or is this simply a special feature of our own scheme for knowledge of objective particulars? Or—to run the two questions into one—is the status of material bodies as basic particulars a necessary condition of knowledge of objective particulars?

Now I have suggested earlier that the fact that material bodies are the basic particulars in our scheme can be deduced from the fact that our scheme is of a certain kind, viz. the scheme of a unified spatio-temporal system of one temporal and three spatial dimensions. If this is correct, then to find a scheme in which material bodies were not basic particulars would be, at least, to find a scheme which was not of this kind. This reflection suggests more than one direction in which we might look. But, in particular, it suggests one very simple, though very radical, direction. We might ask, 'Could there be a scheme, providing for a system of objective particulars, which was wholly non-spatial?' This question reminds us once more of Kant. He spoke of two forms of sensibility or intuition, namely Space and Time. Time was the form of all sensible representations, Space only of some. He regarded it as a matter not of absolute necessity, but of very fundamental fact, that we had both, and only, these two forms of sensible intuition. He would probably think it tautological to say that we cannot *imagine* ourselves possessing other forms, though we could, in some sense, conceive of its possibility. I think he would probably also say that it was in some sense impossible to *imagine* ourselves *not* possessing both these forms. 'We cannot represent to ourselves the absence of space.' [1] I do not know quite

[1] *Critique of Pure Reason*, B38.

what this means. But whether or not we can 'represent to ourselves the absence of space', I do not see why we should not confine ourselves imaginatively to what is not spatial; and then see what conceptual consequences follow. Kant held that all representations were in inner sense, of which Time was the form; but only some representations were representations of outer sense, of which Space was the form. I suggest that we inquire whether there could be a scheme which provided for objective particulars, while dispensing with outer sense and all its representations. I suggest we explore the No-Space world. It will at least be a world without bodies.

[2] Now, as regards what follows, I must sound a note at once apologetic and cautionary. I shall constantly raise questions in a form in which they may well seem quite unanswerable: especially in the form of asking whether a being whose experience was in certain ways quite unlike ours could or could not have a conceptual scheme with certain general features; or whether a being whose conceptual scheme was in certain general ways quite unlike ours could or could not nevertheless reproduce in it certain features of ours. So presented, these questions may well seem at worst nonsensical, and at best to admit of only the most wildly speculative answers. But, in general, this form of question may be seen as simply a convenient, if perhaps over-dramatic, way of raising more evidently legitimate types of question: questions not about hypothetical beings at all, but rather, for instance, about the extent to which, and the ways in which, *we* might find it possible to reinterpret, within a part of our experience, some of the most general conceptual elements in our handling of experience as a whole. How far can we map the structure of this whole within a part of itself? Or what structural analogies can we find between some part and the whole of which it is a part? Or, again, how far can we break down the connexions of certain central concepts with each other and with certain types of experience without seeming to destroy those concepts altogether? Questions which belong to these general kinds are no doubt in some sense idle; but appear to be discussable.

In the ensuing discussion the emphasis will be found to shift in a certain way. For the selected model of a No-Space world something that was taken for granted in the first chapter comes into question: viz. that distinction made by the user of a conceptual scheme between himself and his own states on the one hand, and other particulars of which he has knowledge or experience on the other. The question, whether the conditions of this distinction could be satisfied in the supposed world, will be found to turn in part, but by no means exclusively, on another question, which echoes some themes of the first chapter, viz. the question, whether the conditions of reidentifiability of particulars could be satisfied in the supposed world. But it is not settled by the discussion of this question; and the further attempt to settle it leads us back, in the third chapter, to a direct consideration of our ordinary world, and of the ways in which the conditions of the distinction in question are in fact satisfied there.

So the present chapter acts in part as a bridge between the first and the third. Some illumination of general features of our actual thinking may perhaps be hoped for by thus inquiring how far such features can be reproduced in phenomenal terms of an artificial simplicity, by observing, so to speak, in what ways we have to shape and model our impoverished material in order to reproduce the structure we know.

[3] What does the suggestion that we explore the No-Space world amount to? What is it to imagine ourselves dispensing with outer sense? Traditionally, five senses are recognized as distinguishable modes of perception of public objects. Of these, taste and smell are strikingly more trivial than the others, and taste in addition has a logical complexity which makes it difficult to handle. It does not seem that to suppose our experience free of gustatory or olfactory elements would, by itself, be to invite a significant conceptual revolution. (One does not *see* the world differently if one has a cold.) Let us nevertheless, for simplicity's sake, suppose them eliminated. This leaves us with sight, hearing and touch. Which of these shall we have to suppose eliminated in order to eliminate outer sense? It might at first seem that we

should have to eliminate them all—which would bring the inquiry rather swiftly to an end. For while we can certainly discover
the spatial characteristics and relations of things by sight and
touch, it seems no less certain that we can also discover at least
some spatial features of some things by hearing. Sounds seem to
come from the right or the left, from above or below, to come
nearer and recede. If sounds, the proper objects of hearing,
possess in their own right these direction-and-distance characteristics, does it not follow that we shall have failed to eliminate
spatial characteristics and concepts even if we adopt the radical
hypothesis of a purely auditory experience? This conclusion, however, would, I think, be a mistake, and a fairly obvious one. The
fact is that where sense-experience is not only auditory in character, but also at least tactual and kinaesthetic as well—or, as it is
in most cases, tactual and kinaesthetic and visual as well—we
can then sometimes assign spatial predicates on the strength of
hearing alone. But from this fact it does not follow that where
experience is supposed to be exclusively auditory in character,
there would be any place for spatial concepts at all. I think it is
obvious that there would be no such place. The only objects of
sense-experience would be sounds. Sounds of course have temporal relations to each other, and may vary in character in certain
ways: in loudness, pitch and timbre. But they have no intrinsic
spatial characteristics: such expressions as 'to the left of', 'spatially
above', 'nearer', 'farther' have no intrinsically auditory significance. Let me briefly contrast hearing in this respect with sight
and touch. Evidently the visual field is necessarily extended at any
moment, and its parts must exhibit spatial relations to each other.
The case of touch is less obvious: it is not, e.g., clear what one
would mean by a 'tactual field'. But if we combined tactual with
kinaesthetic sensations, then at least it is clear that we have the
materials for spatial concepts; of the congenitally blind one does
not wonder whether they really know what it means to say that one
thing is above another, or farther from another than a third thing
is. Of a purely visual, or a purely tactual-kinaesthetic, concept of
space, one might feel that it was impoverished compared with
our own, but not that it was an impossibility. A purely auditory

concept of space, on the other hand, is an impossibility. The fact that, with the variegated types of sense-experience which we in fact have, we can, as we say, 'on the strength of hearing alone' assign directions and distances to sounds, and things that emit or cause them, counts against this not at all. For this fact is sufficiently explained by the existence of correlations between the variations of which sound is intrinsically capable and other non-auditory features·of our sense-experience. I do not mean that we first note these correlations and then make inductive inferences on the basis of such observation; nor even that we could on reflection give them as reasons for the assignments of distance and direction that we in fact make on the strength of hearing alone. To maintain either of these views would be to deny the full force of the words 'on the strength of hearing alone'; and I am quite prepared to concede their full force. I am simply maintaining the less extreme because less specific thesis that the *de facto* existence of such cor- relations is a necessary condition of our assigning distances and directions as we do on the strength of hearing alone. Whatever it is about the sounds that makes us say such things as 'It sounds as if it comes from somewhere on the left', this would not alone (i.e. if there were no visual, kinaesthetic, tactual phenomena) suffice to generate spatial concepts. I shall take it as not needing further argument that in supposing experience to be purely auditory, we are supposing a No-Space world. I am not, of course, contending that the idea of a purely auditory world is the only possible model for a No-Space world. There are other and more complex possibilities. I select the idea of a purely auditory uni- verse as one that is relatively simple to handle, and yet has a cer- tain formal richness.

The question we are to consider, then, is this: Could a being whose experience was purely auditory have a conceptual scheme which provided for objective particulars? The question is complex and breaks down into a number of others. Consider first the qualification 'objective' in the phrase 'objective particulars'. It might seem at first that this qualification raises no special diffi- culties. For, as things are at present, different people may cer- tainly be said to hear one and the same particular sound—not just sounds of the same type, instances of the same kind of sound, but exactly the same particular sound. Sounds may be, and most of those that we hear are, public objects. If, when we talk of a sound, we mean a particular sound, then we may, and usually do, mean an objective particular, a public object. So it might seem obvious that if, in a purely auditory world, we could operate with the concept of a particular at all, then we could operate with the concept of an objective particular. But this is in fact not at all clear. For to call a sound a public object, to say that different people may hear one and the same particular sound, seems to mean at least this: that different normal hearers may roughly simultaneously have roughly similar auditory experiences, or auditory experiences systematically related in statable ways, in roughly the same particular surroundings; and perhaps one should add that, in order to fulfil on any particular occasion the requirement that they are hearing the same sound, the causal source of the relevant auditory experiences should be the same for all of them. We may imagine, for example, that the same piece of music is being simultaneously played in two different concert-halls. We may imagine a moment at which a certain chord is played. Then two different normal hearers, each in a different hall, have, roughly simultaneously, roughly similar auditory experiences. But though in one sense the sound they hear is the same—it is the *same chord* for each— in another sense, the sense we are concerned with, the sounds they hear are distinct. They hear different sound-particulars: for the condition of particular-identity of surroundings, and the condition of particular-identity of causal sources, are not fulfilled. Two listeners in the same concert-hall, however, hear the same sound particulars as each other, as well as hearing the same chord, i.e. the same sound-universal; for in their case the conditions of particular-identity of setting and source are both fulfilled.

I do not want to say that the stated conditions for the identity of sound-particulars heard by different listeners are exhaustive. The case of sounds transmitted through various artificial media, for example, suggests other quite interesting possibilities of different criteria for the identity of sound-particulars. I just choose the conditions stated as being the most obvious set, without ruling out the possibility of others.

Of the stated conditions, the last, concerning causation, may perhaps be neglected for our purely auditory universe. The others present an acute problem. For, it seems, to give the idea of publicity of sounds a meaning in the purely auditory world, we must give meaning, in auditory terms alone, to the idea of other people and to the idea of their being in identical particular surroundings. But to *assume* that we could give a sense to the idea of identity of particular surroundings in terms of sound alone would be to beg the question. For the sounds in terms of which we were to give sense to this idea would themselves have to be public sounds; otherwise they could not provide particular-identity of surroundings for the different enjoyers of auditory experiences. But it is precisely the possibility of public sounds, in a purely auditory world, that is in question. So we cannot assume a favourable issue here. Indeed the prospect for a favourable issue begins to look unhopeful.

We might, however, raise our hopes by reducing, or trying to reduce, our demands. I glossed 'objective' particulars just now as 'public' particulars, and that involved the ideas of other enjoyers of experience and of shared surroundings. For this gloss there is, as I have already hinted, much to be said, if a certain general line of thought is correct. A summary, which I hope is not too much of a parody, of this line of thought, might run as follows. We could not talk to one another about the private if we could not talk to one another about the public. We could not talk unless we could talk to one another. Above, at any rate, a very rudimentary level, the limits of thought are the limits of language; or 'what we can't say we can't think'. Finally, there is no experience worth the name, certainly no knowledge, without concepts, without thoughts. Applied to the present question, this line of thought yields the conclusion that the whole idea of a purely auditory experience is empty, unless a sense can be given in purely auditory terms to the idea of public auditory objects which are also topics of discourse between beings who hear them.

I shall not, for the moment, try to pronounce on the merits

of this line of thought. For I earlier introduced the word 'objective' by giving it what is certainly a more traditional, and possibly a less exacting, sense, in terms of the distinction between oneself and one's states on the one hand, and anything on the other hand which is not either oneself or a state of oneself, but of which one has, or might have, experience. So I shall provisionally interpret the question, 'Can the conditions of knowledge of objective particulars be fulfilled for a purely auditory experience?' as meaning: 'Could a being whose experience was purely auditory, make use of the distinction between himself and his states on the one hand, and something not himself, or a state of himself, of which he had experience on the other?' This question, for the sake of a convenient phrase, I shall re-express as follows: 'Can the conditions of a non-solipsistic consciousness be fulfilled for a purely auditory experience?' That is to say, I shall mean by a non-solipsistic consciousness, the consciousness of a being who has a use for the distinction between himself and his states on the one hand, and something not himself or a state of himself, of which he has experience, on the other; and by a solipsistic consciousness, the consciousness of a being who has no use for this distinction.

This question, however, is not the only one we have to answer. There is another which turns out to be closely connected with it, viz.: Can we, in purely auditory terms, find room for the concept of identifiable particulars at all? Would there, in the purely auditory world, be a distinction between qualitative and numerical identity? This seems at first to present no particular difficulty. Could not audible continuity or discontinuity be used as a criterion for distinguishing sounds as particulars? That is to say, suppose, first, that during a certain temporal slice of experience, sound of a certain loudness, timbre and pitch began to be heard, continued without interruption and then stopped. Suppose, second, that during such a slice of experience such sound began, stopped, began again and stopped again. In the first case the number of sounds as particulars would be one; in the second case the number of sounds as particulars would be two. In both cases there would be just one and the same sound in the qualitative sense of 'same', i.e. just one sound as universal. Even when sound of some kind is continuous, as, usually, when music is being heard, we can distinguish qualitatively different sounds within the general sound, and hence, by the criterion of interruption, different particular instances of the same qualitative sound. Also, of course, we can, perhaps more easily, distinguish more complex sound-particulars, composed of sets or sequences of the sound-particulars distinguished by the above method. This seem to show that there could be identifiable, in the sense of *distinguishable*, sound-particulars.

But could there be identifiable, in the sense of *re*identifiable, sound-particulars? Unless this question is answered affirmatively, the concept of a particular with which we are working will be, so to speak, a very thin one. Now, of course, sounds could be reidentified, if 'sounds' is taken in the sense of universals or types. A note could be reidentified, or a sequence of notes or a sonata. But what sense could be given to the idea of identifying a *particular* sound as the same again after an interval during which it is not heard? We cannot turn to the particular-identity of the non-auditory setting of the sounds, to justify our saying, e.g. 'This is the continuation of that same *particular* sequence of sounds which was heard a while ago'; for, by hypothesis, the sounds have no setting but other sounds. The difficulty can be emphasized by considering what might appear to be a possible exception to it. Suppose a sound-sequence of some complexity—and here I am speaking of a type or universal—which has a certain, say, musical unity, and to which I shall refer as M. Suppose within it four 'movements' are distinguishable, A, B, C, D. Suppose an instance of A is heard and then, after a suitable interval, an instance of D is heard. The interval, however, is not occupied by B and C, but by other sounds. May we not suppose that, in this case, when the instance of D is heard, it is identified as a part of the same particular M as that of which the previously heard instance of A was a part; that is, that when D is heard, we have a case of the same particular M, reappearing, so to speak, after an interval; and that thus we have here a case not just of reidentifying a universal, but of identifying a particular as the same again? But, of course, for this suggestion to be of any use, we have to suppose that we have some criterion for distinguishing the case of a reappearance of the same particular M from the case where we just have an instance of A followed after an interval by an instance of D, and where the two are *not* parts of one and the same particular M. This is reminiscent of the case of the two concert-halls, with the same (type or universal) piece of music being played in both simultaneously. Here the criteria for distinguishing between a later part of the same *particular* piece and an instance of a later part of the same *universal* piece were evident enough; they turned, once more, on the non-auditory setting. But in the purely auditory world these criteria are not available; and if *no* criteria are available for making the distinction, then no sense has been given to the distinction and hence no meaning to the idea of reidentification of auditory particulars. The case is perhaps not quite so poor as this suggests. For a criterion of sorts might be suggested. It might be suggested that where the instances of A and D were fairly soft sounds, while the sounds that filled the interval between them were very loud sounds, then we had a clear case of A and D being parts of the same particular; and when this condition was clearly not fulfilled, then we had a clear case of their not being parts of the same particular. But the reasons for such appeal as this suggestion might have for *us* are only too evident. It helps us to think of unheard parts of one particular M being drowned or submerged by the stridencies which intervene between the instance of A and the instance of D; and thus to think that they were there to be heard, would have been heard but for these stridencies. But now we have only to think of the reasons, the evidence, we have for thinking something like this in real life—the visible but inaudible scrapings of the street violinist as the street band marches by—and then we lose interest in the suggested criterion for the case of the purely auditory world.

Nevertheless certain important and interrelated points emerge from these considerations.

The first is the connexion between the idea of a reidentifiable particular, and the idea of the continued existence of a particular while it is not being observed. This connexion conferred whatever appeal it possessed upon the criterion of reidentification of sound-particulars which I have just considered and dismissed. It was not just that the intervening sounds were loud; it was that they were loud enough for us, from within our familiar world, to think of them as *drowning* the unheard sounds which linked the earlier and the later parts of the reidentified particular. But this thought came too evidently from our familiar world, and has no relevance, or has not yet been given any relevance, to our imaginary world. We have yet to show that sense can be given to the idea of continued existence of unobserved particulars in this imaginary world.

This first point leads directly on to the second. The question: Could there be reidentifiable sound-particulars in the purely auditory world? was raised as if it were a further question which had to be considered, over and above another question, viz.: Could a being whose experience was purely auditory make sense of the distinction between himself and his states on the one hand, and something not himself or a state of himself, on the other? But now it seems that these questions are not independent. An affirmative answer to the second entails an affirmative answer to the first. For to have a conceptual scheme in which a distinction is made between oneself or one's states and auditory items which are not states of oneself, is to have a conceptual scheme in which the existence of auditory items is *logically* independent of the existence of one's states or of oneself. Thus it is to have a conceptual scheme in which it is logically possible that such items should exist whether or not they were being observed, and hence should continue to exist through an interval during which they were not being observed. So it seems that it must be the case that there could be reidentifiable particulars in a purely auditory world if the conditions of a non-solipsistic consciousness could be fulfilled for such a world. Now it might further be said that it makes no sense to say that there logically could be reidentifiable particulars in a purely auditory world, unless criteria for reidentification can be framed or devised in purely auditory terms. And if this is correct, as it seems to be, we have the conclusion that the conditions of a non-solipsistic consciousness can be satisfied in such a world only if we can describe in purely auditory terms criteria for reidentification of sound-particulars.

Does the entailment hold in the other direction too? That is, does the existence of the idea of a reidentifiable particular, and hence the idea of a particular which continues to exist while not being observed, entail the existence of the distinction between oneself and states of oneself on the one hand and what is not oneself or a state of oneself on the other? The answer to this question I shall postpone for the moment. Later, I shall suggest a technique for answering it and all similar questions, i.e. all questions about whether something is or is not a sufficient condition for the existence of a non-solipsistic consciousness. Let us merely notice in passing, and dismiss, one temptation to give an affirmative answer to this question on mistaken grounds. One might be tempted to answer affirmatively simply as a result of confusing two different ideas: that of the being with the solipsistic consciousness and that of the philosophical solipsist. But the being with the solipsistic consciousness, whom, for short, I might call the true solipsist, would not think of himself as such; nor as a philosophical solipsist; nor as anything else. He certainly would not think that everything particular which existed was himself or a state of himself. One who claimed to think this might indeed have some difficulty, not necessarily insuperable, in reconciling his doctrine with the idea of a number of particulars which continue to exist unobserved. But the true solipsist is rather one who simply has *no use* for the distinction between himself and what is not himself. It remains to be seen whether a conceptual scheme which allows for reidentifiable particulars must necessarily also make room for this distinction.

Meanwhile let us pass to the next point. Let us inquire how, in our familiar world, the requirements just established are fulfilled. That is to say, with what feature or complex of features of our familiar world is the idea of reidentifiable particulars, existing continuously while unobserved, most intimately, naturally and generally connected? I think the answer is simple and obvious, though the detailed description of the feature in question would be of great complexity. Roughly speaking, the crucial idea for us

is that of a spatial system of objects, through which oneself,
another object, moves, but which extends beyond the limits of
one's observation at any moment, or, more generally, is never
fully revealed to observation at any moment. This idea obviously
supplies the necessary non-temporal dimension for, so to speak,
the housing of the objects which are held to exist continuously,
though unobserved; it supplies this dimension for objects which
are not themselves intrinsically spatial, such as sounds, as well as
for objects that are. Thus the most familiar and easily understood
sense in which there exist sounds that I do not now hear is this:
that there are *places* at which those sounds are audible, but these
are places at which I am not now stationed. There are of course
other senses which can be given to the idea of unheard sounds.
But many of them turn on correlations between auditory phenomena and phenomena of other kinds (e.g., non-auditory phenomena causally associated with auditory phenomena) and on the
extrapolation of these correlations beyond the general limits of
human auditory discrimination. So these do not help us here.
Alternatively they turn on such an idea as that of failing sensory
powers. But why do we think of our powers failing rather than
the world fading? This choice cannot be used to explain a conception it presupposes.

Let us return, then, to the most familiar sense in which we
think of sounds which exist now but are unheard by us, and to
its relation to the idea of places. We have already seen that the
idea of place, and with it that of a spatial system of objects, cannot
be given a meaning in purely auditory terms. Yet it seems we
must have a dimension other than the temporal in which to house
the at present unheard sensory particulars, if we are to give a
satisfactory sense to the idea of their existing now unperceived,
and hence to the idea of reidentification of particulars in a purely
auditory world and hence, perhaps, to the idea of a non-solipsistic
consciousness in a purely auditory world. So our question becomes this. Since we cannot give any literal, even though impoverished, interpretation of spatial concepts in purely auditory
terms, can we at any rate find some sort of variable feature in auditory items which will provide what we might call *an analogy of*

74

Space? And of course—whatever this turns out to mean—a sufficiently close analogy for our purposes?

But how close is sufficiently close? We want the analogy of space to provide for the unperceived, but existing, particular. Roughly, we want it to provide for something like the idea of absence and presence—but not just of absence and presence in the most utterly general sense these words could bear, but absence or presence in a sense which would allow us to speak of something being to a greater or lesser degree removed from, or separated from, the point at which we are. In other words, we want an analogy of distance—of *nearer to* and *further away from*—for only, at least, under this condition would we have anything like the idea of a dimension other than the temporal in which unperceived particulars could be thought of as simultaneously existing in *some kind of systematic relation to each other*, and to perceived particulars. Of course the spatial phenomena with which we are seeking an analogy are infinitely more complex than this. Remote particulars are located, not just in one dimension of distance, but in three; particulars may be unperceived, not because they are too remote, but because they are hidden by others or because, of all the directions we may be looking or feeling in, we are not looking or feeling in theirs. But we may well despair of reproducing analogies for all this complexity in auditory terms. Looking for the simplest feature for which we might find an analogy, it seems that this of distance is the easiest. For the loomings-up and dwindlings and obliterations of perspective we might find an analogy.

It is customary to distinguish three dimensions of sound: timbre, pitch and loudness. Timbre we may discount; for differences of timbre do not seem to admit of any systematic serial ordering. Pitch seems much more hopeful. Indeed, we customarily speak of differences of pitch on analogy with a spatial dimension—we speak of higher and lower notes—and moreover we customarily represent these differences by spatial intervals. If the analogy holds in one direction, may it not also hold in the other? Suppose we imagine that the purely auditory experience we are considering has the following characteristics. A sound of a certain distinctive timbre is heard continuously, at a constant loudness, though with varying pitch. This sound is unique in its continuity. We may call it the master-sound. It may be compared with the persistent whistle, of varying pitch, which, in a wireless set in need of repair, sometimes accompanies the programmes we listen to. In addition to the master-sound, other sounds or sequences of sound of various degrees of complexity are heard. Some of these sequences may be supposed to have the kind of unity which pieces of music have. They recur and are recognized. They are highly complex universals with particular instances. One can imagine that transitions up and down the pitch-range of the master-sound sometimes occur quite fast; while at other times the pitch of the master-sound remains invariant for quite considerable periods. One may imagine, finally, that variations in the pitch of the master-sound are correlated with variations in the other sounds that are heard, in a way very similar to that in which variations in the position of the tuning-knob of a wireless set are correlated with variations in the sounds that one hears on the wireless. Thus suppose a particular instance of one of the unitary sound-sequences I mentioned is being heard. A gradual change in the pitch of the master-sound is accompanied by a gradual decrease, or a gradual increase followed by a gradual decrease, in the loudness of the unitary sound-sequence in question until it is no longer heard. If the gradual change in pitch of the master-sound continues in the same direction, a different unitary sound-sequence is heard with gradually increasing loudness. If it is reversed, the whole accompanying process is reversed too. Here the comparison is with gradually tuning-out one station and tuning-in another—and back again for the reversal. Only of course instead of a tuning-knob being gradually turned, we have the gradual alteration in the pitch of the master-sound. If, on the other hand, the pitch of the master-sound changes very rapidly, the change is accompanied by that kind of cacophonous succession which one gets by twirling the tuning-knob around at top speed. And if the pitch of the master-sound remains constant, then one recognizable unitary sequence of sounds duly completes itself and another begins.

In these circumstances, one might feel, the analogy would be close enough to yield the picture of a sound-world which allowed for reidentifiable particulars. The pitch of the master-sound at any moment would determine the auditory analogue of position in the sound-world at that moment. The sound-world is then conceived of as containing many particulars, unheard at any moment, but audible at other positions than the one occupied at that moment. There is a clear criterion for distinguishing the case of hearing a later part of a *particular* unitary sound-sequence of which the earlier part has been heard previously, from the more general case of merely hearing the later part of the same *universal* unitary sound-sequence of which an earlier part has been heard previously. Suppose for instance a certain unitary sound-sequence, to which we may refer as M (M being the name of a universal) is being heard at a certain pitch-level of the master-sound—say at level L. Then suppose the master-sound changes fairly rapidly in pitch to level L' and back again to L; and then M is heard once more, a few bars having been missed. Then the sound-particular now being heard is reidentified as the same particular instance of M. If, during the same time, the master-sound had changed not from L to L' and back again to L, but from L to L", then, even though M may be heard once more, a few bars having been missed, it is not the same particular instance of M that is now heard, but a different instance. Once again, the wireless supplies the easy comparison: one can tune out a station, and tune it in again while the same piece is being played; or, instead, one might tune in a different station where the same piece is being simultaneously played by a different orchestra.

But, of course, though the analogy, and hence the resultant conceptual scheme which allows for re-identifiable particulars, may be fairly persuasive, fairly attractive, it is not compelling. We could adopt a different scheme of description which allowed for reidentifiable universals but not for reidentifiable particulars. What we cannot consistently do is, as it were, to appear to accept a scheme which allows for reidentification of sound-particulars and then to say that, of course, particular-identity would always be in doubt; that there would be no possibility of *certainty* about

it. This would be the position of philosophical scepticism about
the identity of sound particulars, and ultimately, about the independent reality of the sound-world. It would involve that
kind of inconsistency which I commented on earlier—the
simultaneous acceptance and rejection of a certain conceptual
scheme for reality. Alternatively it could be construed as a kind of
muddled advocacy of a different scheme: in this case, of one which
either did not allow for reidentification of particulars, or which
envisaged more stringent or more complex criteria of reidentification than those which I have described.

Let us briefly pause to compare the situation in the auditory,
and in the ordinary, worlds. In describing a possible scheme which
allows for reidentification of sound-particulars in the auditory
world, I have, obviously, described a scheme which allows for
their reidentification without any kind of reference to particulars
of any other type than their own; for no other type of particular
comes into consideration. In the auditory and in the ordinary
worlds alike, the possibility of reidentification of particulars
depends on the idea of a dimension in which unperceived particulars may be housed, which they may be thought of as occupying. But, for our ordinary world, the word 'housed' is barely a
metaphor and the word 'occupying' is not a metaphor at all. For
in our ordinary world that 'dimension' is, precisely, three-
dimensional space. Now it is the general character of this dimension which, for *any* conceptual scheme, determines the types of
particular which can be reidentified without dependence on particulars of other types. So, in our actual scheme, the particulars
which can be thus independently reidentified must at least be
intrinsically spatial things, occupiers of space; and sound-
particulars, not being of this character, are not independently
reidentifiable. But in the imagined scheme we are now considering, the dimension in question is supplied by variations in
purely auditory phenomena. The dimension is, so to speak, the
pitch-range of the master-sound. So independently reidentifiable particulars may, in this scheme, themselves be purely
auditory.

To return to the auditory analogy of distance, whereby we

tried to allow for a conceptual scheme providing for reidentifiable particulars. I said that the analogy might be fairly persuasive, but was not compelling. Some might find it less persuasive than others. I can imagine one who is not disposed to be at all persuaded by it arguing like this: You have referred to the three characteristic kinds of variation of which sound is capable, viz. loudness, pitch and timbre, and have tried to make them, and in particular pitch, yield between them the analogue of spatial distance. A quite essential element in the construction is the device of the master-sound; whatever was accomplished, was done with the aid of this trick. If we now compare sound with colour—something intrinsically spatial—we see how weak the analogy really is. For colour, like sound, exhibits three characteristic modes of variation—brightness, saturation and hue—of which the first two, like pitch and loudness, admit of serial ordering in respect of degree, while the last, perhaps, like timbre, does not. In the case of a visual scene, we may be presented with coloured areas, exhibiting between them variations of all three kinds simultaneously; and so far there *is* an analogy with sound. But when we are presented with such a scene, we are also and necessarily presented with something which simultaneously exhibits a further principle of ordering of its parts. Suppose we break up the scene, as it were, into its uniform elements, i.e. into elements no one of which at any moment exhibits variations, but each of which is of a definite hue, brightness and saturation. Then these simultaneously presented elements, besides being related to one another in these three respects, are also simultaneously presented as being related in another respect: viz. in a respect which leads us to characterize one as being *above* or *below* or to the *left* or to the *right* of another, or, if there is difficulty over these words at the phenomenal level, which at any rate leads us to characterize one as being further away from another in a certain direction than a third is &c. The point is that relations between elements in respect of the spatial dimension are presented simultaneously, all at once,—we need no changing master-patch to give us the idea of this dimension. But relations between elements in respect of the auditory analogue of the spatial dimension cannot be presented simultaneously, all at

once. They turn essentially on change. Roughly, two visual elements can be seen all at once as at a certain visual distance from one
another; whereas two auditory elements cannot be heard all at
once as at a certain auditory distance from one another. Or, to put
it in another way: the momentary states of the colour-patches of
the visual scene visibly exhibit spatial relations to each other at a
moment; whereas the momentary states of the sound-patches of
the auditory scene do not audibly exhibit the auditory analogue
of spatial relations to each other at a moment. Not in their momentary states, but only in swelling or fading as the pitch of the
master-sound varies in time, could the particular sounds exhibit
such relations. But surely the idea of simultaneous existence of the
perceived and the unperceived is linked with this idea of the
simultaneous presentation of elements, each of a definite character, but simultaneously exhibiting a system of relations over and
above those which arise from the definite character of each.
Surely the former idea is necessarily an extension of the latter, is
just the idea of such a system of relations extending beyond the
limits of observation. So the objector might argue. (So arguing I
think he would, at least in the last sentence, over-reach himself,
by ignoring the importance, for his own doctrine about the extension of the idea of such a system of relations, of the notion of
movement of the scene and the observer relative to each other, and
hence of change. But he might meet this point by saying that he
was stating only a necessary and not a sufficient condition of such
an extension.) If the objector argues so, there is a sense in which
we cannot meet his objections. That is to say, though we might
complicate our auditory world-picture in many ways, we cannot,
while keeping it an auditory picture, incorporate just that feature
which he seems to be insisting on as a condition of regarding the
analogy of space as close enough to satisfy him. Indeed, nothing
but a system of spatial relations, and possibly nothing but spatial
relations as visually perceived, can be conceived by us which
would satisfy this condition. If this is so, then the objector is not
simply criticizing our method of analogy-seeking, but rejecting
the whole idea of any such analogy. This might be a reasonable thing to do if the ground for doing so were that there just

are no formal parallels worth considering between the sensibly spatial and the auditory. But this view would be simply false. One should remember here not only the spatial analogies implicit in our ordinary talk about sounds, but the persistent and in no way irrational tendency of critics of music and the plastic arts to discuss the formal properties of the works they are criticizing in terms which, in their literal application, belong to each other's vocabularies.

The necessary incompleteness of the analogy, then, is not a decisive objection. There remains a doubt about the *meaning* of saying that we have here a possible reinterpretation of the idea of an unperceived and hence of a reidentifiable particular. What are the tests for whether it is a possible reinterpretation or not? I do not think there is any test beyond what we find it satisfactory to say. One can certainly influence the finding by pointing to respects in which the parallel holds or fails to hold—and can also suggest improvements. But no more.

The question, whether we could find room in the purely auditory world for the concept of a reidentifiable particular, was not, however, the only question we set ourselves. There was also the question, whether the conditions of a non-solipsistic consciousness could be satisfied in such a world. An affirmative answer to the first question appeared as at least a necessary condition of an affirmative answer to the second. Whether it was also a sufficient condition, was a point I left undecided. It might appear obvious that it was a sufficient condition. For the concept of a reidentifiable particular was held to entail that of a particular's existing while unobserved and hence, in general, the distinction between being observed and being unobserved, or at least some closely analogous distinction. But how can this distinction exist without the idea of an observer? How, therefore, can the being with the auditory experience make use of any such distinction without the idea of *himself* as an observer? Moreover, when we were preparing to construct our auditory analogue of space, we spoke of ordinary observers as thinking of *themselves* as being at different places at different times. Must not the being with the purely auditory experience similarly think of *himself* as 'at' different places in auditory space? This reasoning is attractive.[1] But, since the entire object of this speculation is to put the maximum pressure on the normal associations of our concepts, it will be consonant with our general programme to resist this attractive reasoning if we can. I think we can resist it. The question essentially is whether a distinction parallel in other respects to the ordinary 'observed–unobserved' distinction can be drawn without the need for any idea such as we ordinarily express by the first person singular pronoun and associated forms. Why should it not be? Let us consider a possible technique for answering such questions. We are to imagine ourselves, our ordinary selves, with all our ordinary conceptual and linguistic apparatus at our disposal, writing reports on a special part of our experience. The part is defined by the description given of the purely auditory world. But the writing of our reports is governed by an important rule. The rule is that we are not, in writing our reports, to make use of any concepts which derive their function from the fact that this special part of our experience is in fact integrated with our experience at large, forms part of a wider whole. All the concepts or expressions we employ must find their justification *within* the part of our experience in question. They must all be concepts or expressions of which we find the use essential or convenient merely in order to do justice to the internal features of this part of our experience. For example, supposing that the description of the purely auditory world is as we have so far given it, then if, in writing our reports, we write the sentence 'I heard M after N at L' (for the purposes of this example it does not matter whether 'M' and 'N' are names of universals or not), we should have broken this important rule. The verb 'to hear' is one we must not use. It is redundant, since the description of the universe of discourse in question specifies that it contains no sensory items other than sounds. And as far as the description so far given is concerned, the personal pronoun appears equally superfluous. The sentence in the report should read simply 'N was observed at L followed

---

[1] We are reminded here of Kant's doctrine of the analytic unity of apperception, of the 'I think' which accompanies all 'my' perceptions. But Kant was very careful to empty this 'I' of referential, identificatory force. He could equally well have left it out altogether, or substituted an impersonal 'it is thought'. See Chapter 3, pp. 102–3.

by M'. That is to say, for the description of the universe so far given, we do not appear, if we follow the rule, to need to make any use of the distinction between oneself and what is not oneself.

It might appear that we should introduce the need for this distinction by modifying the description in the following way. So far we have supposed that movement up and down the range of the master-sound merely occurs. We have introduced no distinction between moving and being moved. Suppose we introduce such a distinction. Suppose, that is to say, that the being whose experience is purely auditory sometimes just suffers change of position —change just occurs—and sometimes initiates it. (If anyone asks how this is to be understood in terms of movement along an auditory scale, I refer him to differences in the way he anticipates what he is going to do and what is going to happen to him— differences in the kinds of *knowledge* he has of these two things.) It might seem that the introduction into our universe of this distinction—the distinction, roughly speaking, between changes that are brought about, and changes that merely occur—would necessitate the introduction of the idea of that which brings about the deliberate changes, and hence of the idea of the distinction between oneself and what is not oneself. Surely, one might say, in a Locke-like phrase, the idea of oneself as an agent forms a great part of the idea of oneself. Indeed, I think that it does so, and perhaps a necessary part. Yet the suggested modification of the imagined universe may be insufficient to necessitate the problematic distinction. Suppose our 'reports' are to be composed with an eye to the future as well as the present and the past. Then we shall need some way, in playing our report-writing game for the revised universe, of marking the distinction between what, in terms of our ordinary conceptual apparatus, we might call announcements of intention on the one hand, and predictions on the other. But this distinction can very well be marked without the use of the first person. We shall need something, perhaps, like a grammatical distinction of voice (such a movement will occur; such a movement will be executed). But there is so far no reason why we should admit also the grammatical distinction of person. We need to distinguish what happens by agency from what does not. But we do not need to distinguish agents. The same applies to the reports proper, that is, those which refer to the present and the past. The impersonal form of scientific papers, in which a distinction is nevertheless made between what was *done*, and what was found to happen, will be perfectly adequate for the reports. More exactly, we shall not need, in the language of the reports, a distinction between a personal and an impersonal form.

If, then, this modification of the purely auditory world will not, on the test suggested, suffice to yield the conditions of a non-solipsistic consciousness, what further or alternative modifications are required to do so? Would any, indeed, be sufficient? These questions start echoes of many others in philosophy which are, in one way or another, connected with the issue of solipsism. Think for a moment of our ordinary conceptions of ourselves, of the kinds of ways in which we talk of ourselves. We do not only attribute to ourselves sense-perception of things other than ourselves, and action and intention. We attribute to ourselves physical characteristics of a kind shared by other basic particulars of our actual conceptual scheme; that is to say, we have material bodies. We attribute to ourselves thoughts and feelings, and pains and pleasures, which we also attribute to others; and we think of ourselves as having transactions with others, as influencing and being influenced by them. It is not obvious which of these features are essential to a non-solipsistic scheme, and which, therefore, we must try to reproduce or find analogues for in the deliberately restricted sensory terms of the auditory world. Could we reproduce all of these features, while not extending the range of sensory experience beyond the auditory? It seems unlikely, but it is perhaps not impossible. We may, for example, suppose our inhabitant of the auditory world to be able not only to initiate movement along the pitch-range of the master-sound, but also to initiate sounds of a different character from those not initiated by him—endow him, so to speak, with a voice. The problem of equipping him with a persistent audible body may perhaps be solved by means of the master-sound itself. It is audible to him all the time, and we may suppose that for each inhabitant of the auditory world, there is a master-sound of a different timbre, though no one hears another's except when it is at the same pitch-level or nearly the same pitch-level as his own. Two hearers are then in the same auditory place. We still seem to be short of what is required; as is evident if we re-think this description in terms of the auditory experience of a single such being. What we have introduced, in introducing different 'voices', is different sets of auditory items of which it may be supposed (*a*) that they are like the sounds initiated by a single such being in a general way; (*b*) that they are unlike other sounds not initiated by him; (*c*) that every such set differs from every other in characteristic ways; (*d*) that each characteristically differing set is associated constantly with a sound which is like his own master-sound in a certain general way, and is never heard by him at a different, or at all widely different, pitch from the pitch of his master-sound at any moment. The most favourable further direction is probably that of simultaneously supposing that (*a*) of the sounds not initiated by a particular being, those which are like those so initiated may be indirectly influenced in certain standard ways by sounds which are initiated by him; and (*b*) that sounds of this character tend to stimulate (provide 'reasons' or 'motives' for) initiated changes either in position or sound-initiation. This seems to open the door to something like communication. We might even further suppose that the ability to initiate movement is a development for the single being, not an original capacity, and follows, as it were, a period of subordination to another master-sound. Evidently, in making such suppositions, one would be trying to produce as close an analogy as possible of the actual human condition. But the fantasy, besides being tedious, would be difficult, to elaborate. For it is too little clear exactly what general features we should try to reproduce, and why. It might be better at this point to abandon the auditory world, and face the issues raised by solipsism in closer connexion with the ordinary world. This task will occupy us in the next chapter.

Before leaving the auditory world altogether, I should consider a possible objection to the whole procedure of this chapter. I raised the question, whether we could make intelligible to ourselves the idea of a conceptual scheme which provided for objective particulars, but in which material bodies were not basic to particular-identification; and I selected the model of the auditory world as one from which bodies were altogether absent. I claimed that some of the conditions of such a scheme could be fulfilled in the terms of the model; but concluded that in order to satisfy ourselves that they would all be fulfilled, we should have to reproduce, in the restricted sensory terms available, more and more general features of the actual human situation. At intermediate stages in the elaboration of the model of a purely auditory experience, I spoke of it as satisfying the conditions for a conceptual scheme which included such-and-such features of our own and excluded such-and-such others. But by what right do I assume the possibility of such types of experience, and of such schemes? By what right, in particular, do I assume that there could be such a thing as a solipsistic consciousness?

The objection is one which I hope I have already anticipated. I make no such assumptions as are here questioned. My real concern is with our own scheme, and the models of this chapter are not constructed for the purpose of speculation about what would really happen in certain remote contingencies. Their object is different. They are models against which to test and strengthen our own reflective understanding of our own conceptual structure. Thus we may *suppose* such-and-such conditions; we may discuss what conceptual possibilities and requirements they can be seen by us as creating; we can argue that they fall short, in such-and-such ways, of being conditions for a conceptual structure such as our own. In all this we need no more claim to be supposing real possibilities than one who, in stricter spheres of reasoning, supposes something self-contradictory and argues validly from it. Indeed we may, if we wish, think of each stretch of argument as preceded by a saving hypothetical clause, by such words as 'If such a being, or such a type of experience, were possible. . . .'

3

PERSONS

[1] Each of us distinguishes between himself and states of himself on the one hand, and what is not himself or a state of himself on the other. What are the conditions of our making this distinction, and how are they fulfilled? In what way do we make it, and why do we make it in the way we do? It might appear a misnomer to refer to this group of questions as the issue of solipsism. But I have no qualms about appropriating the name: for that which customarily bears it is not, as we shall see, a genuine issue at all.

In the discussion of this topic, the notion of identification of particulars is once more crucial: primarily in the sense of distinguishing one particular from others in thought, or observation; but also in the original speaker–hearer senses.

Let me recall some of the steps which led to this issue of solipsism. I had argued that, in our actual conceptual scheme, material bodies, in a broad sense of the expression, were basic particulars: that is to say, that material bodies could be identified and reidentified without reference to particulars of other types or categories than their own, whereas the identification and reidentification of particulars of other categories rested ultimately on the identification of material bodies. I then inquired whether we could make intelligible to ourselves the idea of a conceptual scheme which provided for a system of objective particulars, but in which material bodies were not basic. This led to the construction of a model No-Space world, in which all the sensory items were auditory, but in which it did seem possible to find a place for the idea of a reidentifiable particular, by exploiting certain auditory analogues of the idea of spatial distance. The requirement, however, was for a scheme in which a distinction was made between oneself and what is not oneself. Though it seemed possible that the conditions for this distinction could be fulfilled in such a world, it was not obvious *how* they were to be fulfilled. The introduction of the idea of agency—of a distinction between changes which were deliberately initiated, and those that just occurred—seemed inadequate to compel this crucial distinction; and a final attempt to produce in the auditory world the conditions of a non-solipsistic consciousness seemed just an attempt to copy indiscriminately the features of our ordinary human experience in the very restricted sensory terms available. So, to try to get clearer about what in general those conditions are, it seemed advisable to inquire how in fact they are fulfilled in ordinary human experience.

But though I want to ask this question in relation to our ordinary human experience, yet there is a certain advantage in keeping before our minds the picture of the purely auditory world, the picture of an experience very much more restricted than that which we in fact have. For it may help to sharpen for us the question we are concerned with; it may help to give us a continuing sense of the strangeness of what we in fact do; and this sense of strangeness we want to keep alive in order to see that we really meet it and remove it, and do not just lose or smother it. It helps in this way. We drew a picture of a purely auditory experience, and elaborated it to a point at which it seemed that the being whose experience it was—if any such being were possible at all—might recognize sound-universals and reidentify sound-particulars and in general form for himself an idea of his auditory world; but still, it seemed, he would have no place for the idea of himself as the subject of this experience, would make no distinction between a special item in his world, namely himself, and the other items in it. Would it not seem utterly strange to suggest that he might distinguish himself as one item among others in his auditory world, that is, as a sound or sequence of sounds? For how could such a thing—a sound—be also what *had* all those experiences? Yet to have the idea of himself, must he not have the idea of the subject of the experiences, of that which has them? So it might

begin to look impossible that he should have the idea of himself—
or at any rate the right idea. For to have the idea at all, it seems
that it must be an idea of some particular thing of which he has
experience, and which is set over against or contrasted with other
things of which he has experience, but which are not himself. But
if it is just an item *within* his experience of which he has this idea,
how can it be the idea of that which *has* all of his experiences?
And now we seem to have come upon a form of problem which is
completely general, which applies as much to the ordinary as to
the auditory world. It must, it seems, be soluble for the ordinary
world.

Let us now think of some of the ways in which we ordinarily
talk of ourselves, of some of the things which we do ordinarily
ascribe to ourselves. They are of many kinds. We ascribe to ourselves *actions* and *intentions* (I am doing, did, shall do this); *sensations* (I am warm, in pain); *thoughts* and *feelings* (I think, wonder,
want this, am angry, disappointed, contented); *perceptions* and
memories (I see this, hear the other, remember that). We ascribe to
ourselves, in two senses, position: *location* (I am on the sofa) and
attitude (I am lying down). And of course we ascribe to ourselves
not only temporary conditions, states, situations like these, but
also relatively enduring characteristics, including physical characteristics like height, colouring, shape and weight. That is to
say, among the things we ascribe to ourselves are things of a kind
that we also ascribe to material bodies to which we should not
dream of ascribing others of the things that we ascribe to ourselves. Now there seems nothing needing explanation in the fact
that the particular height, colouring, physical position which we
ascribe to ourselves should be ascribed to *something or other*; for
that which one calls one's body is, at least, a body, a material
thing. It can be picked out from others, identified by ordinary
physical criteria and described in ordinary physical terms. But, so
long as we keep that for the present indispensable sense of strangeness, it can and must seem to need explanation that one's states of
consciousness, one's thoughts and sensations, are ascribed *to the
very same thing* to which these physical characteristics, this physical
situation, is ascribed. That is, we have not only the question:

Why are one's states of consciousness ascribed to anything at all? We have also the question: *Why are they ascribed to the very same thing as certain corporeal characteristics, a certain physical situation, &c.?* It is not to be supposed that the answers to these questions will be independent of one another.

[2] It might indeed be thought that an answer to both of them could be found in the unique role which each person's body plays in his experience, particularly his perceptual experience. All philosophers who have concerned themselves with these questions have referred to the uniqueness of this role. Descartes was well aware of its uniqueness: 'I am *not* lodged in my body like a pilot in a vessel.' In what does this uniqueness consist? It consists, of course, in a great many things. Consider merely some of the ways in which the character of a person's *perceptual experience* is dependent on facts about his own body. Let us take his visual experience. The dependence is more complicated and many-sided than may at first be obvious. First, there is that group of empirical facts of which the most familiar is that if the eyelids of that body are closed, the person sees nothing. To this group belong all the facts known to ophthalmic surgeons. Second, there is the fact that what falls within his field of vision at any moment depends in part on the *orientation* of his eyes, i.e. on the direction his head is turned in, and on the *orientation* of his eyeballs in their sockets. And, third, there is the fact that *where he sees from*—or what his possible field of vision at any moment is—depends on where his body, and in particular his head, is located. I divide these facts into three groups because I want to emphasize that the fact that visual experience is, in all three ways, dependent on facts about some body or bodies, does not entail that the body should be the same body in each case. It is a contingent fact that it is the same body. For it is possible to imagine the following case. There is a subject of visual experience, S, and there are three different relevant bodies: A, B and C. (1) Whether the eyelids of B and C are open or not is causally irrelevant to whether S sees; but S sees only if the eyelids of A are open. And if an operation is performed on the eyes of A, the result affects S's sight, but not if an operation is per-

formed on the eyes of B and C. (2) Where A and B may be, however, is quite irrelevant to where S sees from, i.e. to what his possible field of vision is. This is determined only by where C is. So long as C is in the drawing-room and the curtains are drawn, S can see only what is in the drawing-room. (If one has any difficulty with this idea of 'where one sees from', one may think of the way one tells, from looking at a photograph, where the camera was when it was taken. Just so S's perspective on the world is given by the position of C.) But (3) the direction in which the heads and eyeballs of A and C are turned is quite irrelevant to what S sees. Given the station of C, then which of all the views which are possible from this position is the view seen by S, depends on the direction in which the head and eyeballs of B are turned, wherever B may find himself. I have described now a situation in which the visual experience of S is dependent in three different ways on the state or position of each of the bodies, A, B and C. The dependence in each case will have certain repercussions on the way in which each of those bodies itself can be an object of visual experience to S. Thus S may never see A or B at all: but if S does see A or B, he can never see A with A's eyelids closed and he can never see B's face, though he may sometimes catch a glimpse of B's profile 'out of the corner of his eye' (as *we* say), and will perhaps become quite familiar with the view of the back of B's head. Whenever S is 'looking in' a mirror, i.e. has a direct frontal view of a mirror, he will see the head of C; but he may get *any* view of the head, i.e. he will not necessarily see the face. Now, of course, our actual situation is not like this. Of course, in fact, for any subject of visual experience, S, there is just one body on the state and position of which the character of his visual experience is dependent in all three of these ways; and this triple dependence has its own familiar repercussions on the way in which that body itself becomes an object of visual experience for S. We have noted the contingency and the complexity of this dependence. If we turn to hearing and smell, the other 'distance' senses, the dependence is less complicated, in that orientation is comparatively unimportant. But there is still the double dependence of the character of the experience on both the location and the state of certain organs of one and the same body. Again these could be imagined coming apart. We could e.g. give an independent definition of the point 'from which' a sound is heard as follows: a sound α produced by a given source of sound β is '*heard from*' point P by subject S, if, given that no other changes take place except the movement of β, then α is heard more loudly by S when β is at P than when it is at any other point, and is heard by S with steadily diminishing loudness as β is moved in any direction away from P. Again, then, we might imagine 'the point from which' sound is heard by a given hearer being dependent on the location of one body, while whether that hearer heard anything at all depended on the condition of the ears, the eardrums, &c. of another body. Equally obvious is the special position of one body in relation to all those experiences of a given subject which are assigned to the sense of touch. Countless material bodies may be observed by a given subject to be in, or to come into, contact with others; but there is only one body of which it is true that when that body is a party to such a situation of 'establishing contact', then the subject normally has those experiences to which he alludes when he speaks of *feeling* some material body or other. The subject *feels* the dagger or the feather only when the dagger enters, or the feather lightly brushes, *this* body.

Such points illustrate some of the ways in which each person's body occupies a special position in relation to that person's perceptual experience. We may summarize such facts by saying that for each person there is one body which occupies a certain *causal* position in relation to that person's perceptual experience, a causal position which in various ways is unique in relation to each of the various kinds of perceptual experience he has; and— as a further consequence—that this body is also unique for him as an *object* of the various kinds of perceptual experience which he has. We also noted that this complex uniqueness of the single body appeared to be a contingent matter, or rather a cluster of contingent matters; for it seems that we can imagine many peculiar combinations of dependence and independence of aspects of our perceptual experience on facts about different bodies.

We reminded ourselves of the special position which a person's body occupies in his experience in the hope that it might help to provide an answer to two questions: viz. (1) Why are one's states of consciousness ascribed to anything at all? and (2) Why are they ascribed to the very same thing as certain corporeal characteristics, a certain physical situation &c.? But now I must say straight away that the facts I have been recalling do not seem to me to provide, by themselves, any answer to our questions at all. Of course, these facts explain something. They provide a good reason why a subject of experience should have a very special regard for just one body, why he should think of it as unique and perhaps more important than any other. They explain—if I may be permitted to put it so—why I feel peculiarly attached to what in fact I call my own body; they even might be said to explain why, granted that I am going to speak of one body as *mine*, I should speak of *this* body as mine. But they do not explain why I should have the concept of *myself* at all, why I should ascribe my thoughts and experiences to *anything*. Moreover, even if we were satisfied with some other explanation of why one's states of consciousness, thoughts and feelings and perceptions, were ascribed to *something*, and satisfied that the facts in question sufficed to explain why the 'possession' of a particular body should be ascribed to the *same* thing (i.e. to explain why a particular body should be spoken of as standing in some special relation—called 'being possessed by'—to that thing), yet the facts in question still do not explain why we should, as we do, ascribe certain corporeal characteristics not simply to the body standing in this special relation to the thing to which we ascribe thoughts and feelings, &c., but to the thing itself to which we ascribe those thoughts and feelings. For we say '*I* am bald' as well as '*I* am cold', '*I* am lying on the hearthrug' as well as '*I* see a spider on the ceiling'. Briefly, the facts in question explain why a subject of experience should pick out one body from others, give it, perhaps, an honoured name and ascribe to it whatever characteristics it has; but they do not explain why the experiences should be ascribed to any subject at all; and they do not explain why, if the experiences are to be ascribed to something, they *and* the corporeal characteristics which might be truly ascribed to the favoured body should be ascribed to the same thing. So the facts in question do not explain the use that we make of the word 'I', or how any word has the use that word has. They do not explain the concept we have of a person.

[3] A possible reaction at this point is to say that the concept we have is wrong or confused, or, if we make it a rule not to say that the concepts we have are confused, that the usage we have, whereby we ascribe, or seem to ascribe, such different kinds of predicate to one and the same thing, is confusing, that it conceals the true nature of the concepts involved, or something of this sort. This reaction can be found in two very important types of view about these matters. The first type of view is Cartesian, the view of Descartes and of others who think like him. Over the attribution of the second type of view I am more hesitant; but there is some evidence that it was held, at one period, by Wittgenstein and possibly also by Schlick. On both of these views, one of the questions we are considering—viz. 'Why do we ascribe our states of consciousness to the very same thing as certain corporeal characteristics &c.?'—is a question which does not arise; for, on both views, it is only a linguistic illusion that both kinds of predicate are properly ascribed to one and the same thing, that there is a common owner, or subject, of both types of predicate. On the second of these views, the other question we are considering—viz. 'Why do we ascribe our states of consciousness to anything at all?'—is also a question which does not arise; for on this view it is only a linguistic illusion that one ascribes one's states of consciousness at all, that there is any proper subject of these apparent ascriptions, that states of consciousness belong to, or are states of, anything.

That Descartes held the first of these views is well enough known.[1] When we speak of a person, we are really referring to one or both of two distinct substances, two substances of different types, each of which has its own appropriate types of states and properties; and none of the properties or states of either can be a property or state of the other. States of consciousness belong to one of these substances and not to the other. I shall say no more

[1] Or at least widely enough supposed to justify our calling it the Cartesian view.

about the Cartesian view for the moment—what I have to say about it will emerge later on—except to note again that while it escapes one of our questions, it does not escape, but indeed invites, the other: 'Why are one's states of consciousness *ascribed* at all, to *any* subject?'

The second of these views I shall call the 'no-ownership' or 'no-subject' doctrine of the self. Whether or not anyone has explicitly held this view, it is worth reconstructing, or constructing, in outline.[1] For the errors into which it falls are instructive. The 'no-ownership' theorist may be presumed to start his explanation with facts of the sort which illustrate the unique causal position of a certain material body in a person's experience. The theorist maintains that the uniqueness of this body is sufficient to give rise to the idea that one's experiences can be ascribed to some particular, individual thing, can be said to be possessed by, or owned by, that thing. This idea, he thinks, though infelicitously and misleadingly expressed in terms of ownership, would have some validity, would make some sort of sense, so long as we thought of this individual thing, the possessor of the experiences,

---

[1] The evidence that Wittgenstein at one time held such a view is to be found in Moore's articles in *Mind* on 'Wittgenstein's Lectures in 1930-33' (*Mind*, Vol. LXIV, pp. 13-14). He is reported to have held that the use of 'I' was utterly different in the case of 'I have a toothache' or 'I see a red patch' from its use in the case of 'I've got a bad tooth' or 'I've got a matchbox'. He thought that there were two uses of 'I', and that in one of them 'I' was replaceable by 'this body'. So far the view might be Cartesian. But he also said that in the other use (the use exemplified by 'I have a toothache' as opposed to 'I have a bad tooth'), the 'I' *does not denote a possessor*, and that no Ego is involved in thinking or in having toothache; and referred with apparent approval to Lichtenberg's dictum that, instead of saying 'I think', we (or Descartes) ought to say 'There is a thought' (i.e. 'Es denkt').

The attribution of such a view to Schlick would have to rest on his article, 'Meaning and Verification' (see *Readings in Philosophical Analysis*, ed. Feigl and Sellars). Like Wittgenstein, Schlick quotes Lichtenberg, and then goes on to say: 'Thus we see that unless we choose to call our body the owner or bearer of the data [the immediate data of experience]—which seems to be a rather misleading expression—we have to say that the data have no owner or bearer'. The full import of Schlick's article is, however, obscure to me, and it is quite likely that a false impression is given by the quotation of a single sentence. I shall say merely that I have drawn on Schlick's article in constructing the case of my hypothetical 'no-subject' theorist; but shall not claim to be representing his views.

Lichtenberg's anti-Cartesian dictum is, as the subsequent argument will show, one that I endorse, if properly used; but it seems to have been repeated, without being understood, by most of Descartes's critics. (I do not here refer to Wittgenstein and Schlick.)

as the body itself. So long as we thought in this way, then to ascribe a particular state of consciousness to this body, this individual thing, would at least be to say something that might have been false; for the experience in question might have been causally dependent on the state of some other body; in the present admissible, though infelicitous, sense of the word, it might have 'belonged' to some other individual thing. But now, the theorist suggests, one becomes confused: one slides from the admissible sense in which one's experiences may be said to belong to, or be possessed by, some particular thing, to a wholly inadmissible and empty sense of these expressions, in which the particular thing is not thought of as a body, but as something else, say an Ego, whose sole function is to provide an owner for experiences. Suppose we call the first type of possession, which is really a certain kind of causal dependence, 'having$_1$', and the second type of possession 'having$_2$'; and call the individual of the first type 'B' and the supposed individual of the second type 'E'. Then the difference is that while it is genuinely a contingent matter that *all my experiences are had$_1$ by B*, it appears as a necessary truth that *all my experiences are had$_2$ by E*. But the belief in E and the belief in 'having$_2$' is an illusion. Only those things whose ownership is logically transferable can be owned at all. So experiences are not owned by anything except in the dubious sense of being causally dependent on the state of a particular body; this is at least a genuine relationship to a thing, in that they might have stood in it to another thing. Since the whole function of E was to own experiences, in a logically non-transferable sense of 'own', and since experiences are not owned by anything in this sense, for there is no such sense of 'own', E must be eliminated from the picture altogether. It only came in because of a confusion.

I think it must be clear that this account of the matter, though it contains some of the facts, is not coherent. It is not coherent, in that one who holds it is forced to make use of that sense of possession of which he denies the existence, in presenting his case for the denial. When he tries to state the contingent fact, which he thinks gives rise to the illusion of the 'ego', he has to state it in some such form as 'All *my* experiences are had$_1$ by (i.e. uniquely dependent on the state of) body B'. For any attempt to eliminate the '*my*', or any expression with a similar possessive force, would yield something that was not a contingent fact at all. The proposition that *all* experiences are causally dependent on the state of a single body B, for example, is just false. The theorist means to speak of all the experiences *had by a certain person* being contingently so dependent. And the theorist cannot consistently argue that 'all the experiences of person P' *means the same thing* as 'all experiences contingently dependent on a certain body B'; for then his proposition would not be contingent, as his theory requires, but analytic. He must mean to be speaking of some class of experiences of the members of which it is in fact contingently true that they are all dependent on body B. The defining characteristic of this class is in fact that they are '*my* experiences' or 'the experiences *of* some person', where the idea of possession expressed by 'my' and 'of' is the one he calls into question.

This internal incoherence is a serious matter when it is a question of denying what *prima facie* is the case: that is, that one does genuinely ascribe one's states of consciousness to something, viz. oneself, and that this kind of ascription is precisely such as the theorist finds unsatisfactory, i.e. is such that it does not seem to make sense to suggest, for example, that the identical pain which was in fact one's own might have been another's. We do not have to seek far in order to understand the place of this logically non-transferable kind of ownership in our general scheme of thought. For if we think, once more, of the requirements of identifying reference in speech to *particular* states of consciousness, or private experiences, we see that such particulars cannot be thus identifyingly referred to except as the states or experiences *of* some identified *person*. States, or experiences, one might say, *owe* their identity as particulars to the identity of the person whose states or experiences they are. From this it follows immediately that if they can be identified as particular states or experiences at all, they must be possessed or ascribable in just that way which the no-ownership theorist ridicules; i.e. in such a way that it is logically impossible that a particular state or experience in fact possessed by someone should have been possessed by anyone else. The requirements of identity rule out logical transferability of ownership. So the theorist could maintain his position only by denying that we could ever refer to particular states or experiences at all; and *this* position is ridiculous.

We may notice, even now, a possible connexion between the no-ownership doctrine and the Cartesian position. The latter is, straightforwardly enough, a dualism of two subjects, or two types of subject. The former could, a little paradoxically, be called a dualism too: a dualism of one subject—the body—and one non-subject. We might surmise that the second dualism, paradoxically so called, arises out of the first dualism, non-paradoxically so called; in other words, that if we try to think of that to which one's states of consciousness are ascribed as something utterly different from that to which certain corporeal characteristics are ascribed, then indeed it becomes difficult to see why states of consciousness should be ascribed to, thought of as belonging to, anything at all. When we think of this possibility, we may also think of another: viz. that both the Cartesian and the no-owner-ship theorists are profoundly wrong in holding, as each must, that there are two uses of 'I', in one of which it denotes something which it does not denote in the other.

[4] The no-ownership theorist fails to take account of all the facts. He takes account of some of them. He implies, correctly, that the unique position or role of a single body in one's experi-ence is not a sufficient explanation of the fact that one's experi-ences, or states of consciousness, are ascribed to something which *has* them with that peculiar non-transferable kind of possession which is here in question. It may be a necessary part of the ex-planation, but is not, by itself, a sufficient explanation. The theorist, as we have seen, goes on to suggest that it is perhaps a sufficient explanation of something else: viz. of our confusedly and mistakenly *thinking* that states of consciousness are to be ascribed to something in this special way. But this, as we have seen, is incoherent: for it involves the denial that someone's states of consciousness are anyone's. We avoid the incoherence of this denial, whilst agreeing that the special role of a single body in

someone's experience does not suffice to explain why that experience should be ascribed to anyone. The fact of this special role does not, by itself, give a sufficient reason why what *we* think of as a subject of experience should have any use for the conception of himself as such a subject.

When I say that the no-ownership theorist's account fails through not reckoning with all the facts, I have in mind a very simple, but in this question a very central, thought: viz. that it is a necessary condition of one's ascribing states of consciousness, experiences, to oneself, in the way one does, that one should also ascribe them, or be prepared to ascribe them, to others who are not oneself.[1] This means not less than it says. It means, for example, that the ascribing phrases are used in just the same sense when the subject is another as when the subject is oneself. Of course the thought that this is so gives no trouble to the non-philosopher: the thought, for example, that 'in pain' means the same whether one says 'I am in pain' or 'He is in pain'. The dictionaries do not give two sets of meanings for every expression which describes a state of consciousness: a first-person meaning and a second-and-third person meaning. But to the philosopher this thought has given trouble. How could the sense be the same when the method of verification was so different in the two cases

[1] I can imagine an objection to the unqualified form of this statement, an objection which might be put as follows. Surely the idea of a uniquely applicable predicate, i.e. a predicate which belongs to only one individual, is not absurd. And, if it is not, then surely the most that can be claimed is that a necessary condition of one's ascribing predicates of a certain class to one individual, i.e. oneself, is that one should be prepared, or ready, on appropriate occasions, to ascribe them to other individuals, and hence that one should have a conception of what those appropriate occasions for ascribing them would be; but not, necessarily, that one should actually do so on any occasion.

The shortest way with the objection is to admit it, or at least refrain from disputing it; for the lesser claim is all that the argument strictly requires, though it is slightly simpler to conduct it in terms of the larger claim. But it is well to point out further that we are not speaking of a single predicate, or merely of some group or other of predicates, but of the whole of an enormous class of predicates such that the applicability of those predicates or their negations defines a major logical type or category of individuals. To insist, at this level, on the distinction between the lesser and the larger claim is to carry the distinction over from a level at which it is clearly correct to a level at which it may well appear idle and possibly senseless.

The main point here is a purely logical one: the idea of a predicate is correlative with that of a *range* of distinguishable individuals of which the predicate can be significantly, though not necessarily truly, affirmed.

—or, rather, when there *was* a method of verification in the one case (the case of others) and not, properly speaking, in the other case (the case of oneself)? Or, again—a more sophisticated scruple—how can it be right to talk of *ascribing* in the case of oneself? For surely there can be a question of ascribing only if there is or could be a question of identifying that to which the ascription is made; and though there may be a question of identifying the one who is in pain when that one is another, how can there be such a question when that one is oneself? But this query answers itself as soon as we remember that we *speak* primarily to others, for the information of others. In one sense, indeed, there is no question of my having to *tell who it is* who is in pain, when I am. In another sense, however, I may have to *tell who it is*, i.e. to let others know who it is.

What I have just said explains, perhaps, how one may properly be said to ascribe states of consciousness to oneself, given that one can ascribe them to others. But how is it that one can ascribe them to others? Now one thing here is certain: that *if* the things one ascribes states of consciousness to, in ascribing them to others, are thought of as a set of Cartesian egos to which only private experiences can, in correct logical grammar, be ascribed, *then* this question is unanswerable and this problem insoluble. If, in identifying the things to which states of consciousness are to be ascribed, private experiences are to be all one has to go on, then, just for the very same reason as that for which there is, from one's own point of view, no question of telling that a private experience is one's own, there is also no question of telling that a private experience is another's. All private experiences, all states of consciousness, will be mine, i.e. no one's. To put it briefly. One can ascribe states of consciousness to oneself only if one can ascribe them to others. One can ascribe them to others only if one can identify other subjects of experience. And one cannot identify others if one can identify them *only* as subjects of experience, possessors of states of consciousness.

It might be objected that this way with Cartesianism is too short. After all, there is no difficulty in distinguishing bodies from one another, no difficulty in identifying bodies. Does not this give us an indirect way of identifying subjects of experience, while preserving the Cartesian mode? Can we not identify such a subject as, for example, 'the subject that stands to that body in the same special relation as I stand in to this one', or, in other words, 'the subject of those experiences which stand in the same unique causal relation to body N as *my* experiences stand in to body M'? But this suggestion is useless. It requires me to have noted that *my* experiences stand in a special relation to body M, when it is just the right to speak of *my* experiences at all that is in question. That is to say, it requires me to have noted that *my* experiences stand in a special relation to body M; but it requires me to have noted this as a condition of being able to identify other subjects of experiences, i.e. as a condition of my having the idea of myself as a subject of experience, i.e. as a condition of thinking of any experiences as *mine*. So long as we persist in talking, in the mode of this explanation, of experiences on the one hand, and bodies on the other, the most I may be allowed to have noted is that experiences, *all* experiences, stand in a special relation to body M, that body M is unique in just this way, that this is what makes body M unique among bodies. (This 'most' is perhaps too much—because of the presence of the word 'experiences'.) The proffered explanation runs: 'Another subject of experience is distinguished and identified as the subject of those experiences which stand in the same unique causal relationship to body N as *my* experiences stand in to body M.' And the objection is: 'But what is the word "my" doing in this explanation?' It is not as though the explanation could get on without this word. There is a further objection, to which we will recur.[1] It runs: 'What right have we, in this explanation, to speak of *the* subject, implying uniqueness? Why should there not be any number of subjects of experience—perhaps qualitatively indistinguishable—each subject and each set of experiences standing in the same unique relation to body N (*or* to body M)? Uniqueness of the body does not guarantee uniqueness of the Cartesian soul'.

What we have to acknowledge, in order to begin to free ourselves from these difficulties, is the primitiveness of the concept of a person. What I mean by the concept of a person is the concept of

[1] In the next chapter. See pp. 131–3.

a type of entity such that *both* predicates ascribing states of consciousness *and* predicates ascribing corporeal characteristics, a physical situation &c. are equally applicable to a single individual of that single type. What I mean by saying that this concept is primitive can be put in a number of ways. One way is to return to those two questions I asked earlier: viz. (1) why are states of consciousness ascribed to anything at all? and (2) why are they ascribed to the very same thing as certain corporeal characteristics, a certain physical situation &c.? I remarked at the beginning that it was not to be supposed that the answers to these questions were independent of each other. Now I shall say that they are connected in this way: that a necessary condition of states of consciousness being ascribed at all is that they should be ascribed to the *very same things* as certain corporeal characteristics, a certain physical situation &c. That is to say, states of consciousness could not be ascribed at all, *unless* they were ascribed to persons, in the sense I have claimed for this word. We are tempted to think of a person as a sort of compound of two kinds of subjects: a subject of experiences (a pure consciousness, an ego) on the one hand, and a subject of corporeal attributes on the other. Many questions arise when we think in this way. But, in particular, when we ask ourselves how we come to frame, to get a use for, the concept of this compound of two subjects, the picture—if we are honest and careful—is apt to change from the picture of two subjects to the picture of one subject and one non-subject. For it becomes impossible to see how we could come by the idea of different, distinguishable, identifiable subjects of experiences—different consciousnesses—*if this idea is thought of as logically primitive*, as a logical ingredient in the compound-idea of a person, the latter being composed of two subjects. For there could never be any question of assigning an experience, as such, to any subject other than oneself; and therefore never any question of assigning it to oneself either, never any question of ascribing it to a subject at all. So the concept of the pure individual consciousness—the pure ego—is a concept that cannot exist; or, at least, cannot exist as a primary concept in terms of which the concept of a person can be explained or analysed. It can exist only, if at all, as a secondary, non-primitive concept, which itself is to be explained, analysed, in terms of the concept of a person. It was the entity corresponding to this illusory primary concept of the pure consciousness, the ego-substance, for which Hume was seeking, or ironically pretending to seek, when he looked into himself, and complained that he could never discover himself without a perception and could never discover anything but the perception. More seriously—and this time there was no irony, but a confusion, a Nemesis of confusion for Hume—it was this entity of which Hume vainly sought for the principle of unity, confessing himself perplexed and defeated; sought vainly because there is no principle of unity where there is no principle of differentiation. It was this, too, to which Kant, more perspicacious here than Hume, accorded a purely formal ('analytic') unity: the unity of the 'I think' that accompanies all my perceptions and therefore might just as well accompany none. Finally it is this, perhaps, of which Wittgenstein spoke, when he said of the subject, first that there is no such thing, and then that it is not a part of the world, but its limit.

So, then, the word 'I' never refers to this, the pure subject. But this does not mean, as the no-ownership theorist must think, that 'I' in some cases does not refer at all. It refers; because I am a person among others; and the predicates which would, *per impossibile* belong to the pure subject if it could be referred to, belong properly to the person to which 'I' does refer.

The concept of a person is logically prior to that of an individual consciousness. The concept of a person is not to be analysed as that of an animated body or of an embodied anima. This is not to say that the concept of a pure individual consciousness might not have a logically secondary existence, if one thinks, or finds, it desirable. We speak of a dead person—a body—and in the same secondary way we might at least think of a disembodied person. A person is not an embodied ego, but an ego might be a disembodied person, retaining the logical benefit of individuality from having been a person.

[5] It is important to realize the full extent of the acknowledgement one is making in acknowledging the logical primitiveness of

the concept of a person. Let me rehearse briefly the stages of the argument. There would be no question of ascribing one's own states of consciousness, or experiences, to anything, unless one also ascribed, or were ready and able to ascribe, states of consciousness, or experiences, to other individual entities of the same logical type as that thing to which one ascribes one's own states of consciousness. The condition of reckoning oneself as a subject of such predicates is that one should also reckon others as subjects of such predicates. The condition, in turn, of this being possible, is that one should be able to distinguish from one another, to pick out or identify, different subjects of such predicates, i.e. different individuals of the type concerned. The condition, in turn, of this being possible is that the individuals concerned, including oneself, should be of a certain unique type: of a type, namely, such that to each individual of that type there must be ascribed, or ascribable, *both* states of consciousness *and* corporeal characteristics. But this characterization of the type is still very opaque and does not at all clearly bring out what is involved. To bring this out, I must make a rough division, into two, of the kinds of predicates properly applied to individuals of this type. The first kind of predicate consists of those which are also properly applied to material bodies to which we would not dream of applying predicates ascribing states of consciousness. I will call this first kind M-predicates: and they include things like 'weighs 10 stone', 'is in the drawing-room' and so on. The second kind consists of all the other predicates we apply to persons. These I shall call P-predicates. P-predicates, of course, will be very various. They will include things like 'is smiling', 'is going for a walk', as well as things like 'is in pain', 'is thinking hard', 'believes in God' and so on.

So far I have said that the concept of a person is to be understood as the concept of a type of entity such that *both* predicates ascribing states of consciousness *and* predicates ascribing corporeal characteristics, a physical situation &c. are equally applicable to an individual entity of that type. All I have said about the meaning of saying that this concept is primitive is that it is not to be analysed in a certain way or ways. We are not, for example, to think of it as a secondary kind of entity in relation to two primary kinds, viz. a particular consciousness and a particular human body. I implied also that the Cartesian error is just a special case of the more general error, present in a different form in theories of the no-ownership type, of thinking of the designations, or apparent designations, of persons as *not* denoting precisely the same thing or entity for all kinds of predicate ascribed to the entity designated. That is, if we are to avoid the general form of this error, we must *not* think of 'I' or 'Smith' as suffering from type-ambiguity. Indeed, if we want to locate type-ambiguity somewhere, we would do better to locate it in certain predicates like 'is in the drawing-room' 'was hit by a stone' &c., and say they mean one thing when applied to material objects and another when applied to persons.

This is all I have so far said or implied about the meaning of saying that the concept of a person is primitive. What has to be brought out further is what the implications of saying this are as regards the logical character of those predicates with which we ascribe states of consciousness. For this purpose we may well consider P-predicates in general. For though not all P-predicates are what we should call 'predicates ascribing states of consciousness' (e.g. 'going for a walk' is not), they may be said to have this in common, that they imply the possession of consciousness on the part of that to which they are ascribed.

What then are the consequences of the view as regards the character of P-predicates? I think they are these. Clearly there is no sense in talking of identifiable individuals of a special type, a type, namely, such that they possess both M-predicates and P-predicates, unless there is in principle some way of telling, with regard to any individual of that type, and any P-predicate, whether that individual possesses that P-predicate. And, in the case of at least some P-predicates, the ways of telling must constitute in some sense logically adequate kinds of criteria for the ascription of the P-predicate. For suppose in no case did these ways of telling constitute logically adequate kinds of criteria. Then we should have to think of the relation between the ways of telling and what the P-predicate ascribes, or a part of what it ascribes, always in the following way: we should have to think of the ways of telling as *signs* of the presence, in the individual concerned, of this different thing, viz. the state of consciousness. But then we could only know that the way of telling was a sign of the presence of the different thing ascribed by the P-predicate, by the observation of correlations between the two. But this observation we could each make only in one case, viz. our own. And now we are back in the position of the defender of Cartesianism, who thought our way with it was too short. For what, now, does 'our own case' mean? There is no sense in the idea of ascribing states of consciousness to oneself, or at all, unless the ascriber already knows how to ascribe at least some states of consciousness to others. So he cannot argue in general 'from his own case' to conclusions about how to do this; for unless he already knows how to do this, he has no conception of *his own case*, or any *case*, i.e. any subject of experiences. Instead, he just has evidence that pain &c. may be expected when a certain body is affected in certain ways and not when others are. If he speculated to the contrary, his speculations would be immediately falsified.

The conclusion here is not, of course, new. What I have said is that one ascribes P-predicates to others on the strength of observation of their behaviour; and that the behaviour-criteria one goes on are not just signs of the presence of what is meant by the P-predicate, but are criteria of a logically adequate kind for the ascription of the P-predicate. On behalf of this conclusion, however, I am claiming that it follows from a consideration of the conditions necessary for any ascription of states of consciousness to anything. The point is not that we must accept this conclusion in order to avoid scepticism, but that we must accept it in order to explain the existence of the conceptual scheme in terms of which the sceptical problem is stated. But once the conclusion is accepted, the sceptical problem does not arise. So with many sceptical problems: their statement involves the pretended acceptance of a conceptual scheme and at the same time the silent repudiation of one of the conditions of its existence. That is why they are, in the terms in which they are stated, insoluble.

But this is only one half of the picture about P-predicates. For of course it is true of some important classes of P-predicates, that when one ascribes them *to oneself*, one does not do so on the strength of observation of those behaviour criteria on the strength of which one ascribes them to others. This is not true of all P-predicates. It is not, in general, true of those which carry assessments of character or capability: these, when self-ascribed, are in general ascribed on the same kind of basis as that on which they are ascribed to others. Even of those P-predicates of which it is true that one does not generally ascribe them to oneself on the basis of the criteria on the strength of which one ascribes them to others, there are many of which it is also true that their ascription is liable to correction by the self-ascriber on this basis. But there remain many cases in which one has an entirely adequate basis for ascribing a P-predicate to oneself, and yet in which this basis is quite distinct from those on which one ascribes the predicate to another. Thus one says, reporting a present state of mind or feeling: 'I feel tired, am depressed, am in pain'. How can this fact be reconciled with the doctrine that the criteria on the strength of which one ascribes P-predicates to others are criteria of a logically adequate kind for this ascription?

The apparent difficulty of bringing about this reconciliation may tempt us in many directions. It may tempt us, for example, to deny that these self-ascriptions are really ascriptive at all, to *assimilate* first-person ascriptions of states of consciousness to those other forms of behaviour which constitute criteria on the basis of which one person ascribes P-predicates to another. This device seems to avoid the difficulty; it is not, in all cases, entirely inappropriate. But it obscures the facts; and is needless. It is merely a sophisticated form of failure to recognize the special character of P-predicates, or, rather, of a crucial class of P-predicates. For just as there is not in general one primary process of learning, or teaching oneself, an inner private meaning for predicates of this class, then another process of learning to apply such predicates to others on the strength of a correlation, noted in one's own case, with certain forms of behaviour, so—and equally—there is not in general one primary process of learning to apply such predicates to others on the strength of behaviour criteria, and then another process of acquiring the secondary technique of exhibiting a new form of behaviour, viz. first-person P-utterances. Both these pictures are refusals to acknowledge the unique logical character of the predicates concerned. Suppose we write 'Px' as the general form of propositional function of such a predicate. Then, according to the first picture, the expression which primarily replaces 'x' in this form is 'I', the first person singular pronoun: its uses with other replacements are secondary, derivative and shaky. According to the second picture, on the other hand, the primary replacements of 'x' in this form are 'he', 'that person', &c., and its use with 'I' is secondary, peculiar, not a true ascriptive use. But it is essential to the character of these predicates that they have both first- and third-person ascriptive uses, that they are both self-ascribable otherwise than on the basis of observation of the behaviour of the subject of them, and other-ascribable on the basis of behaviour criteria. To learn their use is to learn both aspects of their use. In order to *have* this type of concept, one must be both a self-ascriber and an other-ascriber of such predicates, and must see every other as a self-ascriber. In order to *understand* this type of concept, one must acknowledge that there is a kind of predicate which is unambiguously and adequately ascribable *both* on the basis of observation of the subject of the predicate *and* not on this basis, i.e. independently of observation of the subject: the second case is the case where the ascriber is also the subject. If there were no concepts answering to the characterization I have just given, we should indeed have no philosophical problem about the soul; but equally we should not have our concept of a person.

To put the point—with a certain unavoidable crudity—in terms of one particular concept of this class, say, that of depression. We speak of behaving in a depressed way (of depressed behaviour) and we also speak of feeling depressed (of a feeling of depression). One is inclined to argue that feelings can be felt but not observed, and behaviour can be observed but not felt, and that therefore there must be room here to drive in a logical wedge. But the concept of depression spans the place where one wants to drive it in. We might say: in order for there to be such a concept as that of

X's depression, the depression which X has, the concept must cover both what is felt, but not observed, by X, and what may be observed, but not felt, by others than X (for all values of X). But it is perhaps better to say: X's depression *is* something, one and the same thing, which is felt, but not observed, by X, and observed, but not felt, by others than X. (Of course, what can be observed can also be faked or disguised.) To refuse to accept this is to refuse to accept the *structure* of the language in which we talk about depression. That is, in a sense, all right. One might give up talking or devise, perhaps, a different structure in terms of which to soliloquize. What is not all right is simultaneously to pretend to accept that structure and to refuse to accept it; i.e. to couch one's rejection in the language of that structure.

It is in this light that we must see some of the familiar philosophical difficulties in the topic of the mind. For some of them spring from just such a failure to admit, or fully to appreciate, the character which I have been claiming for at least some P-predicates. It is not seen that these predicates could not have either aspect of their use, the self-ascriptive or the non-self-ascriptive, without having the other aspect. Instead, one aspect of their use is taken as self-sufficient, which it could not be, and then the other aspect appears as problematical. So we oscillate between philosophical scepticism and philosophical behaviourism. When we take the self-ascriptive aspect of the use of some P-predicates, say 'depressed', as primary, then a logical gap seems to open between the criteria on the strength of which we say that another is depressed, and the actual state of being depressed. What we do not realize is that if this logical gap is allowed to open, then it swallows not only his depression, but our depression as well. For if the logical gap exists, then depressed behaviour, however much there is of it, is no more than a sign of depression. But it can only become a sign of depression because of an observed correlation between it and depression. But whose depression? Only mine, one is tempted to say. But if *only* mine, then *not* mine at all. The sceptical position customarily represents the crossing of the logical gap as at best a shaky inference. But the point is that not even the syntax of the premises of the inference exists, if the gap exists.

If, on the other hand, we take the other-ascriptive uses of these predicates as primary or self-sufficient, we may come to think that all there is in the meaning of these predicates, as predicates, is the criteria on the strength of which we ascribe them to others. Does this not follow from the denial of the logical gap? It does not follow. To think that it does is to forget the self-ascriptive use of these predicates, to forget that we have to do with a class of predicates to the meaning of which it is essential that they should be both self-ascribable and other-ascribable to the same individual, where self-ascriptions are not made on the observational basis on which other-ascriptions are made, but on another basis. It is not that these predicates have two kinds of meaning. Rather, it is essential to the single kind of meaning that they do have, that both ways of ascribing them should be perfectly in order.

If one is playing a game of cards, the distinctive markings of a certain card constitute a logically adequate criterion for calling it, say, the Queen of Hearts; but, in calling it this, in the context of the game, one is ascribing to it properties over and above the possession of these markings. The predicate gets its meaning from the whole structure of the game. So with the language in which we ascribe P-predicates. To say that the criteria on the strength of which we ascribe P-predicates to others are of a logically adequate kind for this ascription, is not to say that all there is to the ascriptive meaning of these predicates is these criteria. To say this is to forget that they are P-predicates, to forget the rest of the language-structure to which they belong.

[6] Now our perplexities may take a different form, the form of the question: 'But how can one ascribe to oneself, not on the basis of observation, the very same thing that others may have, on the basis of observation, reasons of a logically adequate kind for ascribing to one?' This question may be absorbed in a wider one, which might be phrased: 'How are P-predicates possible?' or: 'How is the concept of a person possible?' This is the question by which we replace those two earlier questions, viz.: 'Why are states of consciousness ascribed at all, ascribed to anything?' and

'Why are they ascribed to the very same thing as certain corporeal characteristics &c.?' For the answer to these two initial
questions is to be found nowhere else but in the admission of
the primitiveness of the concept of a person, and hence of the
unique character of P-predicates. So residual perplexities have to
frame themselves in this new way. For when we have acknowledged the primitiveness of the concept of a person, and, with it,
the unique character of P-predicates, we may still want to ask
what it is in the natural facts that makes it intelligible that we
should have this concept, and to ask this in the hope of a non-
trivial answer, i.e. in the hope of an answer which does not *merely*
say: 'Well, there are people in the world'. I do not pretend to be
able to satisfy this demand at all fully. But I may mention two
very different things which might count as beginnings or frag-
ments of an answer.

First, I think a beginning can be made by moving a certain
class of P-predicates to a central position in the picture. They are
predicates, roughly, which involve doing something, which
clearly imply intention or a state of mind or at least consciousness
in general, and which indicate a characteristic pattern, or range of
patterns, of bodily movement, while not indicating at all precisely any very definite sensation or experience. I mean such
things as 'going for a walk', 'coiling a rope', 'playing ball', 'writing a letter'. Such predicates have the interesting characteristic of
many P-predicates, that one does not, in general, ascribe them to
oneself on the strength of observation, whereas one does ascribe
them to others on the strength of observation. But, in the case of
these predicates, one feels minimal reluctance to concede that
what is ascribed in these two different ways is the same. This is
because of the marked dominance of a fairly definite pattern of
bodily movement in what they ascribe, and the marked absence of
any distinctive experience. They release us from the idea that the
only things we can know about without observation or inference,
or both, are private experiences; we can know, without telling
by either of these means, about the present and future movements
of a body. Yet bodily movements are certainly also things we can
know about by observation and inference. Among the things that

we observe, as opposed to the things we know about without observation, are the movements of bodies similar to that about which we have knowledge not based on observation. It is important that we should understand such movements, for they bear on and condition our own; and in fact we understand them, we interpret them, only by seeing them as elements in just such plans or schemes of action as those of which we know the present course and future development without observation of the relevant present movements. But this is to say that we see such movements as *actions*, that we interpret them in terms of intention, that we see them as movements of individuals of a type to which also belongs that individual whose present and future movements we know about without observation; it is to say that we see others as self-ascribers, not on the basis of observation, of what we ascribe to them on this basis.

These remarks are not intended to suggest how the 'problem of other minds' could be solved, or our beliefs about others given a general philosophical 'justification'. I have already argued that such a 'solution' or 'justification' is impossible, that the demand for it cannot be coherently stated. Nor are these remarks intended as *a priori* genetic psychology. They are simply intended to help to make it seem intelligible to us, at this stage in the history of the philosophy of this subject, that we have the conceptual scheme we have. What I am suggesting is that it is easier to understand how we can see each other, and ourselves, as persons, if we think first of the fact that we act, and act on each other, and act in accordance with a common human nature. Now 'to see each other as persons' is a lot of things, but not a lot of separate and unconnected things. The class of P-predicates that I have moved into the centre of the picture are not unconnectedly there, detached from others irrelevant to them. On the contrary, they are inextricably bound up with the others, interwoven with them. The topic of the mind does not divide into unconnected subjects.

I spoke just now of a common human nature. But there is also a sense in which a condition of the existence of the conceptual scheme we have is that human nature should not be common— should not be, that is, a community nature. Philosophers used to discuss the question of whether there was, or could be, such a thing as a 'group mind'. For some the idea had a peculiar fascination, while to others it seemed utterly absurd and nonsensical and at the same time, curiously enough, pernicious. It is easy to see why these last found it pernicious: they found something horrible in the thought that people should cease to have to individual persons the kind of attitudes that they did have, and instead have attitudes in some way analogous towards groups; and that they might cease to decide individual courses of action for themselves and instead merely participate in corporate activities. But their finding it pernicious showed that they understood the idea they claimed to be absurd only too well. The fact that we find it natural to individuate as persons the members of a certain class of moving natural objects does not mean that such a conceptual scheme is inevitable for any class of beings not utterly unlike ourselves. A technique similar to that which I used in the last chapter to decide whether there was a place in the restricted auditory world for the concept of the self, is available to determine whether we might not construct the idea of a special kind of social world in which the concept of an individual person is replaced by that of a group. Think, to begin with, of certain aspects of actual human existence. Think, for example, of two groups of human beings engaged in some competitive, but corporate activity, such as battle, for which they have been exceedingly well trained. We may even suppose that orders are superfluous, though information is passed. It is easy to suppose that, while absorbed in such activity, the members of the groups make no references to individual persons at all, have no use for personal names or pronouns. They do, however, refer to the groups and apply to them predicates analogous to those predicates ascribing purposive activity which we normally apply to individual persons. They may *in fact* use in such circumstances the plural forms 'we' and 'they'; but these are not genuine plurals, they are plurals without a singular, such as occur in sentences like: 'We have taken the citadel', 'We have lost the game'. They may also refer to elements in the group, to members of the group, but exclusively in terms which get their sense from the parts played by these elements in the corporate activity. Thus we sometimes refer to what are in fact persons as 'stroke' or 'square-leg'.

When we think of such cases, we see that we ourselves, over a part of our social lives—not, happily, a very large part—do work with a set of ideas from which that of the individual person is excluded, in which its place is taken by that of the group. But might we not think of communities or groups such that this part of the lives of their members was the dominant part—or was not merely a part, but the whole? It sometimes happens, with groups of human beings, that, as *we* say, their members think, feel and act 'as one'. I suggest it is a condition for the existence of the concept of an individual person, that this should happen only sometimes.

It is quite useless to say, at this point: 'But all the same, even if it happened all the time, every member of the group would *have* an individual consciousness, would embody an individual subject of experience.' For, once more, there is no sense in speaking of the individual consciousness just as such, of the individual subject of experience just as such; there is no way of identifying such pure entities. It is true, of course, that, in suggesting the fantasy of total absorption in the group, I took our concept of an individual person as a starting point. It is this fact which makes the useless reaction a natural one. But suppose someone seriously advanced the following 'hypothesis': that each part of the human body, each organ and each member, had an individual consciousness, was a separate centre of experiences. The 'hypothesis' would be useless in the same way as the above remark, only more obviously so. Let us now suppose that there is a class of moving natural objects, divided into groups, each group exhibiting the same characteristic pattern of activity. Within each group there are certain differentiations of appearance accompanying differentiations of function, and in particular there is one member of each group with a distinctive appearance. Cannot one imagine different sets of observations which might lead us in the one case to think of the particular member as the spokesman of the group, as its mouthpiece; and in the other case to think of him as its mouth, to think of the group as a single *scattered* body? The important point is that as soon as we adopt the latter way of thinking, then we abandon the former; we are no longer influenced by the human analogy in its first form, but only in its second; we are no longer tempted to say: Perhaps the members have consciousness. It is helpful here to remember the startling ambiguity of the phrase, 'a body and its members'.

[7] Earlier, when I was discussing the concept of a pure individual consciousness, I said that though it could not exist as a primary concept to be used in the explanation of the concept of a person (so that there is no mind–body problem, as traditionally conceived), yet it might have a logically secondary existence. Thus, from within our actual conceptual scheme, each of us can quite intelligibly conceive of his or her individual survival of bodily death. The effort of imagination is not even great. One has simply to think of oneself as having thoughts and memories as at present, visual and auditory experiences largely as at present, even, perhaps—though this involves certain complications— some quasi-tactual and organic sensations as at present, whilst (*a*) having no perceptions of a body related to one's experience as one's own body is, and (*b*) having no power of initiating changes in the physical condition of the world, such as one at present does with one's hands, shoulders, feet and vocal chords. Condition (*a*) must be expanded by adding that no one else exhibits reactions indicating that he perceives a body at the point which one's body would be occupying if one were seeing and hearing in an embodied state from the point from which one is seeing and hearing in a disembodied state. One could, of course, imagine condition (*a*) being fulfilled, in both its parts, without condition (*b*) being fulfilled. This would be a rather vulgar fancy, in the class of the table-tapping spirits with familiar voices. But suppose we take disembodiment strictly in the sense that we imagine both (*a*) and (*b*) fulfilled. Then two consequences follow, one of which is commonly noted, the other of which is perhaps insufficiently attended to. The first is that the strictly disembodied individual is strictly solitary, and it must remain for him indeed an utterly empty, though not meaningless, speculation, as to whether there

are any other members of his class. The other, and less commonly noticed point, is that in order to retain his idea of himself as an individual, he must always think of himself as *dis*embodied, as a *former* person. That is to say, he must contrive still to have the idea of himself as a member of a class or type of entities with whom, however, he is now debarred from entering into any of those transactions the past fact of which was the condition of his having any idea of himself at all. Since then he has, as it were, no personal life of his own to lead, he must live much in the memories of the personal life he did lead; or he might, when this living in the past loses its appeal, achieve some kind of attenuated vicarious personal existence by taking a certain kind of interest in the human affairs of which he is a mute and invisible witness—much like that kind of spectator at a play who says to himself: 'That's what I should have done (or said)' or 'If I were he, I should . . .'. In proportion as the memories fade, and this vicarious living palls, to that degree his concept of himself as an individual becomes attenuated. At the limit of attenuation there is, *from the point of view of his survival as an individual,* no difference between the continuance of experience and its cessation. Disembodied survival, on such terms as these, may well seem unattractive. No doubt it is for this reason that the orthodox have wisely insisted on the resurrection of the body.

4

MONADS

I want now to consider briefly some features of a metaphysical doctrine, or system, which serves in an interesting way to connect the problem of the individual consciousness with the general topic of identification. I refer, with a certain qualification, to Leibniz's system of monads. The qualification is this: that when I refer to the system of Leibniz, I shall not be much concerned if the views I discuss are not identical at all points with the views held by the historical philosopher of that name. I shall use the name 'Leibniz' to refer to a possible philosopher at least very similar to Leibniz in certain doctrinal respects; whether or not they are indiscernible in these respects matters little.

To begin with, I must mention two important ways in which the system of Leibniz runs counter, or at least seems to run counter, to theses for which I have been arguing. I discussed at the outset a general theoretical problem of securing uniqueness of reference to a particular. The general theoretical solution of the problem lay in the fact that, for a speaker making references, his own immediate environment supplied common points of reference in relation to which uniqueness of reference to any other item belonging to the single spatio-temporal framework in which he himself was located could be secured. To accept this solution was to accept the general theoretical position that the identification of particulars rests ultimately on the use of expressions with some demonstrative, or egocentric, or token-reflexive, force. For the significance of the theoretically central position of the point of reference in the speaker's vicinity is that ambiguities of reference with regard to this point are ruled out by the use of demonstratives, in conjunction with suitable, though not elaborate, descriptions. It is true that the theoretical problem to which this was the solution appeared as a highly artificial one. It is also true that the solution was nevertheless shown to hold the key to the structure of our actual thinking; that particular-identification was shown to rest in fact on the use of expressions which, directly or indirectly, embody a demonstrative force; for such identification rests upon the use of a unified framework of knowledge of particulars in which we ourselves have a known place. For the purposes of the present chapter, however, the connexion between the theoretical solution and our actual practice is of secondary importance; all that matters is that the general structure of our thought permits the problem, and supplies the solution.

Now the application of this theoretical conclusion about the identification of particulars is not confined to our actual conceptual scheme, in which material bodies are basic. It still holds for the auditory world in which sound-particulars are basic. This is a No-Space world, and the role of demonstratives is correspondingly restricted.[1] Though we had to introduce, in auditory terms, an analogue of space in order to make room for the idea of re-identifiable particulars, it does not seem that demonstratives would be needed for determining a point in the space-analogue; or, at least, it does not seem that they would be needed for this purpose, so long as we confine ourselves to the simple, initial model of the auditory world, with the unique master-sound. For so long as we thus limit ourselves, points in the space-analogue could, it seems, be determined descriptively, as different pitch-levels of the master-sound; whilst the master-sound itself could be identified as *the sound by which no sound is unaccompanied*. But in any case, whether points in the space-analogue could be descriptively determined or not, demonstratives would still be needed for the identification of particulars: demonstratives of time, or, rather, the single demonstrative 'now'. Only by reference

[1] This and the following remarks are to be understood in the light of my general explanations of the way in which discussions of such speculative constructions as the No-Space world are to be understood. Thinking of such constructions as a part of our ordinary experience, we may ask: which of the concepts and modes of expression that we ordinarily employ do we find necessary to do justice to features distinguishable within this part of our experience? See Chapter 2, p. 82, etc.

to their respective positions in the temporal order relative to the present moment could two qualitatively indistinguishable sound-particulars at the same pitch-level of the master-sound be, ultimately and theoretically, differentiated.

This suggests, then, that the theoretical indispensability of a demonstrative element in identifying thought about particulars is not just a peculiarity of this or that conceptual scheme which allows for particulars, but a necessary feature of any conceptual scheme, of any ontology, in which particulars occur. The suggestion is one which I have no hesitation in accepting. In the first place, it necessarily holds for any system incorporating particulars, in which the particulars are spatial or temporal or spatio-temporal entities. This I regard as proved from a consideration of the two example conceptual schemes examined, viz. our own and that of the auditory world. For the arguments adduced would serve just as well for any other sensory terms—if any others are possible—in which a purely temporal, or a spatio-temporal, ontology of particulars could be constructed. The form of the argument is general in each case. As for a purely spatial system—which might be conceived as an instantaneous state of a spatio-temporal world—the fact that, in order to solve the identification problem for the spatio-temporal world, demonstratives must have a spatial as well as a temporal force, seems to be decisive for this case also. In the second place, it seems to me necessarily true—to anticipate a little—that no system which does not allow for spatial or temporal entities can be a system which allows for particulars at all, or at least can be understood by us as such. This point is the same as that made by Kant in saying that space and time are our only forms of intuition. If we take these two points together, it follows that, in general, identifying reference to particulars rests ultimately on the use of expressions which, directly or indirectly, embody a demonstrative force; or, to put it in terms of thought rather than of language, that identifying thought about particulars necessarily incorporates a demonstrative element.

Now the system of Leibniz runs counter, or seems to run counter, to this thesis, in that, for the basic individuals of the system—i.e. for monads—a certain form of the doctrine of the

Identity of Indiscernibles is said to hold. According to this doctrine, in the only form in which it is worth discussing, it is necessarily true that there exists, for every individual, some description in purely universal, or general, terms, such that only that individual answers to that description. Adherence merely to the doctrine as I have just stated it would not alone and directly entail the contradiction of the thesis that identification of particulars requires demonstratives. For it would perhaps be possible, though odd, to accept the doctrine as I have just stated it, and yet think it theoretically impossible to give any general specification of a type of description-in-purely-general-terms such that it was necessarily true that only one individual answered to a description of this type. That is, one might think it impossible to *specify* any type of purely general description which guaranteed uniqueness to any particular it applied to, while thinking it necessary that there should *exist* a uniquely applicable general description for any object. In that case one would have to admit, I suppose, that the solution to the theoretical problem of identification of particulars demanded the admission of demonstrative elements into particular descriptions as a *pis-aller*, that only under this condition could one specify a type of description which guaranteed uniqueness; and of course this would not be a type of description-in-universal-terms. Leibniz, however, did not hold this rather uncomfortable half-way position. He held the much more satisfactory position of believing that he *could* specify a type of purely general description, such that no more than one monad, or basic individual, could answer to any description of that type. He thought that he could specify the type of description in question, but not that he could actually give any such description; for only God could do that. A description of this type was what he sometimes called a 'complete notion' of an individual. It was characteristic of a description of this type that it was a description of an individual, but also, in a certain sense, a description of the entire universe. It was a description, or representation, of the entire universe from a certain point of view. Its being in this way a universally exhaustive description was what guaranteed the uniqueness of its application.

Monads

I shall return to consideration of the merits of this position in a moment. First, I must mention the other of the two ways I spoke of in which Leibniz's system runs counter to theses I have maintained. I have maintained, roughly, that no principle of individuation can be framed for consciousnesses as such, and hence that nothing can be a subject of predicates implying consciousness, unless it is, in that sense of the word which implies also the possession of corporeal attributes, a person, or at least a former person. Now the basic individuals of Leibniz's system are not material; they have no spatial parts; they are, in fact, consciousnesses, subjects of perception and apperception. This statement, if we wanted to be true to the authoritative Leibniz, would call for a great deal of qualification. Even to be true to my possible Leibniz, it calls for some. We had better say not that monads *are* minds, but that minds are the nearest and easiest model for monads of all the categories that we employ. For the historical Leibniz, for instance, only a subclass of monads are said to be conscious, and only a subclass of the states of conscious monads are conscious states; and in the end it turns out that monads, besides being non-spatial entities, are non-temporal entities too. These qualifications, except the last, I shall largely ignore. For my Leibniz, the model for a monad is a mind. So the important respect in which his system runs counter to another thesis I have maintained is the position that these mind-like entities occupy as basic individuals, that is to say, as entities for which a principle of individuation can be framed, without reference to persons or bodies, in terms of their own states alone, i.e. in terms of states of consciousness or of the monadic analogues of these.

Let us see how individuation is said to be secured, how the uniqueness of the monad is supposed to be guaranteed by a certain kind of description. The doctrine we have to examine is the doctrine that each monad represents the entire universe from its own point of view. This doctrine must be unfolded step-by-step. Now what is held to be unique for each monad is its point of view. So let us begin by taking the idea of a point of view literally, i.e. by considering the idea of a point of view from which a spatially extended scene can be examined. Suppose we claimed that such a point of view could be individuated, uniquely determined, by a description, in universal terms, of the character and relations of the elements of the visual field which existed at that point of view. Someone might object that if the scene or area in question were relatively extensive, and the visual field available at different points of view were relatively restricted, such a description of the visual field at a given point of view might by no means apply uniquely to that point of view. For there might be another point of view, at some distance from the first, at which a precisely similar visual field existed. Now it might seem that this objection could be met by providing that the visual fields which existed at all points of view were no less extensive than the whole scene or area, points of view on which were to be individuated; that each visual field comprehended the whole scene In that case, it might seem, there could not be two different points of view at which the visual fields were qualitatively indistinguishable. This, of course, is the point of saying that the monad represents, or reflects, the entire universe from its point of view.

A little further reflection, however, shows that this way of individuating points of view is still utterly unsuccessful. It is necessary only to imagine the universe in question being repetitive or symmetrical in certain ways in order to see that there might be numerically different points of view from which the scenes presented would be qualitatively indistinguishable even though they comprehended the entire universe. Philosophers have imagined various complicated possibilities of this kind. But a very simple illustration will serve. Think of a chess-board. The universe we are to consider is bounded by its edges; the universe consists, therefore, of a limited arrangement of black-and-white squares.   (See illustration on facing page.)

The problem is to provide individuating descriptions of each square, and to do so in terms of the view of the rest of the board obtainable from each square. It is evident that the problem cannot be solved so long as the view from each square is limited to those squares in the immediate vicinity of the given square. With this restriction it would be impossible, for instance, to differentiate square 50 from square 43. But it is only a very little less evident that the problem still cannot be solved even if the view from each square is allowed to comprehend the entire board. It is still impossible, for example, to differentiate square 43 from square 22. The view from each over the whole board is the same: each has two white squares going away from it in one diagonal direction, and five in the other, and so on.

So long, therefore, as we take Leibniz's 'point of view of the whole universe' literally, his problem of individuation without demonstratives is still unsolved. To take it literally is to form the picture of a single world of spatially extended objects, and then to think of the state of each monad as a reflection of this world in

the mirror of that monad's consciousness. It is to think of each monad as occupying a position in this single spatial world, the position defined by 'where this world is seen from' by that monad. When we form the picture, we see that, for the reasons just considered, monads cannot be individuated by the views of the world which they get; for we can think of this world being such that the views from two different positions are indistinguishable. But, of course, the literal-seeming picture is not Leibniz's picture of reality. We obtain the Leibniz picture, or something near enough to it for our purposes, from this one, only by eliminating the single common world of spatially extended objects. All that is real in the Leibnizian system is just the monads, i.e. consciousnesses or potential or quasi-consciousnesses, and their states. There is no common spatial world for them to mirror; there is just a certain correspondence between their states of consciousness;

and spatial characteristics or features belong to the content of those states alone. There are private spaces, but no public space. Since monads, then, are not spatially related to each other, since there is no common spatial world to which they belong, there is no possibility, such as we have been considering, of there being two positions in such a world from which two different monads might have indistinguishable views. The problem of the common *symmetrical* spatial world is eliminated because the common spatial world is eliminated. Space is internal to the monad. The *views* remain, as it were, and correspond to each other in ways which the laws of perspective indicate; but there is nothing of which they are views.

So one objection to the doctrine that individuation can be secured in a way compatible with the principle of the Identity of Indiscernibles falls to the ground as far as the system of Leibniz is concerned. There remains another objection. It, too, can be met in terms of the system; but only at a very high price: the price, namely, of acknowledging that the individuals of the system are not particulars at all, but universals or types or concepts. It is, perhaps, a price that a mathematically-minded metaphysician is quite willing to pay.

This is the point at which the doctrine that monads are analogous to individual consciousnesses becomes crucial. We have already discussed the idea of an individual consciousness, and seen reason to think that this concept must be thought of as secondary to the concept of a person. Once we have accepted the concept of a person as primary, we can readily enough give sense to the idea of distinguishing different subjects of states of consciousness, and can consider the complex question of what the principles of individuation for a person, and hence for a subject of such states, should be. The relevant point at the moment, regarding such principles, is this: that since a person possesses corporeal characteristics (a body), the theoretical problem of individuation admits of a solution, no matter how *alike* the series of states of consciousness of two persons may be. This solution, as in the case of non-animated material bodies, turns ultimately on the use of demonstrative expressions.

But now consider the situation of Leibniz. The objection just now considered, that there might be indiscernible views from different *points* of view, did not arise in his system because monads had no spatial relations or position. It is analytic in the system that if there is a difference in *point* of view, then there is a difference in *view*. The Identity of Indiscernibles holds as a logically necessary principle *for points of view*. But suppose one raises the question: Why should there not be an indefinitely large number of individual consciousnesses or quasi-consciousnesses 'at', or rather with, the *same* point of view? [1] If we are to take the suggested analogy between monads and minds or consciousnesses seriously, we cannot refrain from raising this question. For nothing in our present conceptual scheme rules out as logically impossible the idea that different subjects of states of consciousness, different persons, might be in qualitatively indistinguishable states of consciousness. This question raises a dilemma for Leibniz, and confronts him with a choice of alternatives. To choose one alternative is to abandon the status of the Identity of Indiscernibles as a logical principle, to give up the view that there is a theoretically specifiable class of descriptions-in-general-terms such that it is logically impossible for more than one monad to answer to such a description. If this choice is made, then the analogy between monads and particular consciousnesses can so far be retained. The individuals of the system are particulars. But they are particulars who can only by the grace of God be, even theoretically, identifyingly referred to. For even if it *is* true that there is a uniquely applicable description for every individual, or, in other words, that no two particular consciousnesses have the same point of view, *that* it is true is not a matter of logical necessity, but of the free choice of a God who does not care for reduplication without difference. And, since demonstrative expressions can have no application to the real world of non-spatial, non-temporal monads, even the theoretical possibility of identifying references rests upon this prior theological assurance. Given this assurance, then we know

---

[1] Compare the question: How many angels can stand on the same pin point? If angels are incorporeal and 'stand' is given a suitably angelic sense, there is surely no limit. But not more than one well-balanced *person* could stand there.

that the complete set of predicates which really does define uniquely a 'point of view' will also in fact apply uniquely to the particular consciousness, if any, which has that point of view. This choice, then, appears to preserve the character of the ontology of monads as an ontology of particulars, but destroys the logical integrity of the system. For it makes the possibility of individuation rest upon a *theo*logical principle. Moreover it can only be called an ontology of particulars by courtesy; for the idea of a particular which is analogous to an individual consciousness but is in fact non-temporal is scarcely one that we can understand. Finally—though this is the kind of criticism which may well be held to be irrelevant to such metaphysical systems—it could not possibly be the primary conceptual scheme of any non-divine monad. For, in order to be contemplated as a possible conceptual scheme, it requires at least that the contemplator should attach sense to the idea of distinguishing individual subjects of states of consciousness. We have already discussed the conditions of the possibility of this idea, and they clearly do not allow that the *primary* concept of such a subject should be the concept of a Leibnizian monad. Roughly speaking, the primary conceptual scheme must be one which puts people in the world. A conceptual scheme which, instead, puts a world in each person must be, at least, a secondary product. For all these reasons taken together I shall not allow this alternative to count as an exception to my principle that an ontology which does not allow for either spatial or temporal entities cannot allow for particulars at all. An ontology which could be taken seriously only by God is not to count as a possible ontology.

The other alternative open to Leibniz is in many ways more attractive. It consists in no longer claiming for the basic individuals of the system the status of particulars, the status of particular consciousnesses or something analogous, but allowing them instead the status of types or universals or concepts. On this view, we shall no longer think of each monad as something which, by the grace of God, has and shares with no other monad a 'complete notion', i.e. falls under an exhaustive and uniquely applicable concept. *We shall instead think of the basic individuals of the system as these complete notions, these concepts, themselves.* This has many and immediate advantages from the point of view of the other requirements of the system. The Identity of Indiscernibles is at once guaranteed, in its full logical sense. If one universal differs numerically from another, then it must be possible in principle to *state* the difference in general, i.e. universal, terms. Two universals can share the same *partial* designations: red and blue are both 'colours'. But they cannot share the same *complete* designation. For difference of universals *is* difference of meaning of universal terms. Not only is the individuation of monads in general terms at once secured on this interpretation. The requirement that monads should be non-spatial and non-temporal entities is also immediately intelligible, for concepts are non-spatial and non-temporal entities; and the doctrine that the predicate inheres in the subject of every singular proposition also becomes immediately true. The simplest way to show how these results are secured is the following. The general form of a monad-designation will be the following: 'The concept of an x which . . .'. Several things must be noted about this form of designation. First and foremost, it is not the x's, not the things of which the relative pronoun prepares us for the description, which are the monads. It is the concepts of these things. Consequently, these relative clauses may contain as many spatial and temporal predicates as we please, and it will still make no sense to enquire about the temporal and spatial relations of monads. The concepts designated may have certain *logical* relations; but not any other kind of relations. There is nothing so crude as physical interaction between monads. Secondly, not every designation of the form I mentioned is a possible monad-designation. For example, the phrase 'the concept of a man who killed a man', though it designates a concept or universal, does not designate a possible monad. For it is not a 'complete' concept. If someone kills someone, that cannot be the whole story—I mean, the whole of history. There must be more to be said, e.g. what they were both wearing at the time, what their fathers were like, and so on. We obtain the designation of a 'complete' concept only when the relative clause at the beginning introduces an exhaustive description of, so to speak, the history and geography of a possible world. Here 'world' means spatio-temporal world, and 'possible' means 'capable of being described exhaustively without self-contradiction'.[1] Now, evidently, given these requirements, complete concepts will come in sets, such that two such concepts will belong to the same set if and only if the descriptions introduced by the relative clauses in each case contain identical, though differently ordered, elements. The difference between two concepts belonging to the same set will simply consist in the way the initiating relative pronouns *fit* into this common description of a possible world. Thus, if we select, from among the set of concepts which fit the actual history of the actual possible-world, the Caesar-concept and the Brutus-concept, the descriptions introduced by the relative pronouns in each case, though for the most part identical, will differ in such respects as this: that the designation of the Caesar-concept will contain the phrase '. . . and who was stabbed by a man who . . .' (where the second 'who' is followed by a Brutus-description), while the designation of the Brutus-concept will contain the phrase '. . . and who stabbed a man who . . .' (where the second 'who' will be followed by a Caesar-description). This, on the present interpretation, gives the meaning of the doctrine that every monad mirrors the entire universe from its own point of view. 'Point of view' corresponds roughly, in terms of concept-designations, to 'initial relative pronoun'. It also gives the meaning of the doctrine of the pre-established harmony. Monads harmonize because they belong to the same concept-set. Finally, we can also see why the predicate of every true subject–predicate proposition is included in the subject. For the subject of every such proposition is a monad, and hence, a complete concept, and the proposition merely asserts its membership of a class of concepts to which it analytically belongs. Thus 'Brutus stabbed a man' goes over into 'The concept of a man who F, G . . . and who stabbed a man who . . . is a concept of a man who stabbed a man'.

---

[1] The idea of an 'exhaustive description' is in fact quite meaningless in general; though meaning may be given to it in a particular context of discourse. But this is an objection I shall waive.

Now roughly to complete the sketch of the Leibnizian system on this interpretation. Complete concepts can be ordered in a certain logical respect, which may be called 'richness'. To order complete concepts in this respect is the same as to order *sets* of complete concepts; for any complete concept has the same degree of richness as any other complete concept belonging to the same set. The richest set of concepts is that in which the possible world described from each possible point of view respectively in the descriptions of each concept of the set combines the maximum of diversity in phenomena with the maximum of simplicity in natural laws. The set of monads is identical with this set of concepts. This is the meaning of the doctrine that the actual world is the best possible.

The thing which is most equivocal and uncertain in Leibniz is the question whether or not it is supposed to be purely analytic that the set of actual individuals is identical with the richest set of concepts. If it is analytic, then the whole system approaches to the ideal of logical purity to a degree perhaps unparalleled in any other metaphysical system; for it deals exclusively with the relations of concepts, touching contingency at no point. In this case, where 'C' is the designation of a complete concept, to say 'C is an actual individual' will be to say something which, if true, is itself a conceptual truth; for it will simply *mean* 'C is a member of the richest set of concepts'; and we may allow of the possibility of framing criteria of diversity and simplicity which will make this judgment a matter of calculation. This choice, however, while preserving the purity of the system, may make it seem more remote from actuality than even the purest metaphysician would wish. It would, so to speak, leave even the most sympathetic wondering whether *this* world was *in fact* the best possible, even in the sense of the proffered criteria. The alternative is to allow that 'C is an actual individual' does not mean the same as 'C is a member of the richest set of concepts', but means something like 'C is, as a matter of fact, instantiated'. But if we choose this alternative, a tremendous amount is left to theology, to the good will of God, if we are to get what is, from Leibniz's point of view, a satisfactory result. A number of key propositions become contingent, or at best theological. Suppose 'S' designates the richest set of concepts. Then all of the following propositions must be true for the universe to be satisfactory from Leibniz's point of view, and none of them is logically guaranteed. The propositions are:

1. That no complete concept is instantiated which is not a member of S.
2. That no complete concept which is a member of S is not instantiated.
3. That each instantiated complete concept is uniquely instantiated.

So far as I can see, nothing less than this plurality of requirements will do. For the meaning of 'instantiated' cannot be its most usual philosophical meaning, i.e., very roughly, 'occurring at some time or place in our common spatio-temporal framework'; since this interpretation presupposes a conceptual scheme the ultimate validity of which is denied by the whole system. Spatial and temporal relations and characteristics and things exhibiting them are 'well-founded appearances', not features of reality. Instead, to give a meaning to 'instantiated', we must hark back to the analogy of individual consciousnesses and perceptual views, and think of the instantiation of a complete concept as at least something like the creation of a unitary series of perceptual and other states of consciousness—a private view of a possible world. The creation of one such series, answering to one complete concept— i.e. the creation of one private view of a possible world—does not logically entail the creation of all the others which answer to the other complete concepts of the same set, nor does it entail the non-duplication of itself, nor the non-creation of other series answering to concepts belonging to different sets. So the principles of the Pre-established Harmony and of the Identity of Indiscernibles have to be re-invoked in a different sense, as non-logical principles, when we leave the realm of concepts for that of instantiation of concepts. The claim that a given complete concept C is in fact instantiated will, if things are to be satisfactory, amount to the following: 'C is a member of a set of complete concepts K, such that all and only the members of K are, in fact, each uniquely instantiated, and K is in fact the richest set of concepts'. When Leibniz asserts a singular proposition about the world, he will be committed to all of this, as well as the analytic proposition already distinguished as involved in any subject-predicate proposition.

The conclusion is, then, that even the decision that monads shall be concepts (or types or universals), and not particulars, is not by itself sufficient to preserve the logical purity of the system, once this is imperilled by the question: 'Why should there not be an indefinite number of particular consciousnesses enjoying the same view, the same set of states?' To counter this peril, the decision that monads are concepts must be supplemented by interpreting all the key doctrines of the system as exclusively concerned with the relations of concepts and concept-sets. The interpretation then becomes exclusively Platonistic, and quite divorced from empirical reality; but it retains its attractive purity. If, on the other hand, when the decision has been taken that monads shall be universals or concepts, it is still desired to make the system in some sense descriptive of what is actually the case, then all those extra-logical impurities which would be required on the decision that monads are particulars, are still required, though at one remove. I think it likely that this mixed system, which admits the impurities, though at one remove, is truest, taking everything into account, to the historical Leibniz. This mixed interpretation has the great merit, from the point of view of fidelity to Leibniz, of making it intelligible that monads are non-temporal and non-spatial, while admitting much that is in the texts and would be superfluous on a purely Platonistic interpretation.

This is all I shall have to say directly about Leibniz. I began by treating his system as an attempt at an ontology of particulars in which uniqueness of reference is theoretically secured without demonstratives; and I tried to show how the attempt fails, in spite of its complex ingenuity. I now want to return briefly to what I represented as the crucial difficulty for Leibniz, and connect it more firmly than I have done with the previous discussion of individual consciousnesses. Demonstratives are essentially devices for making references in a world of a spatio-temporal character.

The reason why it seemed, momentarily, as if Leibniz might dispense with them, and yet preserve an ontology of particulars, was that the world of his ultimate entities was not of a spatio-temporal character, and yet the ultimate entities could be thought of as at least courtesy-particulars so long as we told ourselves to think of them on analogy with individual consciousnesses. Even if we succeeded in performing this feat, however—and it is hard indeed to regard it as genuinely possible—Leibniz's difficulty was not solved, but sharpened. For there seemed no reason in logic, as opposed to theology, why there might not be an indefinite number of indistinguishable monad-particulars of a given monad-type; and since demonstratives had no application to entities of this non-spatial, non-temporal kind, the ordinary means of solving identification-problems were not available, even if Leibniz had been prepared to use them. Now it might be felt that even when we return to the common spatio-temporal world of particulars, and have demonstratives at our disposal, there still arises for us a difficulty parallel to the crucial difficulty which arose for Leibniz. For Leibniz the difficulty, I repeat, was that there might be any number of indistinguishable monad-particulars of a given monad-type. For us, is not the difficulty that there might be any number of exactly similar particular consciousnesses associated in the same way with a single particular body?

This difficulty would indeed arise, and would be insoluble, if we tried to construe the notion of a particular consciousness as the notion of a primary or basic type of particular. So the question I have just raised serves merely to provide additional confirmation of the thesis I have previously argued for on other grounds: the thesis that we do not have such a concept, or rather do not have it as a primary concept, the concept of a primary particular. Instead, we have the concept of a person. Persons, having corporeal characteristics, perceptibly occupying space and time, can be distinguished and identified, as other items having a material place in the spatio-temporal framework can be distinguished and identified. They can, of course, also be reidentified; and when all the theses I have argued for have been granted, there remain philosophical questions about the criteria of reidentification for per-

sons: what exactly these criteria are, what their relative weights
are, how we might adjust or further determine our concept in
extraordinary cases. No attempt on these questions is likely to be
successful until the thesis of the previous chapter is clearly understood and admitted; and once that thesis is understood and admitted, the residual problem of personal identity, though still debat-
able, appears as one of relatively minor significance and relatively
little difficulty. I shall not discuss this problem now. But perhaps
I should say one thing. The criteria of personal identity are certainly multiple. In saying that a personal body gives us a necessary
point of application for these criteria, I am not saying that the
criteria for reidentifying persons are the same as the criteria for
reidentifying material bodies. I am not denying that we might, in
unusual circumstances, be prepared to speak of two persons
alternately sharing a body, or of persons changing bodies &c.
But none of these admissions counts against the thesis that the
primary concept is that of a type of entity, a person, such that a
person necessarily has corporeal attributes as well as other kinds
of attributes. Perhaps I should also repeat that once we have
identified a particular *person*, there is nothing to stop us, and nothing does stop us, from making identifying references to a particular of a different type, namely the consciousness of that person.
It is in this way that the concept of a particular consciousness can
exist, as the concept of a non-basic, non-primary type of particular.
And only in this way.

So, then, the problem that does *not* exist is the problem that
seems to have perplexed Hume: the problem of the principle of
unity, of identity, of the particular consciousness, of the particular subject of 'perceptions' (experiences) considered as a primary
particular. There is no such problem and no such principle. If
there were such a principle, then each of us would have to apply
it in order to decide whether any contemporary experience of his
were his own or someone else's; and there is no sense in this
suggestion.[1] Where Hume erred, or seems to have erred, both

[1] This is not to deny, of course, that one *person* may be unsure of his own identity
in some way, may be unsure whether some series of actions had been performed by
him or whether such-and-such a history was his, may be altogether unsure *what* his
history has been. Then he uses what are in principle the same methods to resolve

Kant and Wittgenstein had the better insight. Perhaps neither always expressed it in the happiest way. For Kant's doctrine that the 'analytic unity of consciousness' neither requires nor admits of any principle of unity, is not as clear as one would wish. And Wittgenstein's reported remarks to the effect that the data of consciousness are not owned, that 'I', as used by N in speaking of his own feelings &c., does not refer to what 'N', as used by another, refers to, seem needlessly to flout the conceptual scheme we actually employ. It is needlessly paradoxical to deny, or seem to deny, that when M says 'N has a pain' and N says 'I have a pain', they are talking about the same entity and saying the same thing about it, needlessly paradoxical to deny that N can *confirm* that he has a pain. Instead of denying that self-ascribed states of consciousness are really ascribed at all, it is more in harmony with our actual ways of talking to say this: that, for each user of language, there is just one person in ascribing to whom states of consciousness he does not need to use the criteria of the observed behaviour of that person, though he does not necessarily not do so; and that person is himself. This remark at least respects the structure of the conceptual scheme we employ, without precluding further examination of it. The general lines of such an examination I have already, however inadequately, indicated.

---

the doubt about himself as others use to resolve the same doubt about him; and these methods simply involve the application of the ordinary criteria for *personal* identity. There are merely such differences as this: that he has to *make available* to others certain data which he does not similarly have to make available to himself, e.g. he has to report what he claims to be his memories.

LOGICAL SUBJECTS

SUBJECT AND PREDICATE (1):
TWO CRITERIA

[1] The discussions of Part I have been concerned with identifying reference to particulars. But it is not only particulars that can be identifyingly referred to. Anything whatever can be introduced into discussion by means of a singular, definitely identifying, substantival expression. Yet, among things that can be referred to, i.e. among things in general, particulars have traditionally been held to occupy a special position. It is the doctrine of the special position of particulars among objects of reference, that we have now to investigate.

Since anything whatever can be identifyingly referred to, being a possible object of identifying reference does not distinguish any class or type of items or entities from any other. No doubt there are some things that are actually referred to, and some that are not; but being an object of an actual, as opposed to a possible, reference does not distinguish any philosophically interesting class of entities. Nevertheless 'being an object of reference' does mark some distinction of philosophical interest. It does not distinguish one type of objects from another; but it does distinguish one way of appearing in discourse from another. It distinguishes appearing as a subject from appearing as a predicate. The traditional doctrine we have to investigate is the doctrine that particulars can appear in discourse as subjects only, never as predicates; whereas universals, or non-particulars generally, can appear either as subjects or as predicates. The doctrines might be more fully expressed as follows: particulars, like John, and universals, like marriage, and what we may call universals-cum-particulars, like being married to John, can all be referred to, by the use of referring expressions; but only universals, and universals-cum-particulars, never particulars alone, can be predicated, by means of predicative expressions. I do not wish to suggest that all who embrace the view I have in mind would endorse these ways of expressing it. For the moment we are simply to note the existence of a tradition according to which there is an asymmetry between particulars and universals in respect of their relations to the subject–predicate distinction. We may note also that the most emphatic denial of this asymmetry comes from a philosopher who denies the reality of the subject–predicate distinction altogether. That philosopher is Ramsey.[1] Commenting on doctrines of Johnson's and Russell's, he says that both 'make an important assumption which, to my mind, has only to be questioned to be doubted. They assume a fundamental antithesis between subject and predicate, that if a proposition consists of two terms copulated, the two terms must be functioning in different ways, one as subject, the other as predicate.' Later he says: 'There is no essential distinction between the subject of a proposition and its predicate.'

Right or wrong, the traditional view certainly accords particulars a special place among logical subjects, i.e. among objects of reference, i.e. among things in general. I want to discover the rationale of the traditional view, if it has one. But before we attack the question directly, a great deal of preliminary discussion of the subject–predicate distinction is required. This task will occupy us for the remainder of the chapter. We shall have to consider the views of philosophers who, under one name or another, accept the distinction, while not forgetting the scepticism of a Ramsey, who rejects it. I must re-emphasise the point that the aim of discussion in the present chapter is to set up a problem, and not to solve it. That task is deferred till the next chapter. Ultimately I hope to arrive at an understanding of the general distinction between reference and predication and its connexion with the distinction between particular and universal. These things are not explained in the present chapter; but the ground is prepared for their explanation.

[1] F. P. Ramsey, 'Universals', *Foundations of Mathematics*, pp. 116–7.

Subject and Predicate (1)

I. THE 'GRAMMATICAL' CRITERION

[2] We are to discuss a supposed distinction between two kinds of elements which may be combined to yield a singular proposition of a fundamental sort. I choose the word 'element' for its neutrality. For there are different ways in which the distinction may be thought of, or different aspects under which it may be presented. It may be thought of, first, as a distinction between things that are done in making a statement, a distinction between two complementary *activities* or *functions* involved in the complex activity of asserting a proposition of the kind in question. I list below some of the phrases which philosophers have used to express this functional distinction:

I

A_1		B_1
referring to something	and	describing it
naming something	,,	characterizing it
indicating something	,,	ascribing something to it
designating something	,,	predicating something of it
mentioning something	,,	saying something about it

The list could be extended. If we take any expression from list A and any expression from list B and conjoin them, we obtain an expression—e.g. 'referring to something and predicating something of it', 'mentioning something and characterizing it'—which might serve as a description of the complex activity of making a certain sort of statement, a description which distinguishes two moments, or elements, or functions, in that activity.

In so far as the functions distinguished in List I can be assigned to distinguishable *linguistic* parts of the sentence uttered in making a statement, we clearly have the possibility of a second list. In the second list the elements distinguished are linguistic parts of a statement. Expressions which philosophers have used to present this aspect of the distinction include the following:

II

A₂*	B₂
singular term	predicative expression
referring expression	predicate-expression
subject	predicate
subject-expression	ascriptive expression
proper name (Frege)	

* There are shades of difference here. An expression might be classified as 'refer-ring expression' or 'singular term' or 'proper name' or even 'subject-expression', independently of its appearance in any particular assertion. But we should not perhaps call any expression 'a subject' *tout court*, but rather *the* subject (or one of the subjects) *of* a particular assertion.

The functional distinction and the distinction of linguistic parts do not exhaust the possibilities of distinction. If we look down column A in List I, we see that every activity-expression there represents the activity as having an object: naming *some-thing*, referring to *something* etc. If we look down the expressions in column B, taking each in turn in conjunction with some ex-pression of column A, we find, first, that each activity-expression in column B represents the activity as directed to the same object (referred to by 'it') as our column A activity-word; but we find also that the third and fourth expressions of column B represent the B-activity as having another object—'predicating *something* of' the first object, 'ascribing *something* to' it. (The fifth expression we may, for the moment, neglect.) These expressions, then, sug-gest another sense which we might give to the notion of two elements being combined to yield a proposition. They suggest that we bring together or connect, in some way, two different non-linguistic items, or *terms*, in producing the unified thing, the proposition. The two items are that which we ascribe and that to which we ascribe it, that which we predicate and that of which we predicate it; and to say that we 'bring them together' in producing the proposition is to say no more than that we predicate one of, or ascribe it to, the other. The non-linguistic items which are thus brought together have sometimes been spoken of as the 'con-stituents' of the proposition. The literal implications of the word are, in this connexion, logically grotesque. But we need not necessarily be troubled by those implications; for, even in seeming

to play on them, a philosopher may say nothing which could not
be re-expressed without dependence on them. There is no doubt
that this further distinction is one which philosophers have
acknowledged and used; and it is the one which Ramsey's words
most obviously fit when he says that there is no reason to suppose
that if a proposition consists of two terms copulated, the two
terms must be functioning in different ways, one as subject, the
other as predicate. Ramsey's words were not directed against
nothing. So we may make a third list, a list in which the distinction is drawn neither between speech-functions nor between linguistic parts, but between propositional 'constituents' or terms:

III

A_3	B_3
subject	predicate
subject-term	predicate-term
term referred to	term predicated
	term ascribed

But now, having made the third distinction, we must consider
whether we cannot produce a fourth. The distinctions of List III
are relative, as it were, to a given proposition. In accordance with
List III, we distinguish the term which is in fact the subject of a
given proposition from the term which is in fact predicated of
that subject, and we do this without prejudice to the possibility of
either one of these same terms turning up, in a different proposition, in a different role. The traditional doctrine we are ultimately
to investigate lays it down, indeed, that some terms can appear
only as subjects; but it also allows that others can appear either
as subjects or as predicates. The distinctions of Lists I and II are
not in this way relative to a given proposition, though they are
relative to the idea of a proposition in general. No element
which falls on one side of either of these divisions can ever stray
to the other side. I may refer in the same way to the same thing,
or perform the same act of reference, in different propositions; but
in no proposition can this act of referring to a thing be an act of
predicating that thing. Can we not imagine the possibility of a distinction which preserves the exclusiveness of the divisions of Lists
I and II while being, like the division of List III, not a distinction

of speech-functions or linguistic parts, but a distinction of non-linguistic items in some way corresponding to these? The elements of List III are terms some of which at least may appear in either of two roles. The elements of our further list will have to combine term and role in one. The new elements will be able to figure in different propositions, but not in different roles in different propositions. Whereas the division of elements made in List III itself presupposes a distinction between terms themselves and the roles they appear in, the new division will rest on no such prior distinction, but will divide terms and their roles together, without remainder. It is worth trying to understand such a distinction if we can; for it, or something very like it, was used by a philosopher whose views on this matter we cannot ignore, viz., by Frege. Borrowing his terminology, we record the distinction between

IV

A_4 B_4

object   concept.

The distinction of List IV is a non-linguistic counterpart of the distinctions of List II. Just as no referring expression can be used alone to predicate, so no object can ever be predicated; just as no predicative expression can be used alone as a referring expression, so no concept can ever be an object. This form of the distinction is the least intuitively clear. It will be discussed further below.

[3] So far I have been concerned solely to set out certain associated distinctions, or aspects of one distinction, which have historically been made or recognized by philosophers. I have tried neither to evaluate, nor at all fully to elucidate, them. I have done little more than name them, or record their names.

Now I must try to elucidate them. There is a point on which those writers who recognize the distinctions of List II would agree, and which we may take as our starting-point. It is that the A and B items in these lists are, with a certain qualification, mutually exclusive. No A-expression can be a B-expression, or vice versa; but an A-expression can be a part of a B-expression. Thus Frege says: 'A proper name can never be a predicative expression, though it can be part of one'.[1] Geach makes a less general claim, but one which tends in the same direction. He says: 'The name of an object can . . . be used as logical subject of an assertion about an object. . . . It cannot, without a radical change of sense, be a logical predicate'.[2] Geach here uses the phrases 'logical subject', 'logical predicate', as Frege uses 'proper name', 'predicative expression', to speak of items of List II, i.e. of linguistic parts of a statement. To avoid confusion over variant terminologies, I shall sometimes use code-names derived from my lists and speak of an A_2, a B_2 etc.

The statement I quote from Geach is less general in scope than that which I quote from Frege. Its interest lies in the fact that it is claimed to be a consequence of certain definitions of 'subject' (A_2) and 'predicate' (B_2). So we can assess the adequacy of the definitions in the light of their alleged consequence. It is important to assess their adequacy; for they are *prima facie* attractive. They run as follows:[3]

A B_2 is an expression which gives us an assertion *about* something if we attach it to another expression that *stands for* what we are making the assertion *about*.

An A_2 (of an assertion) is an expression to which there is attached a B_2 so that the two together form an assertion *about* what the A_2 *stands for*.

We have to ask whether these definitions have the consequence that an A_2 can never be a B_2 or at least (to restrict ourselves to Geach's less general claim) whether they have the consequence that the name of an object can be used as an A_2, but cannot, without a radical change of sense, be a B_2. I have italicized the crucial expressions in these definitions. One of them is the word 'about'. Consider the assertions:

Raleigh smokes

Socrates is wise.

[1] 'On Concept and Object' (*Philosophical Writings of Gottlob Frege*, ed. Geach and Black, p. 50).

[2] 'Subject and Predicate' (*Mind*, 1950, p. 463).

[3] op. cit., pp. 461–2. See also the note on p. 140 of this book; Geach's A_2 word is 'Subject'.

In the first of these assertions we should wish to classify the expression 'Raleigh' as an A_2 and the expression 'smokes' as a B_2. Now certainly we could often say of someone who used the sentence that he was talking *about* Raleigh, that he made an *assertion about* Raleigh, that what he asserted about Raleigh was that he smoked. To this extent, at least, the name 'Raleigh' seems to qualify, by the definitions, as an A_2 and the word 'smokes' as a B_2. But it is also plain that there might be circumstances in which it would be correct to say of someone using the sentence that he was talking *about* smoking, and that one of the things he asserted about it was that *Raleigh* smoked or was a smoker. To this extent at least, and as far as the word 'about' is concerned, the name 'Raleigh' seems to qualify, on the definitions, as a B_2. Cook Wilson made much of this point and annexed the pair of expressions 'subject' and 'predicate' accordingly.[1] I do not think it is of great importance for logical theory, but at least it suggests that Geach's definitions rest on sand in so far as they rest on the distinguishing powers of the word 'about'. It might be objected that Geach intends to abstract from the circumstances which lead us to say, of someone who makes such an assertion, sometimes that he is saying something about Raleigh, sometimes that he is saying something about smoking; that we should distinguish between what an assertion is about, and what someone who makes the assertion is making it about, the former being constant in the case of such assertions as this, even if the latter is variable. But if we are to abstract from such circumstances, what is to tell us what an assertion is about? I do not suggest that this question *cannot* be answered; only that it *must* be; only that the required use of 'about' is one that has to be explained, and cannot be used to explain the notions of an A_2 and a B_2.

The other crucial expression in Geach's definitions is the phrase 'stands for'. Does this phrase as it occurs there, prevent our saying that 'Raleigh' is a B_2? No doubt it would do so, if we were prohibited from saying that the expression 'smokes' *stands for* smoking, or the habit of smoking. But I know of no rule or custom which makes it always senseless or incorrect to say this,

[1] *Statement and Inference*, passim, esp. pp. 114 et seq.

any more than I know of any rule or custom which would make it always senseless or incorrect to say that an assertion made in the words 'Raleigh smokes' was an assertion about smoking.[1] There is indeed a certain link between the word 'about', and the phrase 'stand for': in an assertion made *about* a thing we may expect to find an expression which *stands for* that thing. But if we insist on this link, then the insufficiency of 'about' for the purpose of these definitions carries with it the insufficiency of 'stands for'. And if, in view of the insufficiency of 'about', we break the link, we are left with a sense of 'stands for' which is in a different way useless for the purposes of definition, in that it has itself to be explained and cannot be used to explain the notions of an A_2 and a B_2.

In our second example, the expression which we, and Geach, wish to classify as a B_2 has a complexity which the corresponding expression of the first example lacks. It consists of a verb and an adjective ('is wise') instead of a verb alone ('smokes'). This makes no essential difference to the argument. There is no absolute prohibition on our saying that an assertion made in the words 'Socrates is wise' is an assertion about wisdom or about being wise, and no absolute prohibition on our saying, in such a case, or in any case, that the words 'is wise' stand for being wise or for wisdom. The definitions in effect require us to divide the sentence into two parts which together make up the whole of it; and they *allow* us to make the division in the way we want to make it, i.e. between 'Socrates' and 'is wise'. But they do not force us thereupon to classify these parts in the way in which we wish to be forced to classify them.

The words 'stand for' and 'about', then, will not carry the explanatory weight which Geach's definitions require them to carry. In order for the definitions to yield the desired results, we have to interpret the words 'stand for' and 'about' in the light of our knowledge of what is being defined. This is a disabling fact about a definition. If, in view of this disabling fact, we ignore the expressions 'stand for' and 'about', the definitions say no more

---

[1] Geach, indeed, is *required* to say that 'smokes' stands for something. For he commits himself to the view that expressions which are predicable *stand for* properties (op. cit. p. 473).

than this: that a B_2 is an expression which yields an assertion if attached to another expression, and an A_2 is an expression to which a B_2 is attached to form an assertion. But this tells us nothing about the difference between A_2s and B_2s.

Now it certainly seems that it ought to be possible to define, or characterize, a sort, A, of expressions and a sort, B, of expressions such that: (1) given an expression of either sort, one may get an assertion by attaching to it a suitable expression of the other sort; (2) 'Socrates' and 'Raleigh' belong to sort A, 'smokes' and 'is wise' to sort B; (3) an expression of sort A cannot be an expression of sort B, though it might be part of such an expression. We have seen that Geach's definitions, in relying upon 'stands for' and 'about', are so far from differentiating A-expressions and B-expressions, that they may fairly be taken to mention a feature common to both. It will be useful to have another way of speaking of this feature common to both 'Socrates' and 'is wise' in the remark 'Socrates is wise', and common to both 'Raleigh' and 'smokes' in the remark 'Raleigh smokes'. Let us say that the expression 'Socrates' ('Raleigh') serves to *introduce* the particular person, Socrates (Raleigh), into the remark, and that the expression 'is wise' ('smokes') serves to *introduce* the quality, wisdom (the habit, smoking), into the remark. Let us say that anything which is introduced, or can be introduced, into a remark by an expression is a *term*. This piece of terminology has an obvious connexion with some of our earlier lists. By conjoining certain items from the functional distinctions of List I, we obtained such phrases as 'referring to something and predicating something of it' and 'mentioning something and ascribing something to it'. These phrases yielded the distinctions of List III, between the *term referred to* and the *term predicated*. Now we can say that terms referred to and terms predicated are alike *introduced*. So expressions of the two classes distinguished in List II, i.e. A_2s and B_2s, are alike in introducing terms, even though they introduce them in different ways, being used respectively to refer to them and to predicate them. The failure of Geach's definition to distinguish these ways of introducing terms consists essentially in the fact that an assertion may, depending on the context, be said to be *about* any term introduced into it, and not merely about the term or terms introduced in the referring way.

So, then, the expression 'Socrates' and 'is wise' ('Raleigh' and 'smokes') have in common the fact that each serves to introduce a term into the remark 'Socrates is wise' ('Raleigh smokes'); but this does not mean that there is no difference in the style, the manner, of the introduction.

A grammar book of a language is, in part, a treatise on the different styles of introduction of terms into remarks by means of expressions of that language. Such a book deals with many more differences in style of introduction than we are now concerned with. But among the differences it deals with is one which supplies us with the means, or part of the means, of distinguishing A-expressions and B-expressions. This is the difference between the substantival or noun-like style of introduction, and the verbal or verb-like style of introduction. As a first, imperfect attempt at drawing the distinction between A-expressions and B-expressions in an overtly grammatical way, we may consider the following: an A-expression is a singular grammatically substantival expression; a B-expression contains at least one finite form of a verb in the indicative mood which does not, within the limits of the B-expression, form part of a complete sentence or clause; and it is a general requirement of both A- and B-expressions that an expression of either kind should be capable of yielding an assertive sentence when combined with some suitable expression of the other kind. These are obviously not sufficient conditions of an expression's being a subject- or predicate-expression. For, on the one hand, 'nothing' is a singular substantive, yet we should not want to classify it as a subject-expression. On the other hand, 'Socrates is' seems to satisfy the description of B-expressions, since (1) it contains an indicative verb, (2) it is not really a complete sentence, but at most an elliptical form of a complete sentence, and (3) it can be completed into an assertive sentence by the addition of the singular substantival expression, 'a philosopher'; yet we do not want to be committed to saying that 'Socrates is', as it occurs in such a sentence, is a predicate-expression. But though these descriptions do not state sufficient conditions of something's being an A- or a B-expression, we may regard them provisionally as stating necessary conditions. So regarded, they at least secure the consequence which Geach's definitions fail to secure, viz. that an A-expression can never be a B-expression. Moreover, they do not exclude what Frege explicitly allowed, viz. that an A-expression can be part of a B-expression. Finally, in certain simple cases, given a sentence to be exhaustively divided into an A-expression and a B-expression, these descriptions force us to make the division in the way in which we wish to be forced to make it. They allow us no alternative, in the case of 'Socrates is wise', to counting 'Socrates' as the A-expression and 'is wise' as the B-expression; for though 'Socrates is' may be held to satisfy the description of B-expressions, 'wise' does not satisfy the description of A-expressions.

The distinction as it stands is inadequate because it fails to give sufficient conditions of an expression's being an A- or a B-expression. This inadequacy, as we shall later see, is easily corrected by adding further provisions. But, as it stands, the distinction is inadequate in a more important way as well. In relying upon the grammatical phrases, 'substantival expression' and 'expression containing a verb in the indicative mood', the distinction seems both parochial and unexplained: parochial, because grammatical classifications adapted to one group of languages do not necessarily fit others which may be equally rich; unexplained because grammatical classifications do not unequivocally or clearly declare their own logical rationale. That is to say, we have to inquire into the significance of the distinction between the grammatically substantival and the grammatically verb-like modes of introducing terms.

I remarked earlier that a grammar book of a language is in part a treatise on the style of introduction of terms into remarks by means of expressions of that language. One can perhaps imagine, in such a book, a class of expressions being mentioned which *merely* served to introduce terms into remarks, and did not introduce them in any particular style. I do not say that 'Socrates' is such an expression. Still less do I say that grammatical substantives in general are such expressions. But in a comparatively uninflected language like English, an expression like 'Socrates' comes nearest to being such an expression. 'Socrates is wise', 'Socrates, be wise', 'Let Socrates be slain', 'Slay Socrates,' 'Plato admired Socrates'. Here are very different kinds of remark. In all of them, however, the expression 'Socrates' is invariant. The fact that the expression 'Socrates' occurs in a remark gives us no reason for expecting it to be one kind of remark rather than another (e.g. assertion, exhortation, command, instruction, &c.). In a highly inflected language, like Latin, the situation is different in one respect, but similar in a more important respect. That the name 'Socrates' appears in a particular grammatical case in a remark tells us *something* about the way in which the term, Socrates, is introduced into the remark. But it still tells us nothing about what general kind of remark it is. That 'Socrates' is in the vocative does not tell us whether the following remark is an assertion or a request or an undertaking; 'Socrates' is in the nominative case in 'Let Socrates be slain' as well as in 'Socrates is wise', in the accusative case in 'Kill Socrates' as well as in 'Plato admired Socrates', in the ablative case in 'Let the talk be about Socrates' as well as in 'The talk was about Socrates'.

It is different with 'is wise'. This expression introduces being wise just as 'Socrates' introduces Socrates. But it does not *merely* introduce its term, or introduce it with *merely* such an indication of the style of introduction as is given by the case-ending of a noun. It introduces its term in a quite distinctive and important style, viz. the assertive or propositional style. Now it will surely be objected that the fact that words 'is wise' occur in a remark do not guarantee that the remark is an assertion. For I might pronounce the words 'Socrates is wise' is an interrogative tone of voice and thereby ask a question instead of making an assertion. Or I might use the words 'is wise' in framing a different kind of question, in asking 'Who is wise?'. Or again I might make a remark which begins with the words '*If* Socrates is wise . . .' or '*If* Raleigh smokes . . .'; and in these cases I am certainly not asserting that Socrates is wise or that Raleigh smokes, and may not be asserting anything at all, but, e.g., giving somebody conditional permission to do something. These points are certainly correct. Yet we must remember that questions demand answers; that questions such as 'Socrates is wise?' invite us to pronounce on the truth-value of *propositions* which the questions themselves supply; that questions such as 'Who is wise?' invite us to complete and assert *propositions* of which the questions themselves supply the propositional form and half the content. And we must remember that it is part of the function of conditional clauses to bring before us *propositions*, though without commitment as to their truth-value. So even if we cannot say that the distinctive style in which 'is wise' 'smokes', etc. introduce their terms, is simply the assertive style, we can at least say that it is a propositional style, a style appropriate to the case where the term is introduced into something which has a truth-value. This is why I employed the alternation, 'the assertive or propositional style'. But I think it can be argued that the apparent weakening (by broadening) of the characterization of the style of introduction is really no weakening of it at all. For the standard way of insulating a propositional form of words from that commitment as to its truth-value which consists in asserting it is to *add* to it, to add, for example, the conjunction 'that'. This gives us a reason for saying that the *primary* function of the propositional symbolism of the indicative verb is assertive, a reason for saying that what is *primarily* the assertive style of introduction of terms is also a broader thing, a propositional style of introduction. So I shall continue to speak *indifferently* of the 'assertive' or the 'propositional' style of introduction of terms.

We should further note that the indicative mood of the verb is, in standard English, a necessary mark of assertion, whilst it is not, even in English, and still less in other languages, a necessary mark of other, secondary appearances of propositions. The propositions brought before us in the clauses of conditional sentences may be framed in the subjunctive mood; grammar may demand, or permit, a subjunctive, or accusative-and-infinitive, construction for the propositions of indirect speech; and there are other possibilities. From one point of view, these facts may seem merely to strengthen the case for characterizing B-expressions as 'expressions which introduce their terms in the *assertive* style'.

From another point of view, they may seem to raise difficulties. For if, in the desire for greater generality, we wish rather to characterize B-expressions by reference to the *propositional* style of term-introduction, must we not agree that the presence of a verb in the indicative mood is not a necessary condition of an expression's being a B-expression? Yet if we do give up this putative necessary condition, we shall have to pay, for a grammatical description, a daunting price in complexity. I think the practical answer to these difficulties is that we can perfectly well preserve the idea of the assertive or propositional style without encumbering ourselves with further grammatical classifications. The central fact to cling to is that the primary mode of appearance of *propositions* is assertion; and this gives us a reason for saying that, of many propositional styles, the primary one is what is also primarily the assertive style. We have to acknowledge the two facts, that the symbolism of assertion is also a way of symbolizing something broader, viz. the appearance of a proposition, and that this broader thing is not always or only symbolized by the symbolism of assertion. Neither fact, however, gives a decisive reason for abandoning an approach which, so far, accords well with the received views of the distinction under consideration.

So, then, the use of the indicative form of a verb characteristically involves the introduction of a term in such a way as to show that what it is introduced into is a proposition. The use of the substantival form, on the other hand, has no such implications; it is the form we should naturally use if we merely wanted to make *lists* of terms. In the remark 'Socrates is wise', both the expressions 'Socrates' and the expression 'is wise' introduce terms, viz. Socrates and being wise. But—to borrow a phrase of W. E. Johnson's—the expression 'is wise' not only introduces being wise, it also carries the assertive or propositional tie; or, in still older terminology, it not only introduces its term, it also copulates it.

This contrast of styles does not give us the materials for a strict definition of 'A-expression' and 'B-expression'. But, like the grammatical description on which it in part depends, it yields a characterization which is sufficient to guarantee both Frege's dictum, and Geach's alleged consequence of his own definition. An A-expression does not introduce its term in the typically assertive style, a B-expression does. No expression which does not introduce its term in this style can be an expression which does; and vice versa. So no A-expression can be a B-expression, or vice versa. Yet an A-expression can be part of a B-expression. 'John' is an A-expression, and 'is married to John' is a B-expression; for it introduces its term, viz. being married to John, in the assertive style.

We have, then, two new ways of describing a distinction between A-expressions and B-expressions. One way is overtly grammatical. The other attempts to get behind the grammatical distinction to its rationale. Neither description gives a fully adequate account of the distinction. But both yield the consequence which Geach desires and which Frege asserts. These ways of drawing the distinction, then, enable us to understand some of the things that are said about the items of List II. By the same token, they enable us to understand some of the things that Frege says about the items of List IV. We have just seen that, and why, an A_2 can never be a B_2 or vice versa. It is for the same reason that Frege maintains that an A_4 can never be a B_4 or vice versa, that an object can never be a concept or a concept an object. In order to present a concept as an object we should have to introduce the concept by means of a substantival expression; but Frege wishes to think of a concept as essentially something that can be represented *only* by a non-substantival expression, by an expression that introduces its term in the verb-like, coupling, propositional style. Hence the paradox that the concept *wise* is an object, not a concept.[1] All this means is that the expression 'the concept *wise*' is an A-expression, not a B-expression, that what it introduces it does *not* introduce in the assertive style. We can, at least so far, understand Frege's doctrine of A_4s and B_4s only as a curiously infelicitous way of expressing the distinction between A_2s and B_2s.

Frege characterizes the distinction between A_4s and B_4s by means of a metaphor. Objects, he says, are *complete*, concepts *incomplete* or *unsaturated*. 'Not all the parts of a thought can be

[1] op. cit. p. 45.

complete; at least one must be 'unsaturated' or predicative; otherwise they would not hold together'. [1] Of B_2s he says that it is only because their sense is unsaturated that they are capable of serving as a link. Russell, too, used this metaphor, though he applied it more narrowly: he held that in the proposition there was one constituent which was in its own nature incomplete or connective and held all of the constituents of the proposition together. Ramsey quarrelled with this metaphor, saying that there was no reason why one part of a proposition should be regarded as more incomplete than another: any *part* equally fails to be the whole. But we might now say something in defence of the metaphor. Returning to the items of List II, we might say, first, that the expression 'is wise' ('smokes') seems more incomplete than the expression 'Socrates' ('Raleigh') just because it is, in a sense, nearer completion. The name 'Socrates' might be completed into *any* kind of remark, not necessarily a proposition; but the expression 'is wise' demands a certain kind of completion, namely completion into a proposition or propositional clause. The latter expression looks fragmentary just because it suggests a particular kind of completion; the former expression looks nonfragmentary just because it carries no such suggestion. What holds for items of List II holds also, if we follow Frege, for items of List IV; since the distinctions in the latter list parallel the distinctions in the former.

Whether we like the metaphor or not matters little, so long as we recognize its basis. But Ramsey's utter lack of sympathy with it gives us a clue to which we shall return.

[4] Let us now test these conclusions by turning from Frege and Geach to consider another writer, W. V. Quine, whose views are in some respects similar to theirs. The main thing which I wish to carry away from consideration of Frege and Geach is the fact that both writers make an absolute distinction between two mutually exclusive classes of expressions, members of each of which can be combined with suitable members of the other to yield an assertion. Members of the two classes of expressions alike

---

[1] op. cit. p. 54.

introduce terms; but members of one class introduce them assertively, and members of the other class do not. The List IV
distinction of non-linguistic items merely mirrors, in a confused
way, this distinction in the style of introduction. Essentially the
distinction we have arrived at is a distinction between styles of
introduction of terms. It says nothing of any distinction between
types or *categories* of terms, between *kinds* of object. Hence it
says nothing about the distinction between particulars and
universals.

A distinction made by Quine which seems to correspond to
some extent with the List II distinction of these writers is the distinction between singular terms and general terms.[1] The correspondence is not exact. Quine gives, as examples of general terms,
adjectives like 'wise' and 'human' and common nouns like 'man'
and 'house'; whereas the corresponding B-expressions of List II
would be such phrases as 'is wise' and 'is a house'. A more striking
respect of difference between Quine and the other two writers
is to be found in what Quine clearly regards as the essential
characterization of his distinction. It runs: 'Singular terms are
accessible to positions appropriate to quantifiable variables,
while general terms are not.' When we look a little more closely,
however, these differences in approach appear much less significant.

Let us note, to begin with, that Quine explicitly contrasts
distinctions between kinds of objects (non-linguistic terms) with
the distinction between singular and general terms. Thus the substantives 'piety' and 'wisdom' are as much singular terms—the
names of abstract objects—as are the substantives 'Socrates' and
'the earth'—the names of concrete objects. Distinctions of types
of object have, on the face of it, nothing essentially to do with the
distinction between singular and general terms. This agrees with
the point we have just noted about our own interpretations of the
List II distinctions of other authors. It is, Quine goes on to say,
the distinction between singular and general terms which is the

---

[1] *Methods of Logic*, esp. pp. 203–8. Quine uses the expression 'term' in application
to linguistic items only, whereas I apply it to non-linguistic items. The word is
always to be understood in the second way, except when I am actually speaking of
Quine's doctrines or using it in the context of the phrase 'singular term'.

more vital one 'from a logical point of view'. His initial characterization of this vital distinction is admittedly vague. He says
that the singular term purports to name one and only one object,
while the general term does not purport to name at all, though it
may 'be true of' each of many things. This is clearly an unsatisfactory way of explaining a classification according to which, for
example, the word 'philosopher' is a general term and not a
singular term. For though we should not want to say, without
further ado, that the word 'philosopher' purported to name only
one object, i.e. we should not want to call it a singular term on this
explanation, it also seems that we should not want to say, without
further ado, that the word 'philosopher' was true of each of many
things or persons, i.e. we should not want to call it a general term
on this explanation. Certainly we might understand the remark
that the word 'philosopher' was true of each of many things, but
we should surely understand it as an abbreviated way of saying
something else, such as: it is true of each of many things, e.g.
Socrates, *that he is a philosopher*. That is to say, it is true of *that he
is a philosopher* rather than of *philosopher* that it is true of Socrates.
But if we are allowed thus to supplement the word 'philosopher'
to make it fit what Quine says of general terms, it is not clear why
we should not also supplement it to make it fit what he says of
singular terms. Thus it is certainly the case that the expression 'the
philosopher' may in a suitable context purport to name, or refer
to, one and only one person; and Quine would himself classify
'the philosopher' as a singular term.

Quine himself helps us out of these difficulties and shows us
that the distinction he is really concerned with is not so much the
distinction between singular terms and the expressions he lists as
general terms but the distinction between singular terms and expressions he calls 'predicates'. Thus he says: 'The positions occupied by general terms have indeed no status at all in logical
grammar, for we have found that for logical purposes the predicate recommends itself as the unit of analysis; thus "Socrates is a
man" comes to be viewed as compounded of "Socrates" and
" ① is a man", the latter being an indissoluble unit in which "man"
merely stands as a constituent syllable comparable to the "rat" in

"Socrates".' [1] Now we are back once more in the territory of the
List II distinctions, in the Frege–Geach–Russell atmosphere.
Quine's ringed numeral signifies in part, though not only, the
'incompleteness' of the predicate-expression, its demand to be
completed into a proposition by, e.g., the addition of a term-
introducing substantive. And the attraction of the phrase 'is true
of' is now readily understood; for only propositions are true, and
it is the characteristic of predicate-expressions to introduce their
terms in the propositional style.

What now of the characterization in terms of quantification?
Evidently we should not expect mere 'constituent syllables',
either of singular terms or of predicate-expressions, to be 'accessible to positions appropriate to quantified variables'. The important point must be that singular terms have such access, while
predicate-expressions do not.

But how are we to understand this doctrine? Is it, as Quine
seems to claim, a more profound and essential characterization
than that which we have given? Or does it, rather, presuppose the
latter, and appear merely as a consequence of it? Let us consider
the grammatical character of those expressions of ordinary language which are said to correspond to the quantifiers and bound
variables of logic. These are expressions such as 'everything',
'something' and (when, e.g., the existential quantifier is preceded
by the negation sign), 'nothing'; or 'everybody', 'somebody', 'nobody'; or 'There is something which . . .', 'There is nothing
which . . . not . . .', 'There is nobody who . . .' &c. Now all
these expressions either are grammatically singular substantives
or terminate in a singular relative pronoun with no accompanying
clause and, hence, from the point of view of their possible completion into sentences, have exactly the same character as grammatically singular substantives. They therefore do not have the
character of B-expressions and cannot figure grammatically in the
places in sentences in which B-expressions can figure. Given, then,
the grammatical structure of the ordinary phrases of quantification, Quine's doctrine follows immediately from our own earlier
characterization of A- and B-expressions; but if we are to take the

[1] op. cit. p. 207.

doctrine in this grammatical spirit, then it seems to add nothing to that earlier characterization and indeed to rest upon it.

It might be said that this is the wrong spirit in which to take this doctrine. We should think primarily, not of the grammatical structure of the phrases of quantification, but of the kind of meaning they have; and should then interpret, in the light of this thought, the doctrine that subject-expressions do, and predicate-expressions do not, have access to the positions in sentences occupied by the phrases of quantification. It is no easy thing to follow this recommendation. But let us try. We may suppose the existence of statements of a fundamental kind, such that each statement of this kind contains two elements, one of each of two different sorts, an A-sort and a B-sort. These elements are such that there can be both a range of statements of which each member contains the same A-element and different B-elements, and also a range of statements which contain the same B-element and different A-elements. The difference between B-elements and A-elements is as follows. We can form the idea of a statement which is entailed by, but does not entail, any member of a range of statements with a constant B-element and varying A-elements, and which itself contains the same B-element but no A-element. We may in this case speak of the A-element-expressions giving place to the variables of existential quantification in the entailed statement. We cannot, however, coherently form a corresponding idea (replacing 'A' by 'B' and 'B' by 'A' throughout) of a statement entailed by any member of a range of statements with the same A-element and different B-elements.

On such lines as these we might make, or begin to make, a serious attempt to interpret the doctrine in the recommended spirit. But would such an interpretation make immediately clear the difference between A-expressions and B-expressions? I am sure that it would not. Such a doctrine might have its place at the end, but not at the beginning, of our explanations.[1] We need not lose sight of the possibility of such an interpretation of Quine's view. But let us, for the time being, content ourselves with the superficial, grammatical interpretation, and note merely

[1] See Chapter 8, Section [3].

its concordance with the distinction as we have so far understood it.

[5] When I first drew the distinction between A-expressions and B-expressions in an overtly grammatical way, I remarked that the resulting statement of conditions was by no means adequate. It was required of an A-expression, for example, that it should be a grammatically singular substantival expression; and this description was satisfied by the word 'nothing'. To some extent the deficiencies of the overtly grammatical mode of drawing the distinctions have already been implicitly met. It is required of an A-expression, as of a B-expression, that it should introduce a term; and there is no term which 'nothing' introduces. What of the other grammatically singular substantives of quantification, such as 'something' and 'everything'? Let us say that for the purpose of this discussion an expression does not introduce a term unless it has, as part of its standard use, the aim of distinguishing that term from others, of definitely identifying it. There is no doubt, I think, that this requirement is in line with the intentions of the authors whose views we have been discussing: that Quine, for example, confronted with two ordinary statements made respectively in the words, 'Peter struck a philosopher', and 'Peter struck the philosopher', would count the expression, 'the philosopher', but not the expression, 'a philosopher', as a singular term; that Frege would similarly apply, and withhold, the designation, 'proper name'. This restriction, then, we adopt. Evidently, it excludes not only indefinite descriptions such as 'a philosopher', but also the just-mentioned substantives of quantification. 'Everything' does not distinguish, and 'something' does not definitely identify, anything.

This restriction helps also to correct certain deficiencies of the grammatical characterization of B-expressions. We noted that the requirement for a B-expression (viz., that it should include a finite form of the verb in the indicative mood, which did not, within the limits of the B-expression, form part of a complete sentence or clause with introducing conjunction) did not definitely exclude 'Socrates is . . .' from the class of B-expressions. A general requirement of both A- and B-expressions is that an expression of either kind should be capable of yielding an assertive sentence when combined with some suitable expression of the other kind. This requirement, together with the restriction imposed in the previous paragraph, rules out 'Socrates is . . .' in all cases except in those in which it is in any case admissible. Thus though 'Socrates is . . .' can be completed into such assertions as 'Socrates is wise' or 'Socrates is a philosopher', neither 'wise' nor 'a philosopher' counts as an A-expression. The phrase 'the philosopher who taught Plato' is indeed an A-expression, and 'Socrates is . . .' can be completed into the assertion 'Socrates is the philosopher who taught Plato'. But here, where 'is' has the force of 'is the same as' or 'is identical with', there is perhaps no objection to counting 'Socrates is' as a B-expression.[1]

The distinction, as it stands, requires that any expression of either kind, A or B, should, as a whole, introduce a term. This requirement may give rise, in the case of B-expressions, to a certain objection. For what terms are we to say are introduced by such expressions as 'is a philosopher' or 'is the philosopher who taught Plato'? Surely it is highly forced and unnatural to speak of such terms as *being a philosopher* or *being the philosopher who taught Plato*. To this objection there is more than one reply. In the first place, one can simply deny that there is in fact anything forced or unnatural in these locutions. Being a philosopher is certainly something one can and does talk about; and being the philosopher who taught Plato is something that at least Socrates might talk about. Both these terms are definitely identified by the substantival expressions I have just used, and hence by the corresponding B-expressions. In the second place, even if talk of the terms introduced by B-expressions is in some cases strained and unnatural, it does not immediately follow that it is either illegitimate or useless. Whether it is so or not can be determined only by examining the use that is made of it. Finally, it may turn out that we have no need, in what follows, to exploit any applications of the terminology of 'terms' to which the objection of strain and unnaturalness might be made. If, using our machinery, we can establish explanatory connexions at a fundamental level, we may

[1] See Chapter 8, Section [5].

also come to see by what analogies and extensions the distinctions we are concerned with can range from simple to more complicated levels at which, perhaps, the explanatory apparatus we use for the simple cases may indeed wear an artificial look.

[6] The distinction, as we now have it, encourages a scepticism such as Ramsey's. We have a vaguely expressed contrast between A-expressions which introduce their terms in the substantival style, and B-expressions which introduce their terms in the assertive style. This contrast derives from, and in part depends on, familiar grammatical classifications, particularly the classification 'substantive', about which we have said independently, little enough, except that it is the form which we naturally use when we want merely to *list* terms. We may well now ask, with Ramsey: How could such a distinction be of fundamental importance for logic and philosophy? Since both A-expressions and B-expressions introduce terms, and the difference is merely that B-expressions also carry the assertive indication, the propositional link, could we not undermine the whole distinction by merely making the propositional link something separate in the sentence, not part of a term-introducing expression? Could we not imagine simple sentences in which term-introducing expressions *merely* introduce terms, in no particular style, and in which the syntactical jobs at present performed by variations in the style of term-introduction were allotted to linguistic devices other than term-introducing expressions? Should we not thereby undercut the subject-predicate distinction completely? So thinking, we echo Ramsey's remark that one has only to question, in order to doubt, the assumption 'that if a proposition consists of two terms copulated, the two terms must be functioning in different ways, one as subject, the other as predicate'. And when we think further of the grammatical sources of our distinction, we may recall another remark of Ramsey's: 'Let us remind ourselves that the task on which we are engaged is not merely one of English grammar; we are not schoolchildren analysing sentences into subject, extension of the subject, complement and so on'.[1]

[1] op. cit. pp. 116–7.

We shall experiment with this scepticism in a moment. Before we do so, let us entertain a thought on the other side. Ramsey, having denied that there was any fundamental distinction to be drawn between subject and predicate, proceeded to take the undeniably valid step to the conclusion that no fundamental distinction between particular and universal could be *based on* a subject–predicate distinction—such a foundation, he imagined, being precisely what is attempted in the traditional doctrine that particulars, unlike universals, can appear as subjects only, never as predicates. But what if matters were really the other way about? It would indeed be a mistake to try to *found* the particular–universal distinction on the subject–predicate distinction. It might also be a mistake to think that the subject–predicate distinction could be explained independently of the particular–universal distinction. The correct way to think of the matter might, for example, be along such lines as these. There undoubtedly are propositions of a simple kind in which a particular term and a universal term are each introduced and assertively linked; the foundation of the subject–predicate distinction lies in the difference of type or category of the terms introduced into this kind of proposition; and that distinction is somehow extended by analogy to cases not of this simple kind, and becomes associated with grammatical forms and distinctions which obscure its foundation and make it appear a trivial and easily undermined affair. If any line of thought such as this is right, then our whole approach so far has been, if not wrong, at least misleading. For we have tried—and in this appeared to be following our authorities—to elucidate the distinctions of List II without reference to differences between types of terms. We have spoken of differences in the style of introduction of terms, not of differences between types of introduced terms. Frege's contrast between unsaturated and complete constituents merely seemed a metaphorical variation on a distinction between styles of introduction. And Quine's apparently different test for a logical subject-expression, i.e. replaceability by quantifier and variable, appeared after all to rest upon the distinction between substantive and verb.

Still, Quine seemed to offer the possibility of a deeper

interpretation; and there might be more in Frege's metaphor than we have yet found. Though the approach we have so far followed appears to be in harmony with the authorities, it is not clear that a different approach would clash with them; and we have always to bear in mind the thought that the key to our problems may not be in any one thing, but in the more or less complex interplay of several.

[7] Before we consider other possible approaches, let us develop briefly the scepticism prompted by the present approach. We return to that characterization of the subject–predicate distinction which finds, first, a likeness between subject-expression and predicate-expression in that both introduce terms and, second, the essential difference in the fact that the predicate-expression, but not the subject-expression, carries the symbolism which, in the primary case, differentiates a proposition from a mere list of terms. Returning to this characterization, we return to the doubt which it prompts about the fundamental importance of the distinction. Granted that we have assertions divisible into two term-introducing parts, why should it matter which term-introducing part carries the assertive symbolism? Could it not as well be one part as the other in every case? Or why should it be either? Why should not the propositional indication be carried by something extraneous to *any* term-introducing expression in the sentence? Thus we might represent our sample assertion, 'Socrates is wise', by merely writing down two expressions, one to introduce each term (say, the expressions 'Socrates' and 'Wisdom')[1] and then differentiating the result from a simple list by means of an extraneous proposition-indicator: say, a bracket round the two substantives, thus

(Socrates Wisdom).

So far, at least there seems to be nothing wrong with the notation; the types of the terms safeguard us from any ambiguity. Now from the vantage-point of this suggestion, we can, it seems, re-

---

[1] The expressions I here use are, of course, in fact nouns; but in a language of sentences such as those here imagined, we could not make *just the same* grammatical classifications into noun, verb, adjective &c. as we are familiar with.

gard as a mere alternative convention the ordinary grammatical technique of making one of the term-introducing expressions the carrier of the propositional link. It would be as if we adopted the rule that instead of representing the fact that we had an assertion, and not a list or a command, by means of a bracket round *both* the term-introducing expressions, we should represent this fact by bracketing one and not the other. Consistently with the adoption of this rule, we could, by way of stylistic variety, allow ourselves the choice between

(Socrates) Wisdom

and

Socrates (Wisdom)

whereas

Socrates Wisdom

would be simply a list, and

(Socrates) (Wisdom)

would be just ungrammatical. Many of the doctrines we have been considering could be re-expressed as very evident truths: e.g. the doctrine that bracketed expressions yield assertions when put alongside suitably chosen unbracketed expressions, or the doctrine that no bracketed expression was unbracketed and conversely (i.e. no subject-expression was a predicate-expression and vice versa).

But what of the traditional doctrine that no particular can appear as a predicate? *Prima facie*, this doctrine would look like a proposal to adopt a totally arbitrary convention. It would be as if someone who used both the long bracket convention and the short bracket convention should say: 'When using the short bracket convention, always write the assertion

(Socrates Wisdom)

in the form

Socrates (Wisdom)

and never in the form

(Socrates) Wisdom

and observe a similar restriction for all expressions introducing particular terms; in general, the assertive symbolism is never to be applied to an expression merely introducing a particular'. Now of course a convention in itself arbitrary may acquire prestige through being long observed. It may come to seem part of the order of things, even expressive of a profound truth or necessity. So it might come to seem to people utterly senseless to write '(Socrates) Wisdom'; for, it might seem, an expression introducing a particular term just *cannot* have the assertive bracket put around it alone.

It is important to note the limitations of this sceptical line of argument. At most it shows that *if* we think of the subject–predicate distinction in a certain way and *if* we confine our attention to a very simple kind of assertion, *then*—under these two conditions—the doctrine that a particular can never appear as a predicate appears to lack a rationale and to express an arbitrary prejudice. The argument does not show that the doctrine would continue to appear in this light if either one of these conditions were not fulfilled: if, for example, we thought of the subject–predicate distinction in some other way or if, while still thinking of it in the same way, we began to consider more complicated cases of assertion. Still, it is worth making this limited point. For it at least shows us that we must look for the rationale of the traditional doctrine, if it has one, outside these limits. That we should have to do this is not made immediately clear by the treatment accorded to the subject–predicate distinction by the writers we have been considering.

There is a possible objection, which should be mentioned now, to the procedure I have just been following. The objection is, roughly, that in trying, as it were, to abolish the distinction between the noun-like and the verb-like parts of a simple statement, by separating the assertion-indicating function from the term-introducing function of the verb-like part, I have overlooked another important function of the verb-like part: the function, to which Aristotle particularly directed attention, of indicating time, by means of variation in tense. The answer to the objection is that here again there seems to be nothing compelling about the association of this function with a particular range of term-introducing expressions. We have just seen that we can theoretically detach the assertive function from a variation in the grammatical style of a term-introducing expression and associate it with a separate piece of symbolism; and that we can then arbitrarily reassociate it, if we wish, with a part, rather than the whole, of the assertion, as when we make the transition from the symbolism of the coupling bracket around the whole sentence to the short bracket convention. Similarly for time-indication. An arrow running above the whole sentence and pointing to the left might be used to indicate a past time-reference, an arrow running to the right future time-reference and the absence of an arrow present time-reference. Thus for 'Socrates was wise', we should have

$$\overset{\longleftarrow}{(\text{Socrates Wisdom})}$$

As before, the adoption of a short-arrow convention would give us the alternatives of

$$\overset{\longleftarrow}{(\text{Socrates Wisdom})} \text{ and } (\text{Socrates } \overset{\longleftarrow}{\text{Wisdom}})$$

and we might even choose to exploit this flexibility in symbolism to mark a certain kind of difference which may sometimes go unmarked in ordinary written language, though there are various ways in which we can there mark it if we choose. For, as things are, we *might* say 'Socrates was wise' indifferently in the case where Socrates used to be wise and is no longer wise, and in the case where Socrates has ceased, not to be wise, but to be. We might feel that

$$(\text{Socrates } \overset{\longleftarrow}{\text{Wisdom}})$$

was more appropriate for the first case and

$$\overset{\longleftarrow}{(\text{Socrates Wisdom})}$$

for the second.[1] It must be admitted that if we systematically took advantage, in the way I have suggested, of the notational flexibility of the short-arrow convention, then no doubt we

[1] It is worth noting what a natural economy it would be to eliminate the assertive bracket in favour of an assertive *line*, i.e. to combine the assertive indication with the time-indication.

should more often attach the short arrow to the expression introducing the universal term than to the expression introducing the particular terms in assertions of the kind we are considering; for, in general, there is more to say about events in which particular persons or objects participate or about their short-term states or conditions than there is to say about their permanent characteristics. Granted that we were going to have a rule *either* to the effect that expressions simply introducing particulars *or* to the effect that expressions simply introducing universals should never have the time-indication associated with them, then the fact I have just mentioned would be a reason for applying the restrictive rule to terms introducing particulars. But that fact is evidently not a compelling reason for having such a restrictive rule at all.

The above remarks are, of course, not intended as a contribution to the study of tense-differences and their functions. They are designed simply to indicate one way in which a possible objection to my procedure might be met. There are many other ways of meeting it. We have to recognize that the List II expressions distinguished as B-expressions are, in fact, often time-indicators as well as assertion-indicators. But neither separately nor together, it seems, do these facts about them give an immediately compelling reason for regarding the distinction as fundamental, or essential to any symbolism for assertion; for both functions, it seems, could be performed independently of any such distinction between term-introducing expressions. Nor, consequently, do these facts seem to give a firm basis for the traditional association between the particular–universal distinction and the subject–predicate distinction.

It is time to consider a different approach to the subject–predicate distinction. Having set out a version of that distinction which takes no account of difference of type or category of terms, we are now to set out a version of the distinction which is directly based upon a difference of type or category of terms.

2. THE CATEGORY CRITERION

[8] Any term, particular or universal, must be capable of being assertively tied to some other term or terms so as to yield a significant result, a proposition. A term may be thought of as a principle of collection of other terms. It may be said to *collect* just those terms such that when it is assertively tied to any one of them, the result is not only a significant, but also a true, proposition. Now it is convenient to have, and we do have, names for different kinds of assertive tying, based partly on differences in the types or categories of terms, partly on differences in the purpose or context of assertion. Thus we say of a speaker that he *characterizes* an object as such-and-such, or *instances* something as a so-and-so, or *attributes* something to something else. Corresponding to some of these names of different kinds of assert*ive* tying, we have names for different kinds of assert*ed* tie. Thus we use such forms as '... is an instance of ...', '... is characterized by ...', '... has the relation of ... to ...'. I shall appropriate some of these expressions, using them as the names of different kinds of asserted tie, where the differences concerned are merely differences in the types of the tied terms and have nothing to do with the context or purpose of assertion. It is important that we should not think of these two- or three-place expressions as themselves the names of terms of a certain kind, viz. relations. Something analogous to Bradley's argument against the reality of relations may be used, not indeed to show that relations are unreal, but to show that such assertible links between terms as these are not to be construed as ordinary relations. Let us speak of them as non-relational ties.[1]

Non-relational ties may bind particulars to universals; universals to universals; and particulars to particulars. Among those universals which apply to, or collect, particulars, I shall draw a rough distinction between two types; and hence also between two kinds of non-relational tie which bind particulars and universals.

[1] See further, p. 174 *et. seq*. There are many differences between non-relational ties and genuine relations besides that which I have just hinted at. Non-relational ties, for example, demand of the terms they bind a degree of type-heterogeneity greater than that which relations will generally suffer.

This is the distinction between *sortal* and *characterizing* universals, and hence also between the sortal, or *instantial*, tie and the characterizing tie. A sortal universal supplies a principle for distinguishing and counting individual particulars which it collects. It presupposes no antecedent principle, or method, of individuating the particulars it collects. Characterizing universals, on the other hand, whilst they supply principles of grouping, even of counting, particulars, supply such principles only for particulars already distinguished, or distinguishable, in accordance with some antecedent principle or method. Roughly, and with reservations, certain common nouns for particulars introduce sortal universals, while verbs and adjectives applicable to particulars introduce characterizing universals. Now it is not only characterizing universals which have the power to supply principles of grouping for particulars already distinguishable in accordance with some other principle or method. This power they share with particulars themselves. Thus, just as among particulars already distinguished as historical utterances, or catches at cricket, we may further group together those which are wise utterances, or difficult catches, so among such particulars we may further group together those which are Socrates' utterances, or Carr's catches. Socrates, like wisdom, may serve as a principle of grouping of particulars already distinguished as such in accordance with some other principle or method. I shall accordingly assume the right to speak of non-relational ties between particulars and particulars; and to this kind of tie I shall, in memory of Cook Wilson, give the name, 'the attributive tie'. (Of course, particulars tied by the attributive tie will be of different types from each other.) In general, whenever a particular is bound to a universal by the characterizing tie, we can frame the idea of another particular bound to the first by the attributive tie; so to the characterizing tie between Socrates and the universal, *dying*, there corresponds the attributive tie between Socrates and the particular, his death.[1]

---

[1] We have more use for some of the ideas of particulars that we can frame in this way than we have for others. In general, we perhaps have most use for the ideas of particular events so framed, less use for the ideas of particular conditions or states,

Let us now compare the ways in which terms may collect each other by these three kinds of tie.

(1) One and the same particular may be sortally or instantially tied to a number of different sortal universals: thus Fido is a dog, an animal, a terrier. In general, the universals to which one and the same particular is sortally tied will have a characteristic relation to each other, which is sometimes described as that of sub- or super-ordination. Again, one and the same sortal universal may be instantially tied to a number of different particulars: Fido, Coco and Rover are all dogs. Such particulars will have to each other a general, or sortal, resemblance. We may say that while one particular may collect several universals by the instantial tie, and one universal may collect many particulars by the instantial tie, the principle of collection in each case is of quite a different kind. We may mark this difference by employing, in addition to the symmetrical form, 'x is instantially tied to y' (where x or y can be either particular or universal, so long as one is each), also the asymmetrical form, 'x is an instance of y' (where x must be particular and y universal).

(2) One and the same particular may be tied by a characterizing tie to many characterizing universals: thus Socrates is wise, is warm, is cold, fights, talks, dies. And one and the same characterizing universal may be tied by a characterizing tie to many different particulars: Socrates, Plato, Aristotle are all wise, all die. *Via* the characterizing tie, again, then, one particular collects, at different times, many universals, and one universal, at different times, many particulars. But again the principle of collection is different in each case. The principle on which one particular collects different characterizing universals at different times is supplied by the continuing identity of the particular, in which the most widely and generally, though not universally, distinguishable factor is what is vaguely referred to as spatio-temporal

---

least use for the ideas of particulars which are simply cases of qualities or properties. But we do say such things as 'His anger cooled rapidly', 'His cold is more severe than hers', even 'The wisdom of Socrates is preserved for us by Plato'. Some philosophers, no doubt, made too much of the category of particularized qualities. But we need not therefore deny that we acknowledge them.

continuity; the principle on which one characterizing universal collects different particulars, at the same or different times, involves a certain characteristic resemblance between those particulars at those times. We may mark this difference by adding to the symmetrical phrase, 'x is joined by a characterizing tie to y', the asymmetrical phrase, 'x is characterized by y' (where x must be particular and y universal).

(3) When we come to consider the attributive tie, there is a difference in the situation. A given particular, say Socrates, may collect, by the characterizing tie, an enormous number of characterizing universals; correspondingly it may collect, by the attributive tie, an enormous number of particulars. Thus Socrates collects, by the characterizing tie, say *smiling* and *orating*, and correspondingly, by the attributive tie, a particular smile and a particular oration. But whereas the universals, *smiling* and *orating*, can collect, by the characterizing tie, any number of particulars of the same kind as Socrates, the particular smile and the particular oration cannot, by the attributive tie, collect any other particulars of the same kind as Socrates. Let us express this feature of attributive ties by speaking of the dependent member and the independent member of any such tie: the independent member may in general collect many particulars similar to the dependent member, but the dependent member cannot collect any other particulars similar to the independent member. In addition to the symmetrical form, 'x is attributively tied to y', we may employ the asymmetrical form, 'y is attributed to x' (where y must be the dependent member).[1]

---

[1] There are some particulars which are the independent members of all the attributive ties they enter into. These may be called, simply, independent particulars. Aristotle seems to have thought that the only independent particulars (of an at all familiar kind) were fairly substantial things like horses and men. But there seems no reason for denying that some phenomena or occurrences less substantial than these may also rank as independent particulars. No doubt there will be borderline cases, i.e. cases where we should hesitate between saying that one particular is dependently attributed to another and saying that it is genuinely (e.g. causally) related to another. But it seems difficult to force the border quite as far as Aristotle would wish in the direction of the satisfyingly substantial particular; unless indeed we reinforce the present notion of an independent particular with further criteria such as those employed in Part I of this book as tests for the status of *basic* particular.

[9] The object of this discussion of different kinds of non-relational ties was to prepare the ground for setting up another criterion for the subject–predicate distinction. Now there is an obvious analogy between the ways in which sortal and characterizing universals respectively collect the particulars they collect. This analogy does not extend to the ways in which particulars collect universals by instantial or characterizing ties; nor does it extend to the ways in which particulars collect other particulars by the attributive tie. Suppose now, on the strength of these analogies and disanalogies, we adopt the following ruling: the primary sense of '*y* is predicated of *x*' is '*x* is asserted to be non-relationally tied to *y* either as an instance of *y* or as characterized by *y*'. In view of the senses we have given to 'is an instance of' and 'is characterized by', this amounts to *ruling* that universals can be predicated of particulars, but not particulars of universals. The next step is to extend the sense of '*y* is predicated of *x*', while preserving the analogies on which the primary sense is based. Thus, to allow that universals may be predicated of universals, we have to show that there are non-relational ties between universals and universals analogous to the characterizing or sortal ties between universals and particulars. And, of course, it is easy to find such analogies. Is not thinking of different species as species of one genus analogous to thinking of different particulars as specimens of one species? Again, the tie between different musical compositions, themselves non-particulars (types), and their common form, say, the sonata or the symphony, is analogous to the sortal tie between a particular and a universal. Or again, thinking of different hues or colours as bright or sombre, thinking of different human qualities as amiable or un-amiable, is analogous to thinking of different particulars as characterized in such-and-such ways. In all these cases we think of universals collecting other universals in ways analogous to the ways in which universals collect those particulars which are instances of them or are characterized by them. But we cannot think of particulars collecting *either* universals *or* other particulars in ways at all analogous to these. A further slight extension of the sense of '*y* is predicated of *x*' is required, to allow for

the doctrine that particulars, though not simply predicable, may be parts of what is predicated. This may be most readily secured by a slight modification of the rules for 'is an instance of' and 'is characterized by'. The phrases, 'is an instance of' and 'is characterized by', as I have introduced them, are properly followed by, respectively, the designation of a sortal universal and the designation of a characterizing universal. We now rule that so long as the proper successors of these phrases are present, the principles of grouping which they introduce may be further modified in any way whatsoever, without detriment to the appropriateness of 'is an instance of' or 'is characterized by'. Thus one particular may be an instance, not only of a smile, but of a smile of Socrates, and another may be characterized, not only by being married, but by being married to John. So Socrates and John may be part of what is predicated, though not themselves predicable.

In this way, by taking as the fundamental case of y being predicated of x, the case in which x (a particular) is asserted either to be an instance of, or to be characterized by, y (a universal), and by proceeding thence to develop other cases by analogy or extension, we can build up a sense of 'to predicate' for which it is true that universals can both be simply predicated and have things predicated of them (i.e. be subjects), whereas particulars can never be simply predicated, though they can have things predicated of them (i.e. be subjects) and can be parts of what is predicated.

This procedure, then, yields us the second, or 'categorial', criterion for the subject–predicate distinction. In developing the first, or 'grammatical', criterion, I made no use of any distinction between types of terms, but concentrated solely on the presence or absence of the propositional symbolism, i.e. of the propositional style of term-introduction. In developing the categorial criterion, on the other hand, I make no reference to the location of the assertive symbolism, but build up the criterion solely on the basis of a distinction between types of terms. To all appearance, therefore, the two criteria are independent of each other. We must now inquire how far there is, in practice, a correspondence between what is predicated in the sense of the first criterion, and what is predicated in the sense of the second; and then seek to explain the degree of correspondence we find. If we can both find and explain a correspondence, we shall have found the rationale of the traditional doctrine.

3. TENSIONS AND AFFINITIES BETWEEN THESE CRITERIA

[10] It is obvious enough that the correspondence between the grammatical and categorial requirements for a predicate works well in general. It is all the more instructive to consider certain special cases where tension develops between these requirements and where we find a rather remarkable linguistic resolution of the tension. We approach these cases indirectly, by way of some cases where there is no such tension.

Among characteristic linguistic forms of grammatically predicative expression are the following: an indicative form of a verb; an adjective preceded by an indicative form of the verb 'to be'; a noun preceded by the indefinite article preceded by an indicative form of the verb 'to be'. Thus we have 'Socrates smiles', 'Socrates is wise', 'Socrates is a philosopher'. In each of these examples a predicated universal is introduced by one of the characteristic linguistic forms. Both the categorial test and the grammatical test for what is predicated yield the same answer. In so far as these two tests are always to yield the same answer, we might expect that proper names of particulars would never admit of appearance in any of these simple forms. In practice, of course, we find that names of particulars admit quite freely of adjectival forms which can follow the verb 'to be': e.g. 'is English, Victorian, Napoleonic, American, Russellian, Christian, Aristotelian' &c.; they admit fairly freely of use as nouns after the indefinite article and the verb 'to be': e.g. 'is a Hitler, a Quisling' &c.; and they even sometimes admit of a verb-form: e.g. it might be jocularly said of a philosopher that he Platonizes a good deal. These cases, however, present no difficulty for one who wishes to insist on the correspondence between the category requirements and the grammatical requirements for predicates. Suppose 'N' is the relevant proper name of a particular. Then it does not generally seem that we use the forms 'x is N-ic (N-ian)', 'x is a N', 'x N-izes', to assert a non-relational tie between x and N. What, in such cases, the grammatical predicate-expression introduces and assertively links to x is not just the particular, N, but either a characterizing or sortal universal to which the particular has, for historical reasons, given its name (e.g. *being Napoleonic*) or one of those compounds of relational universal and particular which the extended category criterion allows us to count as predicable (e.g. in some contexts, 'being American' has the force of 'being manufactured in America' and 'being British' means 'being subject to the sovereign of Great Britain').

The point here is that language freely allows the use of proper names of particulars in simple grammatically predicative forms, just in those cases where the use of these forms has no tendency to make us say that we are predicating the particular, in the cases, in fact, where we can say that the term introduced by the grammatically predicative expression is a universal or a universal-cum-particular. Should anyone object to the use of the word 'universal' here, we can say instead: the principle of collection supplied in such a case by, e.g., Napoleon, is a resemblance principle of the kind which universals supply, and not a principle of the kind which the continuing identity of a particular supplies. The non-relational tie asserted by 'The gesture was Napoleonic' is a characterizing tie rather than an attributive tie: the things asserted to be bound by the tie are not the gesture and Napoleon, but the gesture and resemblance principle of collection supplied by Napoleon. Generally, we are prepared to use such predicate-forms as 'is Napoleonic' only when we can regard Napoleon as supplying a principle of collection at least analogous to those supplied by universals. Thus the analogy on which our category-notion of predication is built up is preserved.

But now let us compare cases where we are prepared to use these forms with cases where we are strikingly unprepared to use them. Let us take first Ramsey's pair of sentences:

(1) Socrates is wise
(2) Wisdom is a characteristic of Socrates.

We should notice, first, that if we start off with the substantive, 'wisdom', to say what (1) says, then we do *not* proceed to 'is

Socratic' or 'Socratizes', but proceed instead somewhat as in (2). Now the category test and the grammatical test alike requires us to say of (1) that wisdom is predicated of Socrates, the subject of the predication. The category test seems to require us to say exactly the same thing of (2). For both sentences assert a characterizing tie binding the particular, Socrates, and the universal, wisdom. The grammatical test does not require us to say the same thing of (2). But language safeguards us from having, on this test, to say the *opposite* thing (i.e. that Socrates is predicated of wisdom) by introducing, as it were, a dummy universal, *being a characteristic (of)*. If we take this at its face value, we are able, adhering to the grammatical test, to purchase immunity from saying that Socrates is predicated of wisdom, and to say instead that what is predicated of wisdom is the compound of universal and particular, viz. *being a characteristic of Socrates*. What we find here is, as it were, an anxiety to preserve the grammatical predicate-place for the categorially predicable, even at the cost of faking universals to keep up appearances. For the general grammatical requirements of verb-like plus substantival elements would be satisfied by writing (2) in a form such as 'Wisdom is Socratic (Socratizes)', which, since it interposes no dummy universal, would, on the grammatical criterion, require us to say that Socrates is predicated and would thus lead to an overt clash between the grammatical criterion and the category criterion.

Why do I speak of *faking* universals to avoid the overt clash? The answer was foreshadowed in the previous section. It becomes clear enough, if we ask why we do not similarly insist on

> Socrates is characterized by wisdom

instead of

> Socrates is wise.

To any such insistence we could raise an objection. It is a necessary feature of any term, particular or universal or particular-cum-universal, that it is capable of entering into a non-relational tie with (some) other terms, and any subject–predicate proposition is an assertion of a non-relational tie between terms. If we promote the tie to a term, or a part of a term, then we must regard the proposition as asserting a non-relational tie between the new terms, e.g. *Socrates* and *being characterized by wisdom*. But if we *insist* on the promotion at the first stage, why not at the second, thus: 'Socrates is characterized by being characterized by wisdom'? And so on. We must stop at some point if we are to have a proposition. Why insist on starting?

But does not the same objection apply to the insistence on (2) as an alternative to 'Wisdom Socratizes'? It would, of course, apply, if we discounted the reason, the motive, for the preference. But we cannot discount it: the question of justification, or explanation, of the drive to keep up appearances is still *sub judice*. Besides, we have an alternative way, permitted by the grammatical criterion, of looking at the matter. We can construe 'Wisdom is a characteristic of' as predicate-expression, and 'Socrates' as subject-expression, and see the whole sentence, not as an insisted-on alternative to 'Wisdom Socratizes', but as a permitted periphrasis for 'Socrates is wise'. But if we make this choice, then we must be clear that the other analysis which the grammatical criterion leaves open (viz. Subject; 'Wisdom'; Predicate: 'is a characteristic of Socrates') is no longer admitted to be an open alternative at all. That is, we must give up, grammar notwithstanding, the ambition so to frame this proposition that wisdom appears as a subject.

Faced with (2), then, either we can take the grammatical criterion at its face value, call 'wisdom' a subject-expression and then note that, in order to keep in line with the category criterion, we have to fake the dummy universal, *being a characteristic (of)*; or we can keep in line without faking anything—but in that case we have directly to strengthen the grammatical criterion with the category criterion and say that, appearances notwithstanding, no analysis of (2) is permissible which makes 'wisdom' the subject-expression.

[11] Let us consider now another set of cases, in some respects analogous, in others more complicated. Sometimes, if we asked which of the kinds of non-relational tie I have distinguished was actually asserted by a proposition, the natural answer would be

the attributive tie. But this seems to raise difficulties. For the attributive tie joins only particulars to particulars. So it seems that in the assertion of attributive ties either nothing appears as a predicate or a particular does. But the idea that nothing appears as a predicate goes against the grammatical requirements, and the idea that a particular appears as a predicate goes against the category requirements. How does language deal with this situation? We are concerned, it must be remembered, with assertions in which one particular is asserted to be attributively tied to another, in which, as we sometimes actually say, one particular is attributed to another.

Examples of sentences of this kind are:

The blow which blinded John *was struck by* Peter
The catch which got Compton out *was made by* Carr.[1]

The particulars asserted to be attributively tied are the blow and Peter in one case, the catch and Carr in the other. And appearances are this time saved by promoting the tie between the particular action and the particular agent into a quasi-relational-universal. The general scheme of such sentences is roughly:

The particular action—is performed/executed/done by—the
particular agent.

It is easy to see that the would-be relational universal is no such thing, no genuine term. We cannot, for example, form a further term by compounding the particular action with the quasi-universal. The agent and his action are two different particulars; but his action and his doing of his action are not two different particulars. As before, if we insist, for its own sake, on the erection of tie into term at one stage, why not at another, i.e. why not insist on moving to 'The doing of the action—was executed by—the agent', and so on?

It might seem that, again as before, we have available another way of looking at these sentences. Must we see them as supplying dummy universals to keep up the façade of agreement between the grammatical requirements and the category requirements for

[1] Sometimes the genitive case is used in such constructions: thus, 'The blow was Peter's', 'The catch was Carr's'.

a predicate? Can we not see them as permitted periphrases for sentences which raise no such problems, i.e. for sentences which are not naturally seen as assertions of attributive ties at all? In some simple cases, this choice is obviously open: e.g. 'He effected his escape' is simply a periphrastic way of saying 'He escaped'. And it is true that sentences are available which are, in a broad sense, variants on our problem sentences. Thus we can say: 'Compton was caught out by Carr', and 'John was blinded by being struck by Peter'.

But do these sentences do quite the same job as the problem sentences? We can *speak* them so that they do—by stressing 'Carr' in one and 'Peter' in the other. The point is that the grammatical structure of the problem sentence is appropriate to the cases where the corresponding assertions carry certain presuppositions: that there was a catch which got Compton out, a blow which blinded John. The structure of the variant sentences is not similarly appropriate to these cases, though the force of presupposition can be preserved by suitable stressing of elements in the variant sentences. This means that there is a certain strain in construing the problem sentences as permitted periphrases for other sentences, sentences in which 'The blow which blinded John' and 'The catch which got Compton out' do not appear as claimants for the position of subject-expression. It is not merely whim which induces us to cast the terms these phrases introduce for the role of subjects of predication. In this fact we may detect the germ of another criterion for the subject-predicate distinction, a criterion which may turn out to form a bridge between those other two whose real and feigned correspondences we have been considering. This idea I shall develop in the next chapter.

I have described my examples crudely and questionably enough, and there is, I think, a rich field of interesting matter here towards which I have only gestured. But it is, I think, unquestionable that these examples show, to speak metaphorically, a kind of effort on the part of language to keep, or to seem to keep, in line two criteria for something being predicated, or appearing as a predicate: the grammatical criterion, according to which that which is predicated is introduced by a part of the sentence which carries assertive symbolism; and the category criterion according to which only universals, or complexes containing universals, never particulars *simpliciter*, can be predicated. It is as if there were felt to be a certain appropriateness in these two criteria corresponding, yielding the same result. It is the tendency which I thus metaphorically speak of in terms of effort or feeling, which we now have to try to explain.

6

SUBJECT AND PREDICATE (2): LOGICAL SUBJECTS AND PARTICULAR OBJECTS

I think it is possible to give a complete theoretical explanation of this association, of the affinity, so to speak, which the grammatical criterion and the category criterion appear to have for each other. I think, moreover, that the general lines of the explanation are clear and indisputable. Its detailed elaboration, however, seems to me a matter of great difficulty, in which mistakes are easy to make, and clarity hard to preserve. The total explanation I offer is advanced in the form of two theories developed respectively in the first and second parts of this chapter. The two theories are independent of each other, in that they operate at different levels and either could be accepted without the other. The essentials of the explanation offered are contained in the first theory; but the theories are connected in this sense, that if both are accepted, the second can be seen to reinforce the explanation given in the first. The second has also an independent interest, which is developed in the succeeding chapter. At the end of these explanations it becomes clear that the 'grammatical criterion' for the subject–predicate distinction is, as one would expect, of secondary theoretical importance, being mainly a mark of the presence or absence of a more fundamental kind of completeness.

1. THE INTRODUCTION OF PARTICULARS INTO PROPOSITIONS

[1] Part of the answer to our question is to be found in a contrast between the conditions of introducing particular and universal terms respectively into propositions. The notion of term-

introduction, which I have used throughout, is, of course, neutral as between the introduction of a term as a subject of predication and the introduction of a term as predicated. *But term-introduction, in either mode, essentially involves the idea of identification.* The term-introducing expression indicates, or is meant to indicate, what term (*which* particular, *which* universal) is introduced by its means. When we say 'John smokes', the first expression indicates what particular it is that is referred to, the second expression indicates what characteristic it is that is ascribed to him.

Let us first consider the conditions of introducing a particular into a proposition; and here I shall temporarily revert, for the sake of its familiarity, to the non-neutral terminology of 're-ferring'. We are to inquire into the conditions which must be satisfied in order for it to be the case that an identifying reference to a particular is made by a speaker and correctly understood by a hearer. One condition, evidently, is that there should be a particular which the speaker is referring to; another is that there should be a particular which the hearer takes him to be referring to; a third is that the speaker's particular should be identical with the hearer's. Let us pay attention to the first of these conditions. What does it involve? What is concealed by the phrase, 'to which he is referring'? Well, at least it involves this requirement, that (in the standard case—we need not consider others) there should be a particular answering to the description used by the speaker, if he uses a description. What if he uses a name? One cannot significantly use a name to refer to someone or something unless one knows who or what it is that one is referring to by that name. One must, in other words, be prepared to substitute a description for the name. So the case of name-using calls for only a minor modification of the condition stated. There must be a particular answering to the description which the speaker uses, or to the description which he is prepared to substitute for the name he uses, if he uses a name. But this condition is not enough. He is referring to just one particular. If we abstract from the force of the definite article in a given speech-situation, there may be many particulars which are fitted by the description the speaker uses or the description he would substitute for the name he uses. Of course the speaker, rightly, relies heavily on the context of the speech-situation. He says no more than is necessary. But we are now considering, not simply what he says, but the conditions of his doing what he does by what he says. For him to be referring to just one particular, it is not enough that there should be at least one particular which his description fits. There must be *at most* one such particular *which he has in mind*. But he cannot, for himself, distinguish the particular which he has in mind by the fact that it is the one he has in mind. So there must be some description he could give, though it need not be the description he does give, which applies uniquely to the one he has in mind and does not include the phrase, 'the one I have in mind'.[1] It might be maintained that this remark requires qualification by the addition of some such phrase as 'as far as he knows' after 'uniquely'; and this on the ground that the speaker's subsequent knowledge might embrace a second and distinguishable particular which, however, also answered to any putatively identifying description which he was able to give at the time of the original putative reference. But this argument is mistaken. If the situation as described should really arise (it would be a rare, but not impossible, one), then it would follow that the speaker really did not know at the time of the original putative reference what particular he was speaking

[1] Such a description—let us call it an 'identifying description'—may, of course, include demonstrative elements, i.e. it need not be framed in purely general terms. In general, indeed, it could not be so framed; it is impossible, in general, to free all identification of particulars from all dependence upon demonstratively indicatable features of the situation of reference. It should be added, moreover, that the identifying description, though it must not include a reference to the speaker's own reference to the particular in question, may include a reference to another's reference to that particular. If a putatively identifying description is of this latter kind, then, indeed, the question, whether it is a genuinely identifying description, turns on the question, whether the reference it refers to is itself a genuinely identifying reference. So one reference may borrow its credentials, as a genuinely identifying reference, from another; and that from another. But this regress is not infinite.

It is perhaps prudent to make certain other qualifications explicit. For example here, as elsewhere, I use the word 'description' in an extended, though philosophically familiar, sense. A 'description' of a thing need not tell one what it is *like*; 'The city I spent last year in' might be an identifying description of Chicago. Again, when I speak of 'preparedness to substitute a description for a name', this requirement must not be taken too literally. It is not required that people should be very ready articulators of what they know.

The requirements here set out are, of course, essentially the same as the requirements for 'hearer's identification' set out in Chapter 1, Section [3], p. 23.

of, that he really did not satisfy the conditions of making a genuine identifying reference, though he thought he did; for there would now be no answer to the question, *which* particular he was then referring to. If, on the other hand, he can now answer this question, then it follows that he could then have supplied some detail which would differentiate the particular referred to to from the one his subsequent knowledge embraces, i.e. the situation as described would not really have arisen.

We may summarize all this by saying that in order for an identifying reference to a particular to be made, there must be some true empirical proposition known, in some not too exacting sense of this word, to the speaker, to the effect that there is just one particular which answers to a certain description. *Mutatis mutandis*, a similar condition must be satisfied for a hearer, in order for it to be the case that there is some particular which the hearer takes the speaker to be referring to. (The third condition of those I listed requires, not indeed that the speaker's and hearer's descriptions should be identical, but that each description should apply—uniquely—to one and the same particular.)

I have been using the terminology of identifying reference for the sake of its familiarity and convenience. We can substitute the neutral terminology of term-introduction without in any way altering the substance of what has been said.

Let us now inquire what similar conditions, if any, must be satisfied in order for a universal term (such as particulars may either be characterized by, or be instances of) to be successfully introduced into a proposition. *We find that there are no such parallel conditions which can be generally insisted on.* Suppose there is an adjectival form of expression, 'ϕ', for the universal in question. We are to look for some empirical proposition, if any can be found, which must be true in order for the universal term putatively introducible by 'ϕ' to be introduced at all. A sufficient condition of its introducibility would be the truth, known to the speaker, of the general empirical proposition that *something or other is* ϕ. But this cannot be generally insisted on as a necessary condition. For another equally sufficient condition, indeed one that is satisfied in the case of some universals, would be the truth of the empirical proposition that *nothing is* φ. If we form the disjunction of these two sufficient conditions, we may indeed be said to obtain a necessary condition: viz. that *either something is* φ *or nothing is* φ. But now we no longer have an empirical proposition, a fact about the world. We have a tautology.

It might be objected that we can find an empirical condition of the successful introduction of the universal term by means of the expression 'φ': viz. the condition that the proposition expressed in the words, 'something is φ' is, whether true or false, a significant empirical proposition, and is unambiguously understood by both speaker and hearer. But now the condition is in no sense parallel to, or on the same level as, that which we found to be necessary for the introduction of a particular. The required fact is not, in the required sense, a fact about the world. It is a fact about language. Parallels for it, i.e. facts about the significance and understanding of the words used, could be mentioned for the case of particular-introduction; but no parallels to the additional empirical requirements for the case of particular-introduction can be generally found for the case of universal-introduction.

It might again be objected that, in practice, empirical propositions of the form, 'something is φ', would not acquire their significance unless at least a preponderant proportion of them were also true. Therefore, it might be argued, the contrast between the conditions of particular-introduction and the conditions of universal-introduction is by no means as marked as I have claimed. The situation is, rather, that the introduction of a particular term universally presupposes, whilst the introduction of a universal term in general presupposes, the truth of some empirical proposition. But to this objection, apart from any cavils about the structure of the argument, there are two replies, of which the second, at least, is decisive.

The first reply consists in emphasizing differences between the kinds of presupposed empirical propositions. The kind of proposition the truth of which is universally required for the introduction of a particular term is a kind of proposition which states a quite definite fact about the world, something that might, as it were, belong to history. But the kind of proposition the truth of which may, in general, though not universally, be required for universal-introduction to be possible is a quite indefinite sort of proposition, the fact it states is a quite indefinite sort of fact. That something, somewhere, at some time, is or was red, or round, or wise, is not a fact which could belong to history.

The second reply nullifies the effect of the objection altogether. It is not only universally necessary that an empirical proposition of a sharply definite kind should be true in order for the introduction of a particular to be effected. It is also necessary for a proposition of that kind to be known to be true. For only so are the conditions of identifying reference to just one particular fulfilled; only so are the conditions of identification, on the speaker's or the hearer's part, fulfilled. Consider now how different it is with universal-introduction. It may be the case that the words used for identifying the universal terms introduced could acquire their meaning only if most of the universals so introduced were in fact instantiated. But once the words have acquired their meaning, however they acquire it, it is by no means necessary, in order for them to perform the function of identifying the universal term they introduce, that their users should know or believe empirical propositions to the effect that the universal terms in question are in fact instantiated. The users *will* generally know, or think, this. But *that* they should, is not a necessary condition of the expressions in question performing their identifying function. All that is necessary is that the users should know *what* the expressions mean, not *that* they acquired their meaning in virtue of the truth of some empirical proposition.

The vital contrast, then, may be summarily stated as follows. The identifying introduction of either a particular or a universal into discourse entails knowing what particular or what universal is meant, or intended to be introduced, by the introducing expression. Knowing what particular is meant entails knowing, or sometimes—in the case of the hearer—learning, from the introducing expression used, some empirical fact which suffices to identify that particular, other than the fact that it is the particular currently being introduced. But knowing what universal is meant does not in the same way entail knowing any empirical fact: it merely entails knowing the language. (This is a *very* summary statement; it should not be regarded as a substitute for what it summarizes.)

But now a qualification must be made. I have said that it is a universally necessary condition of the introduction of any particular term into discourse, that there should exist, and be known, a true empirical proposition of a certain very definite kind, whereas it is not a necessary condition of the introduction of a universal term into discourse that there should exist, and be known, a true empirical proposition of any parallel kind. The qualification concerns the way in which the universal term is introduced. For if the universal term is introduced, not by means of some expression which identifies the universal term in virtue of its meaning, but by means of some expression which gives a description of the universal, then, indeed, for the introduction to be successfully so effected, it may be necessary that some empirical proposition is true. Thus the universal term, wisdom, may be introduced, not by means of the adjective, 'wise' or the substantive, 'wisdom', but by such a description as 'the quality most frequently attributed to Socrates in philosophical examples'. Or, again, a type of illness might be introduced, not as, say, 'influenza', but as 'the disease which kept John from work last week'. For this method of introduction to be successful, it must indeed be the case that there was a disease, just one disease, which, last week, kept John from work. The importance of this qualification will emerge shortly. It obviously does not contradict the main thesis, which, in the case of universal terms, has the form of the denial of a universal proposition.

[2] Now let us cease, for a moment, to speak of particulars and universals, and speak instead, and in general, of this distinction between: (1) expressions such that one cannot know what they introduce without knowing (or learning from their use) some distinguishing empirical fact about what they introduce; (2) expressions such that one can very well know what they introduce

without knowing any distinguishing empirical fact about what they introduce. Both kinds of expression are in a certain sense incomplete. For introducing a term is not making a statement; it is only *a part* of making a statement. Yet expressions of the first kind have evidently a completeness, a self-sufficiency, which expressions of the second kind lack. Of expressions of class (1), one might say: although they do not explicitly state facts, they perform their role only because they present or represent facts, only because they presuppose, or embody, or covertly carry, propositions which they do not explicitly affirm. They necessarily carry a weight of fact in introducing their terms. But expressions of class (2) carry no weight of fact in introducing their terms. They can only *help* to carry a fact, and even this they can do—unless they form a part of a class (1) expression—only by being coupled with some other expression into an *explicit* assertion.

Let us now recall the grammatical criterion for a predicate-expression. The predicate-expression introduces its term in the coupling, propositional style, in the explicitly incomplete style which demands completion into an assertion. Now surely the manifest incompleteness of the assertive style of introduction—the demand to be completed into an assertion—answers exactly to the incompleteness of the second of the two kinds of expression I have just distinguished; it answers exactly to the failure of this kind of expression to present a fact on its own account. We have a contrast between something which in no sense presents a fact in its own right but is a candidate for being part of a statement of fact, and something which does already in a sense present a fact in its own right and is also a candidate for being part of a statement of fact. It is appropriate enough that in the explicit assertion constituted by both taken together, it should be the former which carries the propositional symbolism, the symbolism that demands completion into an assertion.

What we here propose, in effect, is a new, or mediating, criterion for the subject–predicate distinction. A subject-expression is one which, in a sense, presents a fact in its own right and is to that extent complete. A predicate-expression is one which in no sense presents a fact in its own right and is to that extent incomplete. We find that this new criterion harmonizes admirably with the grammatical criterion. The predicate-expression, on the new criterion, is one that can be completed only by explicit coupling with another. The predicate-expression, on the grammatical criterion, is precisely the expression which carries the symbolism demanding completion into an explicit assertion. We emphasize the harmony, the affinity, of these two criteria; and by fusing them, we return to, and enrich, that contrast between the 'complete' and the 'incomplete' parts of the sentence which we discussed in expounding the 'grammatical' sense of the subject-predicate distinction. We find an additional depth in Frege's metaphor of the saturated and the unsaturated constituents.

Not only does the new criterion harmonize admirably with the grammatical distinction. It also harmonizes, as the whole of the preceding section shows, with the category criterion. For, in the first place, the whole burden of that section was that particular-introducing expressions can never be incomplete in the sense of the new criterion, *and thus can never be predicate-expressions on that criterion.* This is part of what the category criterion requires. In the second place, it was shown in that section that many universal-introducing expressions are incomplete in the sense of the new criterion and thus qualify, on that criterion, as predicate-expressions; but also that certain universal-introducing expressions, e.g. some of those which identify the universal term they introduce by description, are complete in the sense of the new criterion and thus qualify, on that criterion, as subject-expressions. Both these results are consistent with the category criterion.

These considerations seem to me to explain in part the affinity between the grammatical criterion and the category criterion for subjects and predicates. They explain, or help to explain, the traditional, persistent link in our philosophy between the particular–universal distinction and the subject–predicate (reference-predication) distinction. When once that association has been firmly established and explained at a fundamental level, we can allow a certain flexibility to enter our classifications at a more sophisticated level. Thus, in the statement, 'Generosity is a more amiable virtue than prudence', may we not want to say that generosity and prudence appear as subjects, and the universal-characterizing universal, *being a more amiable virtue* (*than*), appears as a predicate? Yet the expressions, 'generosity' and 'prudence', do not possess the kind of completeness which our mediating criterion requires of subject-expressions; they do not covertly present any fact. The solution of this problem is that, once the fundamental association has been made, the analogies I spoke of earlier [1] may be allowed to carry the burden of further extensions and modifications of the problematic distinction. The analogies I mean in this case are those that hold between non-relational, characterizing ties binding particulars and universals on the one hand, and non-relational ties binding universals and universals on the other.

This is but one case, and a simple one. There are others, requiring different treatment, which I shall not now discuss. But there is one further piece of explanation which must be given. Another persistent element in the traditional theory is the doctrine that expressions introducing complex terms such as I have referred to as 'universals-cum-particulars', may be classified as predicate-expressions (e.g. 'is married to John'). Yet do not such expressions, by virtue of containing a part which introduces a particular, possess the completeness which—making all allowance for flexibility—I must presumably insist on counting as a disqualification for the status of predicate? The answer is that such expressions do not themselves, as wholes, possess this completeness, though each contains a part which does. The expression 'is married to John' does not, *as a whole*, present any fact; for it performs its term-identifying function just as successfully if no one is married to John as it does if someone is married to John. The expression 'John' carries, in use, its own presupposition of fact; but the expression 'is married to John' carries no further presupposition of fact of *its* own. All *it* presupposes is the tautology that either someone is married to John or no one is. So such complex expressions, taken as wholes, have the incompleteness that qualifies them to rank as predicates.

[1] See Chapter 5, p. 171.

[3] The general account I have sketched raises many problems. In the first place, the crucial idea of completeness remains vague. I have said that term-introducing expressions which are, in the relevant sense, complete present or represent facts, or presuppose or embody or covertly carry propositions. The variety of terminology may well seem suspicious. What precise account can be given of the relations between term-introducing expressions which are, in the relevant sense, complete, and the facts or propositions which confer upon them their completeness? How is the content of these facts or propositions determined by, or otherwise related to, the actual term-introducing expressions used?

The variety of cases is too great to allow of a single answer to this question. In certain simple cases, the answer is simple enough. Suppose I say, pointing, 'That person there can direct you'. The expression, 'That person there', introduces, or identifies, a particular. It is clear enough both what the fact is upon which the term-introduction rests, and what its relation is to the words used. The term-distinguishing fact is that there is just one person there, where I am pointing; if there is no one at whom I could be taken to be pointing, my putatively term-introducing expression fails of a reference and my statement fails of a truth-value. In such cases, then, we have a clear enough sense of presupposition, and a clear enough indication of what is presupposed by the use of the term-introducing expression. But now consider a less simple case. What if our term-introducing expression is the proper name (ordinarily so called) of a particular? Clearly it is not required, for term-introduction by such means, that there should be just one object or person which bears the name. Nor can we be satisfied with the answer that the presupposed fact is the fact that there is just one object or person which both bears the name and is being currently referred to by its means. For—to consider the case of the speaker alone—the previous argument requires the 'presupposed' fact to be some true empirical proposition known to the speaker which he might cite in order to indicate *which* particular he has in mind; and this cannot be the fact that there is just one he has in mind. But now if we find a fact which answers to this specification, i.e. which might serve to distinguish the one he has in mind, there is no longer any guarantee that the fact we find can be said to be presupposed, by the statement containing the term-introducing expression, in the simple sense of presupposition which we have just seen illustrated in the case of the statement beginning 'That person there'. It might, for example, be the case that there is just one child whom I saw before breakfast yesterday, and this might be the child whom I currently refer to as 'John'. But it will certainly not be the case that just this existential fact is presupposed, in the sense illustrated, by the statement I currently make about John.

Nevertheless I think it would be a mistake to conclude that the notion of presupposition is irrelevant to our question in the case of names. Consider the situation in which a reference is made, by name, to Socrates. By the argument of the previous section, both speaker and hearer, in this situation, satisfy the conditions for successful term-introduction if each knows some distinguishing fact or facts, not necessarily the same ones, about Socrates, facts which each is prepared to cite to indicate whom he now means, or understands, by 'Socrates'. But what is the relation between these facts and the name? Or, to put what is really the same question in another form, what are the conditions of my correctly describing them as 'facts about Socrates', where I use, and do not mention, the name? It is in relation to this question that the notion of presupposition is once more relevant. Suppose we take a group of speakers who use, or think they use, the name, 'Socrates', with the same reference. Suppose we then ask each member of the group to write down what he considers to be the salient facts about Socrates, and then form from these lists of facts a composite description incorporating the most frequently mentioned facts. Now it would be too much to say that the success of term-introduction within the group by means of the name requires that there should exist just one person of whom all the propositions in the composite description are true. But it would not be too much to say that it requires that there should exist one and only one person of whom some reasonable proportion of these propositions is true. If, for example, it should be found that there was just one person of whom half the propositions were jointly true, and just one person, a different one, of whom the other half of the propositions were jointly true, then, unless some indication were given of which Socrates was meant, it would become impossible to give a straightforward answer to the question, whether any particular 'proposition about Socrates' was true or false. It is true, perhaps, of Socrates$_1$ and not of Socrates$_2$. It is neither true nor false of Socrates *simpliciter*, for, it turns out, there is no such person.

We do not need, then, to give up, but rather to refine, the notion of a presupposition. To give a name to the refinement I have just illustrated, we might speak of a presupposition-set of propositions. The propositions making up the composite description of Socrates would form such a set. Neither the limits of such a set, nor the question of what constitutes a reasonable, or sufficient, proportion of its members will in general be precisely fixed for any putatively term-introducing proper name. This is not a deficiency in the notion of a presupposition-set; it is part of the efficiency of proper names.

It will be obvious that the range of actual cases is by no means exhausted by the two examples I have chosen: the example of a simple demonstrative-cum-descriptive indication, on the one hand, and that of a proper name, such as 'Socrates', on the other. It cannot even be claimed that the proper name, in that use of it which I discussed, is quite typical of its class, or that the account given can be quite simply extended to other cases of name-using. There is, accordingly, no hope of giving a simple general account of the relation between 'complete' term-introducing expressions and the term-distinguishing facts which must be known in order for term-introduction to be effected by their use. But, then, it is no part of my thesis that such an account can be given.

Having said this, we can safely, for the sake of a name, speak of such term-distinguishing facts or propositions as 'presupposed' by the use of those term-introducing expressions; and turn, in conclusion, to consider one more point. I have said that the success of any putatively term-introducing expression in introducing a *particular* term rests upon knowledge of some term-distinguishing fact. Very often, if we formulated such facts, the resulting statements would themselves contain expressions introducing particular terms. This need not fill us with fear of infinite regression. For we can always count on arriving, in the end, at some existential proposition, which may indeed contain demonstrative elements, but no *part* of which introduces, or definitely identifies, a particular term, though the proposition *as a whole* may be said to *present* a particular term. (The simplest form of such a proposition is: 'There is just one so-and-so there'.) But though the fact that the immediate presuppositions of most expressions introducing particular terms will themselves contain expressions introducing particular terms is not a fact that need fill us with fear of infinite regression, it is a fact that may well fill us with salutary caution. What it should caution us against is the idea that we are in any way bound, by adopting the explanations I have given, to consider presupposed propositions which contain no parts introducing particulars as the *only* presupposed propositions which are relevant to our theory. This is certainly not the case. All the theory requires is that expressions introducing particulars, unlike expressions introducing universals, should *always* be complete in a certain sense; and that sense is explained when it is shown how those expressions must always carry an empirical presupposition. The requirement that they should carry such a presupposition is satisfied just as fully in the cases where the presupposed propositions themselves contain expressions introducing particulars as in the cases where they do not. It is no doubt reassuring to learn that, if we should embark on a journey through successive presuppositions, we can be sure of reaching an end. But it is not to be supposed that such an end must, or can, be reached in a single step.

It might still be thought, however, that the position we have arrived at is theoretically unsatisfactory, in the following way. I have claimed to investigate the conditions of introducing a particular term into a proposition by means of a definitely identifying expression. I have asserted that the possibility of such term-introduction rests upon knowledge of some term-distinguishing fact. If we formulated propositions expressing such knowledge, they would be found either to contain expressions themselves introducing other particular terms, or at least to involve quantification over particulars; and it can plausibly be argued that sentences involving quantification over particulars (e.g. 'There is just one so-and-so there') could have no place in language unless definitely identifying expressions for particulars (e.g. 'That so-and-so') also had a place in language. But if this is so, how can I claim to have stated the conditions which must be satisfied for the introduction of a particular by means of a term-introducing expression? For I cannot formulate my statement of conditions without tacitly supposing that language contains term-introducing expressions for particulars. So the account suffers from circularity.

This objection fails. It fails through not distinguishing between (1) an account of the conditions-in-general of the use in language of expressions introducing particular terms, and (2) a doctrine concerning the conditions of the use, on any particular occasion, of an expression introducing a particular term. Alternatively, the distinction overlooked by the objection might be described as that between (1) an account of the conditions of the introduction of particulars into *discourse* in general, and (2) an account of the identifying introduction of a particular into a given *piece* of discourse. It is, of course, the second of these, and not the first, which I have advanced. Viewed in the first way, my account would indeed suffer from circularity; viewed in the second, it does not. It may well be felt, however, that a doctrine of the second kind should be supplemented with some account of the first kind; and such an account I attempt to give in Part II of this chapter.

[4] Before we turn to this further problem, however, it is worth considering a certain philosophical proposal which, in the present connexion, has great attractions. Though the motives for which it has been made are different from those which prompt the present inquiry, it seems to offer a seductive way of simplifying the results of the last three sections. I do not think the proposal is acceptable; but it is important to see why it is not.

The proposal in question may present itself as a form of

analysis of propositions containing expressions which introduce particular terms; or it may present itself in the guise of a description of an ideal language in which referring expressions for particulars do not occur, their place being taken by the bound variables of existential quantification. Such a language, to give W. V. Quine's description, would be a language from which all singular terms are eliminated.[1] The sentences in which they occur are replaced by existentially quantified sentences with a uniqueness condition. By the theory of the previous section of this chapter, we should indeed find such sentences at the end of the regress of presuppositions, if we chose to pursue that regress to its end. By Quine's proposal, on the other hand, such sentences are incorporated *as a part* of all those ideal sentences which replace ordinary sentences containing singular terms.

One must, I think, acknowledge that in the present connexion this idea really has great force and attractiveness. In place of the vague and qualified discussions of the previous section, it enables us to give an absolutely precise sense to the idea of that mixture of 'completeness' and 'incompleteness' which expressions introducing particulars necessarily have. Such expressions are complete in that they carry presuppositions of fact, incomplete in that they are not assertions on their own account, but parts of assertions. When we look to their counterparts in the ideal language, we find, first, the completeness represented by a fully explicit assertion of the form:

There is something which uniquely F

and, then, the incompleteness represented by the addition of a further relative pronoun, thus:

There is something which uniquely F *and which.* . . .

The second relative pronoun is followed by the predicate-expression which completes the whole assertion and which, in the

[1] See *Methods of Logic*, pp. 220–24, also *From a Logical Point of View*, pp. 7 f, 13, 146, 166 f. Quine's programme is an extension of Russell's Theory of Descriptions; it consists, one might say, in carrying through this theory to the limit, while simultaneously dropping the notion of the true subject-expression, the logically proper name. I hope, in what has gone before, that I have preserved what is true in this theory, whilst avoiding its ultimately self-destructive over-simplifications.

ordinary singular-term-encumbered language, follows the singular term. A referring expression of ordinary language, a logical subject-expression, is whatever thus dissolves, in the ideal language, into a quantified assertion, plus a relative pronoun. A predicate-expression is what does not thus dissolve, and so has an absolute incompleteness, i.e. a propositional incompleteness which cannot be removed by the simple expedient of dropping a relative pronoun. Now all expressions introducing particulars dissolve in the way described, and hence cannot but be logical subject-expressions. Some expressions introducing universals may dissolve in this way; but many do not. So universals may appear either as subjects or as predicates.[1]

In spite of the attractive simplicity of this analysis, however, and its harmony with the spirit of the previous sections, I think the form in which it is presented makes it unacceptable; and if the form of the analysis is rejected, then the whole analysis, as a distinctive and intelligible account, is rejected too. For what distinguishes it as a separate theory from, say, the account given in the previous section, is precisely the claim that all subject-expressions are strictly superfluous, because eliminable in favour of quantification, variables of quantification and predicate-expressions. Yet the linguistic terms in which the analysis is couched are terms which, if we are to understand them in the way we are invited to, presuppose the existence of subject-expressions, of linguistic singular terms. There are, in ordinary speech, various forms of indefinite reference to particulars, and various ways of making, on behalf of particulars, an existential claim followed by a relative pronoun. The device of existential quantification over particulars is to be understood as corresponding roughly to these forms of ordinary speech. These forms have a place, a role, in language which is to be brought out or elucidated in contrast with the place, or role, in language which linguistic singular terms have. No sense can be attached to the idea that they can have the place they have even if there is no such place. But this is the idea we are invited to accept when we are invited to see all subject-

---

[1] Quine's preoccupation is to ensure, where possible, that universals appear only as predicates. This he refers to as 'nominalism'. See Chapter 8 below.

expressions dissolving into, or being replaced by, such forms. We are invited to see this dissolution as explaining the place which subject-expressions have in language! Or again, consider that we are invited to look on the expressions which replace the '*F*'s and '*G*'s in the quantified sentences as ordinary predicate-expressions. This invitation in itself is perfectly in order; for ordinary predicate-expressions can of course be coupled with those various forms of indefinite reference, and of existential claim followed by a relative pronoun, which appear in ordinary language. But, once again, these forms have the place they have in ordinary language only because singular terms, subject-expressions, have the place *they* have there. So we cannot *both* accept the invitation to look on the expressions which replace the '*F*'s and '*G*'s in the quantified sentences as ordinary predicate-expressions *and* at the same time acquiesce in the total dissolution of subject-expressions into the forms of the quantified sentences. In brief, the doctrine is exposed to precisely that charge of circularity against which I defended the theory of the preceding sections. For, just because it envisages the total elimination of linguistic singular terms for particulars, it necessarily offers itself as an account of the conditions-in-general of the use of these expressions, and not merely of the conditions of the use of such an expression on a particular occasion; yet it depends on forms which themselves presuppose the use of these expressions.

To these objections the following answer might be made. It is parochial, it might be said, to concern ourselves about the actual ways in which we use the expressions in terms of which we are invited to read the quantified sentences. Even the invitations so to read them must not be taken too seriously. The analysis must rather be seen as an attempt, hampered by the difficulty of getting away from the forms of ordinary speech, to get us to see what is fundamentally the case about expressions introducing particulars. We must be liberal and imaginative in our interpretation of it.— One may well feel some sympathy with such a point. If so, one has also the obligation to ask what *is* conveyed by a doctrine which, taken at its face value, is unacceptable. In the next chapter we shall consider some possibilities which might, if we are very liberal and imaginative indeed, seem to indicate possible interpretations of the doctrine here in question, or at least to be in the spirit of that doctrine. But we need not pursue the matter now. For any such interpretation is remote indeed from the overt sense of the doctrine, and far from being a possible alternative answer to those questions which we attempted to answer in the previous sections.

2. THE INTRODUCTION OF PARTICULARS INTO DISCOURSE

[5] One 'introduces a particular' into a proposition if one makes an identifying reference to that particular in that proposition. In the first part of this chapter I have discussed the conditions of the introduction of particulars into propositions. The outcome of this discussion was, summarily, the doctrine that every introduction of a particular carried a presupposition of empirical fact. The propositions of fact thus presupposed could be thought of, without circularity but not without regression, as themselves involving the introduction of (identifying reference to) particulars, as well as quantification over particulars; and the ultimately presupposed propositions of fact could be thought of, without either circularity or regression, as involving quantification over particulars, though not the introduction of (identifying reference to) particulars.

Now the phrase 'introduction of particulars' might also reasonably bear a very different sense. The introduction of particulars in this second sense would be the introduction of the *custom* of introducing them in the first sense. It is individual particulars which are introduced in the first sense. It is at least *kinds* of particulars, or even particulars in general, which are introduced in the second sense. We may mark the difference in sense, where necessary, by the use of subscripts. Individual particulars are introduced$_1$ into propositions. Kinds of particular are introduced$_2$ into discourse.

At the end of section [3] of this chapter I remarked that it might well be felt that a doctrine concerning the conditions of introducing$_1$ particulars ought to be supplemented with a doctrine concerning the conditions of introducing$_2$ particulars. Apart from any intrinsic interest of such a theory, might it not round off or reinforce the 'completeness' theory of sections [1]–[3]? That theory was defended against the charge of circularity just on the ground that it was not a theory of introducing$_2$ particulars; and this defence points to some of the requirements that a theory of introducing$_2$ particulars would have to fulfil. If, for example, the theory represents the introduction$_2$ of particulars of a certain class as presupposing or resting upon the existence of facts of a certain class, then these must be facts such that stating them involves neither introducing$_1$ nor quantifying over particulars of that class. If a *general* theory, on these lines, of the introduction$_2$ of particulars is advanced, then at least the ultimately presupposed facts must be such that the statement of them does not involve introducing$_1$ or quantifying over any particulars at all.

Let us, where necessary, distinguish by means of subscripts two uses of 'presupposition' parallel to the two uses of 'introduction' already distinguished. The truth of some presupposed$_1$ proposition is a condition of the successful introduction$_1$ of a certain particular, and hence a condition of the presupposing statement's having a truth-value. The existence of facts of a presupposed$_2$ kind is a condition of the introduction$_2$ of a certain kind of particulars, i.e. is a condition of there being any propositions at all into which particulars of that kind are introduced$_1$.

Now, it might be asked, whatever the independent interest of a theory of presuppositions$_2$, how could it in any way reinforce or complement a theory of presuppositions$_1$? For it is required of presupposed$_2$ facts that their statement does not involve introducing$_1$ or quantifying over particulars of the kind for which they supply a basis. But it is a direct consequence of this requirement that the statement of these facts does not involve introducing any sortal universals of which those particulars are instances. Therefore presupposed$_2$ facts, in so far as they provide a basis for the introduction$_2$ of certain kinds of particular equally provide a basis for the introduction$_2$ of certain kinds of universal. Where, here, is the asymmetry between particulars and universals which was characteristic of the theory of presuppositions$_1$?

We may first reply here that the objection is overstated, since the existence of facts presupposed$_2$ by the introduction$_2$ of a certain range of particulars is not thereby shown to be a necessary condition of the introduction$_2$ of the sortal universals of which particulars of that range are instances. To think so would be to limit too much the power of human imagination. But this answer does nothing to show how a theory of presuppositions$_2$ could in fact in any way add to or complement a theory of presuppositions$_1$.

We may begin to see how the one theory may deepen and reinforce the other when we consider a certain special type of case. This is the case in which a dependent particular is introduced as attributively tied to a relatively independent particular, as in such phrases as 'The death of Socrates', 'The blow which Peter gave John', 'The catch which got Compton out'. If such a phrase as any of these introduces a particular, then there is some true proposition in which no particulars of the relevant kind are either introduced or quantified over, but which serves as a basis for the introduction of that particular. Thus *Socrates died, Peter struck John, Compton was caught out*. Here the presupposed propositions do not contain the sortal universals of which particular deaths, catches and blows are instances; but they do contain the characterizing universals, *dying, striking* and *being caught out*, universals which characterize particulars of a different type from those which they supply the basis for introducing. So the facts these propositions state are not only presupposed$_1$ by propositions into which the particular death, or blow, or catch is introduced$_1$ by one of the quoted expressions; they also belong to the range of facts presupposed$_2$ by the introduction$_2$ of particulars of this kind. Such cases show how, at least sometimes, the requirements of a theory of presuppositions$_1$ and a theory of presuppositions$_2$ may be satisfied simultaneously. They show, how, in some cases, the proposition presupposed$_1$ by a particular-introducing expression is not such as itself to presuppose the existence of other propositions into which particulars of the kind in question are introduced$_1$.

Cases of this kind provide an untypically easy bridge between the two kinds of theory. We certainly shall not always expect a presupposed$_1$ proposition (or a member of a presupposed$_1$ proposition-set) to belong to the appropriate class of presupposed$_2$

propositions. *The general nature of the connexion between the theories is, rather, this: if we accept the theory of presuppositions₁, then saying that the existence of a certain class of particular-introducing expressions presupposes₂ the existence of a certain class of facts involves claiming that we can think of some introduction₁ of a particular of the relevant class as presupposing₁ a fact of the presupposed₂ class.* There is no need to suppose that we must, or can, see *every* introduction₁ of a particular in this light. What makes the cases we have just considered so untypically easy is just that we can here see every such introduction₁ in this light. Part of the reason why we can do so is that the transition from the characterizing universals which the presupposed propositions contain to the sortal universals of which the particular deaths, blows &c. are instances is a very easy conceptual transition indeed.

If, then, the theory of presuppositions₂ can be made out in general, its connexion with the theory of presuppositions₁ can be left to take care of itself. But can it be made out? There are, certainly many types of particular which raise no great difficulties. I have in mind those items which are introduced at a relatively sophisticated stage of thought, such as the particular entities of scientific theory or particular social institutions. Philosophers have correctly abandoned the hope of 'reducing' propositions in which such items are introduced or quantified over to propositions in which they do not figure. But there is no reason why they should give up the more modest aspiration to find classes of facts in the statement of which only more primitive kinds of particulars figure, yet which supply a basis for the introduction of these more sophisticated entities. For example, propositions about nations cannot be reduced to propositions about men; but propositions about men are presupposed₂ by propositions about nations. This aspiration is so obviously reasonable that it needs no general argument to support it; and I shall supply none.

Our difficulties really begin only when we approach the end of the regress of presuppositions₂, when, that is to say, we start looking for the classes of facts which supply a basis for the introduction of those particulars upon which the introduction of all others directly or indirectly rests. I remarked just now upon the requirement that propositions stating the facts which supply the basis for the introduction₂ of a certain kind of particulars must not contain universals of which those particulars are instances. This negative requirement holds at all stages of the regress of pre-suppositions₂. At the last stage, it means that the universals contained in the presupposed₂ propositions must not function as sortal or characterizing universals at all. This seems indeed a severe requirement. Where are we to find propositions which both have this character and are adequate to supply a basis for the introduction of the fundamental kinds of particular?

[6] We had better begin by inquiring whether there is *any* familiar kind of universal, and *any* familiar kind of statement introducing such universals, which at least exhibit the required character, even if they do not by themselves supply an adequate basis for particular-introduction on the required scale. Now there certainly is such a kind of universal, and there certainly is such a kind of statement. I have in mind what I shall call *feature-universals* or *feature-concepts*, and what I shall call *feature-placing statements*. As examples I suggest the following:

> Now it is raining
> Snow is falling
> There is coal here
> There is gold here
> There is water here.

The universal terms introduced into these propositions do not function as characterizing universals. *Snow*, *water*, *coal* and *gold*, for example, are general kinds of stuff, not properties or characteristics of particulars; though *being made of snow* or *being made of gold* are characteristics of particulars. Nor are the universal terms introduced into these propositions sortal universals. No one of them of itself provides a principle for distinguishing, enumerating and reidentifying particulars of a sort. But each can be very easily modified so as to yield several such principles: we can distinguish count and reidentify *veins* or *grains*, *lumps* or *dumps* of coal, and *flakes*, *falls*, *drifts* or *expanses* of snow. Such phrases as 'lump of coal' or 'fall of snow' introduce sortal universals; but 'coal' and 'snow' *simpliciter* do not. These sentences, then, neither contain any part which introduces a particular, nor any expression used in such a way that its use presupposes the use of expressions to introduce particulars. Of course, when these sentences are used, the combination of the circumstances of their use with the tense of the verb and the demonstrative adverbs, if any, which they contain, yields a statement of the incidence of the universal feature they introduce. For this much at least is essential to any language in which singular empirical statements could be made at all: viz. the introduction of general concepts and the indication of their incidence. But it is an important fact that this can be done by means of statements which neither bring particulars into our discourse nor presuppose other areas of discourse in which particulars are brought in.

Languages imagined on the model of such languages as these are sometimes called 'property-location' languages. But this is an unfortunate name: the universal terms which figure in my examples are not properties; indeed the idea of a property belongs to a level of logical complexity which we are trying to get below. This is why I have chosen to use the less philosophically committed word 'feature', and to speak of 'feature-placing' sentences.

Though feature-placing sentences do not introduce particulars into our discourse, they provide a basis for this introduction. The facts they state are presupposed, in the required sense, by the introduction of certain kinds of particular. That there should be facts statable by means of such sentences as 'There is water here', 'It is snowing', is a condition of there being propositions into which particulars are introduced$_1$ by means of such expressions as 'This pool of water', 'This fall of snow'. In general, the transition from facts of the presupposed kind to the introduction of the particulars for which they supply the basis involves a conceptual complication: it involves the adoption of criteria of distinctness and, where applicable, criteria of reidentification for particulars of the kind in question, as well as the use of characterizing universals which can be tied to a particular of that kind. A *basis* for criteria of distinctness may indeed already exist at the feature-placing level. For where we can say 'There is snow here' or 'There is gold here', we can also, perhaps, say, 'There is snow (gold) *here*—and *here*—and *here*.' Factors which determine multiplicity of placing may become, when we introduce particulars, criteria for distinguishing one particular from another. Of criteria of reidentification I shall say more later.

It might now reasonably be said that it is by no means sufficient, for the general theory of presuppositions, to find just some class of presupposed facts which qualify for the terminal stage of the regress, the stage at which no particulars are introduced at all. For if the theory is to work in general, then any route, and not merely specially chosen routes, through the regress, should lead, in the end, to facts of such a class. It is reasonable enough to claim that facts of the class just illustrated supply a basis for the introduction of certain kinds of particulars. But it would be highly unplausible to claim that particulars of these kinds supply, together with the characterizing universals which attach to them, a basis for the introduction of all other kinds of particulars whatever. In the first chapter of this book, it was argued that certain kinds of particular are, from the point of view of identification, the basic particulars of our conceptual scheme. These were, roughly, those directly locatable particulars which were or possessed material bodies. If we could find, for a reasonable selection of particulars of this class, presupposed facts in the statement of which particulars were not introduced, then, perhaps, we might regard the general theory as vindicated. For facts involving basic particulars may be presumed to provide, directly or indirectly, a basis for the introduction of most types of non-basic particular. The apparent exceptions are those non-basic particulars, such as public auditory or visual phenomena like flashes and bangs, which are directly locatable, but are not conceived of by us as necessarily e.g. events happening to, or states of, particulars of other types. But if these raise any problem, it is likely to be a problem of secondary importance.

It appears, however, that basic particulars themselves raise a serious problem. For whilst particulars like pools of water, lumps of gold etc. do certainly belong to the class of basic particulars, they can scarcely be said to constitute a fair or reasonable selection from that class. The sortal universals of which they are instances (*pool of water*, *lump of gold*) are alike in this: that their names incorporate, as a part, the names of kinds of stuff (*water*, *gold*) which seem supremely, or even uniquely, well adapted to be introduced as universal terms into feature-placing sentences. That is why it is so easy to find, in ordinary language, convincing examples of cases where we operate, not with the notion of particular instances of, e.g., gold or snow, but merely with the notion of the universal feature itself and the notion of placing. But the sortal universals of which basic particulars are more characteristically instances (e.g. men, mountains, apples, cats, trees) do not thus happily separate into indications of a particularizing division, such as *pool* or *lump*, on the one hand, and general features, such as *water* or *gold*, on the other. It is easy to see the ground of this difference. For particulars such as heaps of snow could be physically lumped together to yield one particular mass of snow; but we could not lump particular cats together to yield one enormous cat. It must surely be more difficult, therefore, to envisage a situation in which, instead of operating with the notion of the sortal universal, *cat* or *apple*, and hence with the notion of particular cats or apples, we operate with the notion of a corresponding feature and of placing. Ordinary language does not seem to provide us with a name for a universal term which could count as the required feature in the case of, say, cats. Is it not perhaps the essential difference between, say, cats and snow, that there *could* be no concept of the 'cat-feature' such as the theory seems to require, that any general idea of cat *must* be the idea of *a* cat, i.e. must already involve criteria of distinctness and re-identification for cats as particulars?

These difficulties, though important, are not decisive. For they do not show that it is logically absurd to suppose that there might be a level of thought at which we recognize the presence of cat, or signs of the past or future presence of cat, yet do not think identifyingly of particular cats. Let us suppose that the idea of such a level of thought is coherent; and let us introduce, as its linguistic counterpart, the idea of a form of linguistic activity which, if we are to speak of language-games, might be called 'the naming-game'. Playing the naming-game may be compared with one of the earliest things which children do with language—when they utter the general name for a kind of thing in the presence of a thing of that kind, saying 'duck' when there is a duck, 'ball' when there is a ball &c. Now it may be said that these utterances have the force of 'There is a duck', 'There is a ball' &c., i.e. they have the force of forms which have the place in language which they do have only because expressions used to make identifying references to particulars have the place in language which *they* have. But anyone for whom these utterances have this force is not playing the naming-game. This remark indeed deprives me of the right to appeal to the alleged fact that the naming-game is played. But no such appeal is necessary. All that is required is the admission that the concept of the naming-game is coherent, the admission that the ability to make identifying references to such things as balls and ducks includes the ability to recognize the corresponding features, whereas it is logically possible that one should recognize the features without possessing the conceptual resources for identifying reference to the corresponding particulars. Granted this, it does not matter whether naming-game utterances, or feature-placing utterances in general, are common or ordinary or not. We can readily enough acknowledge that the introduction of particulars is so fundamental a conceptual step as to leave the primitive pre-particular level of thought as, at most, no more than vestigial in language.

But is the idea of the naming-game a coherent and distinct idea —distinct, that is, from the idea of bringing a particular under a sortal universal? To answer this, we must say more about the criteria of distinctness and reidentification involved in the conceptual move to particulars. I referred just now to a possible argument to the effect that there *could* be no idea of a cat-feature which would be distinct from, yet yield a basis for, the sortal universal, *cat*, as the general feature, *snow*, is distinct from, yet yields a basis for, the sortal universals, *patch of snow* or *fall of snow*; for in the case of cats there is no general feature which can be thought of as divided in different ways to yield different sortal universals, as the general feature, snow, can be thought of as divided in different ways to yield different sortal universals. What this argument shows, however, is not that the required type of general concept of cat is impossible, but rather that the concept must already include in itself the *basis* for the criteria of *distinctness* which we apply to particular cats. Roughly, the idea of the cat-feature, unlike that of snow, must include the idea of a characteristic shape, a characteristic pattern of occupation of space.

But now what of the criteria of reidentification? Does the concept of the cat-feature include a *basis* for this? If so, what is the substance of the phrase, 'a basis for criteria'? Is it not merely an attempt to persuade us that there is a difference, where there is none, between the concept of the cat-feature and the sortal universal, cat? This is the crucial question. I think the answer to it is as follows. The concept of the cat-feature does indeed provide a basis for the idea of reidentification of particular cats. For that concept includes the idea of a characteristic shape, of a characteristic pattern for the occupation of space; and this idea leads naturally enough to that of a continuous path traced through space and time by such a characteristic pattern; and this idea in its turn provides the core of the idea of particular-identity for basic particulars. But this is not to say that the possession of the concept of the cat-feature entails the possession of this idea. Operating with the idea of reidentifiable particular cats, we distinguish between the case in which a particular cat appears, departs and reappears, and the case in which a particular cat appears and departs and a different cat appears. But one could play the naming-game without making this distinction. Someone playing the naming-game can correctly say 'More cat' or 'Cat again' in both cases; but someone operating with the idea of particular cats would be in error if he said 'Another cat' in the first case, or 'The same cat again' in the second. *The decisive conceptual step to cat-particulars is taken when the case of 'more cat' or 'cat again' is subdivided into the case of 'another cat' and the case of 'the same cat again'.*

It might still be objected that, even if the concept of the cat-feature is not identical with that of the sortal universal, cat, yet it is identical with the concept of another sortal universal, namely that of a temporal slice of a cat; that one who, playing the naming-game, says 'Cat!' at least says something which has the force of 'There is *a* cat-slice here'. This objection must be considered carefully, for the idea of temporal slices of substantial things is a peculiarly philosophical idea, which has scarcely been adequately explained. We must ask: What are the temporal limits of a cat-slice? When are we to say that we still have *the same* cat-slice? Shall we say that we have a different cat-slice when what we should ordinarily call the *attitude* of the cat changes? Or its *position*? Or both? Or shall we say that the limits of a cat-slice are given by the temporal limits of a period of continuous observation of the cat-feature? It does not seem that the concept of the cat-feature determines the answer to these questions. If it does not, then it is false that the possession of the concept of the cat-feature entails the possession of the concept of these peculiarly philosophical particulars. We may note, moreover, that the last of the suggested answers would deprive the resultant particulars of the status of objective particulars. They would better be called 'cat-sights' than 'cat-slices'. We have sufficiently seen the subordinate position occupied in our conceptual scheme by such particulars as these.

Nevertheless I think some limits must be acknowledged to the generality of our theory. When, for example, the particulars for which we are seeking a basis are sharply defined and short-lasting events such as the flashes and bangs of which we spoke in the first chapter, then it seems difficult to insist on a parallel conceptual distinction between the possession of the feature-concept and the possession of the concept of the sortal universal. There would still be a *formal* distinction between speaking of particular bangs or flashes and speaking, e.g., of times at which it banged or flashed. But the introduction$_2$ of particular bangs would not seem to involve, in the adoption of criteria of identity for bangs, the kind of conceptual innovation discussed in the other cases. The feature-concept would not simply supply a *basis* for those criteria; it would determine them completely. This limitation on the generality of our theory, however, is one which we can accept with some equanimity. For the position, as generally identifiable particulars, which ephemeral items like flashes and bangs occupy in our conceptual scheme is, as I showed in the first chapter of this book, dependent on the general identifiability of basic particulars. It is enough if the theory holds for basic particulars themselves. How large and simplifying a conceptual step is involved in *their* introduction₂ is something I shall try to make clear in the following chapter.

I suggest, then, that in feature-placing propositions, in propositions demonstratively indicating the incidence of a general feature which is not, or not yet, a sortal universal, we can find the ultimate propositional level we are seeking. We do not have to make separately plausible the idea of feature-placing propositions corresponding to every specific kind of basic particular of which we speak. It is enough if we can do so for specimen instances of very broad categories of basic particular. Concepts of other sortal universals within the same broad categories can be thought of as framed on the model of the selected instances.

I have spoken throughout of the *introduction* of notions, of conceptual *steps* or *transitions*, as if I were speaking of a development in time, of steps which had a temporal order. Perhaps there are such stages in the history of the individual person's conceptual development. Perhaps there are not. I do not know and it does not matter. What is in question is not an order of temporal development, but an order of explanation; what finally, after argument, appears to us, the users of the conceptual scheme, a coherent and intelligible ordering of its elements. Of course, there is a point at which argument must end, and the appeal is simply to our understanding of what we do. But there can be no better kind of evidence for a view about the structure of our conceptual scheme than the fact that we eventually find such-and-such arguments compelling. I must acknowledge that, judged by this criterion, the theory of this section has a speculative and uncertain character from which the 'completeness' theory of the first part of this chapter is, I think, free. Fortunately, the acceptability of the latter does not depend on the soundness of the former.

[7] The theory of presuppositions$_1$ and the theory of presuppositions$_2$ are independent of each other. But if both are accepted, they can be woven together to yield a certain logico-metaphysical picture. By way of summary, I sketch its outlines.

I have wanted to develop a sense in which the thought of a particular is a complete thought, while the thought of a universal is not, or need not be; to show how the particular has a logical complexity, a completeness for thought, which the universal does not or need not have. We may be tempted to express this idea by saying such things as: 'The particular is a construction from facts, whereas the universal is an abstraction from facts'. But this is altogether too vague. So we try to get at the complexity of the particular by resolving it. But there are different ways of trying to resolve it.[1]

I began by showing how every introduction$_1$ of a particular into a proposition rests upon a definite fact about the world other than the fact stated by the proposition into which it is introduced, whereas the introduction$_1$ of a universal into a proposition need rest upon no such definite prior fact. Here the thought of the definitely identified particular is resolved into that of a proposition which *as a whole* individuates the particular, but contains no part introducing it. Such a proposition individuates the particular for the introduction of which it supplies a basis by describing it either (*a*) as uniquely related to some other definitely identified particular or (*b*) as uniquely exemplifying some complex of universal and demonstrative elements. But such propositions themselves involve at least quantifying over particulars and may involve introducing$_1$ particulars as well. This is not a logical defect in the method, since it is a theory of the introduction$_1$ and not the introduction$_2$ of particulars. But it leaves us with a certain sense of incompleteness.

We cast around, therefore, for some method which we can apply at some point—we do not have to apply it at every point—

---

[1] One way is quite wrong: it is the attempt to resolve the thought of the particular into, on the one hand, the thought of the particular itself, and, on the other hand, the thought of the sortal universal which it instantiates. I have described this way so that its wrongness, its self-contradictoriness, is obvious. It is the way which leads to the unknowable substratum.

to supplement the first method of resolving the complexity of the particular. Here we have a clue in the recognition of the existence of different types of particular, and especially of the distinction between dependent and independent particulars. For this gives us the idea of a type of resolution such that no sortal universal which the resolved particular instantiates shall figure in this resolution, though a universal in some way corresponding to such a sortal universal may. We are to find a type of fact which can be seen as underlying the particular, but of which no sortal universal which the particular instantiates is a constituent. In the case of dependent particulars it is relatively easy to see how this is done. There must be a fact about a relatively independent particular underlying any thought of a dependent particular. But if we are to press the method to the limit, it seems that we must ultimately find facts which supply a basis for some particulars, but in which neither particulars of any kind, nor sortal universals instantiated by particulars of any kind, are constituents. We *can* find, or can make intelligible to ourselves the idea of, facts of this kind with a wide enough range for our purposes. These are those facts the statement of which involves the demonstrative placing of universal features which are not sortal universals; and facts of this feature-placing kind we can see as what ultimately underlie our talk of the basic particulars.

So the fundamental picture, or metaphor, I offer is that of the particular resting on, or unfolding into, a fact. It is in this sense that the thought of a definite particular is a complete thought. But the thought of a definite particular, while in one sense complete, is also in another sense incomplete. For when we make the transition from the thought of the fact into which the particular unfolds to the thought of the particular itself, then we are thinking of it as the constituent of some further fact. Just as the particular rests upon, or unfolds into, a fact, so the non-general fact may be folded up into, or supply the basis for, a particular, provided that we are ready with criteria of identity for particulars of that class and with a range of characterizing universals for them, i.e. with a range of possible facts for them to be constituents of.

If any facts deserve, in terms of this picture, to be called ultimate or atomic facts, it is the facts stated by those propositions which demonstratively indicate the incidence of a general feature. These ultimate facts do not contain particulars as constituents but they provide the basis for the conceptual step to particulars. The propositions stating them are not subject–predicate propositions, but they provide the basis for the step to subject–predicate propositions. Why this step should be taken, is a question we shall consider later.

To sum up, then. The aim has been to find a foundation for the subject–predicate distinction in terms of some basic antithesis between 'completeness' and 'incompleteness'. This antithesis was was to explain the traditional association of the subject–predicate distinction with the particular–universal distinction. We find this antithesis by, as it were, putting pressure on the idea of a particular till it gives way to the idea of a fact. At the limit of pressure we find the feature-placing fact in which no particular is a constituent, though a universal is. At this limit, then, the universal appears as still something incomplete for thought, a constituent of a fact, whereas the particular does not appear at all; and at this limit, we say, the antithesis, subject–predicate, disappears. So we set up, as a paradigm for reference, as a paradigm for the introduction of a subject, the use of an expression to introduce a particular, to introduce, that is, something which is both complete for thought in that it unfolds into a fact, and incomplete in that, so introduced, it is thought of as a constituent of a further fact; and we set up as a paradigm of description, of the introducduction of a predicate, the use of an expression to introduce a universal, to introduce, that is, something which has the same kind of incompleteness as the particular but lacks its completeness. The two introduced terms are to be such that the assertion of a non-relational tie between them constitutes something once more complete, a complete thought; and the association of the symbolism of this assertion with the universal rather than the particular we see, in the end, as no more than a mark of the former's lack of that completeness which the latter possesses.

Once the fundamental association is made, more than one way is available of explaining those further extensions of the problematic distinction which, for example, allow universals too to appear as logical subjects. But on this matter I shall have more to say in Chapter 8.

7

LANGUAGE WITHOUT PARTICULARS

[1] From the discussion at the end of the previous chapter a number of questions arise. By attempting to answer them we may get a firmer grasp of the notions of a particular and of a logical subject. First, we may ask what exactly is involved in the 'step' from feature-placing sentences to the introduction₂ of particulars. I have spoken of the introduction of particulars as involving the readiness to operate with criteria of distinctness and reidentification for the introduced entities. But what exactly does this mean? If the theory of the end of the previous chapter is correct, then ordinary discourse of that fundamental kind in which singular statements of empirical fact are made contains *some* forms which do not involve the introduction₁ of, or quantification over, particulars. We might wonder how far, in theory, empirical discourse could be carried without reference to particulars, how far, at least theoretically, we can devise means of saying what we want to say, especially at the level of discourse about *basic* particulars, without in fact introducing such items. By considering what means we should have to employ in thus attempting to dispense with particulars, we shall better be able to understand the conceptual effect of their introduction. One thing at least is obvious: that in order to carry through the project of eliminating particulars, as far as possible, from discourse, we shall have to eliminate all predicates of particulars, all characterizing and sortal universals, in favour of corresponding feature-concepts. But evidently much more than this will be required.

Another question which might be raised is this. By what right do we rule that feature-placing sentences are not subject–predicate sentences? Is not a question thereby begged in favour of the 'completeness' theory of the last chapter? Of course the ruling gets some support from ordinary grammar. The sentence, 'It is snowing', for example, has no grammatical subject; it would be senseless to ask 'What is snowing?' But, apart from the fact that ordinary grammar is an unreliable support here—for one can also say, for example, 'Snow is falling'—it may well be said that this appeal is quite superficial. 'It is snowing', spoken in a suitable context, has some such force as 'It is snowing here and now'. What is to prevent us from reckoning 'here' and 'now' as subject-expressions denoting a time and a place, and the rest of the sentence as a predicate-expression ascribing a character to this subject-pair? This question becomes more urgent if we remember one of those descriptions of a logical subject-expression which we earlier considered, viz. the one given by Quine. For are not these adverbial demonstratives accessible to positions in sentences which may also be occupied by the variables of quantification? At least this much is true: that where we can say 'here', 'now' &c., by way of demonstrative placing of a feature, we can often also say 'somewhere', 'nowhere', 'everywhere', 'wherever' and 'sometime', 'never', 'always', 'whenever'. Are we not to say that 'It never rains but it pours' is a sentence involving quantification? We could write it as 'Wherever and whenever it rains, there and then it pours', or, using 'p' and 't' as time- and place-variables respectively, as 'For every p and t, if it rains at p at t, then it pours at p at t'. Similarly we could write 'Wherever it rained yesterday, it rained again today' as follows: 'For every p, if there is a t such that t lies within yesterday and it rained at p at t, then there is a t such that t lies within today and it rained at p at t'. If, then, we are to accept what might be called the 'quantification test' as final, there appears at least to be a case for saying that the demonstrative adverbs of place and time are subject-expressions, and, correspondingly, that phrases such as 'it rains' are predicate-expressions. What then becomes of the theory of the previous chapter?

But here we must make a distinction. I have throughout made it a condition of an expression's being a singular logical subject-expression, that it should introduce, i.e. definitely identify, a term. The grammatical criterion for the subject–predicate distinction rested upon distinguishing modes of introduction of terms, the category criterion upon distinguishing types of terms introduced. Now there can indeed be no question of ruling out places and times in advance as candidates for the position of logical subjects. For it is possible definitely to identify times and places in language, possible to introduce them as definitely identified terms; they can be referred to by name or by definite description. But though times and places *can* be introduced as terms into propositions, they are not so introduced by the adverbial demonstratives which are here in question. These demonstratives do not introduce terms at all. They serve indeed to indicate the incidence of the general feature introduced by the rest of a feature-placing sentence; but it cannot be maintained that 'now' or 'here' independently identifies a time or a place. 'Now' and 'here', by themselves, set no boundaries at all; nor is it their function to introduce extensionless points or durationless instants. They merely act as pointers to some extent of space and time which they do not, by themselves, delimit. So the fact that they may be said to pass the 'quantification test' cannot be accepted as decisive. Since they do not introduce terms, they are not logical subject-expressions.

Still, it might be said, this does not settle the question, whether feature-placing statements are to be counted as subject–predicate statements, in favour of the ruling that they are not. Demonstrative adverbs are disqualified as subject-expressions because they do not introduce terms. But what of the expression which introduces the universal feature to be placed? That introduces a term. Why should it not be counted as subject-expression and the demonstrative indications, together with the propositional symbolism, as predicate-expression? It is easy enough to square the grammar, to employ a noun designating the feature and to eliminate impersonal verbs. In general, we can say 'ϕ is here' instead of either 'It ϕ-s here' or 'There is ϕ here'.

Our response to this suggestion must depend, so to speak, on the spirit in which it is made. Interpreted dogmatically, it would amount to a proposal to ignore the whole of the discussion of the last two chapters, to ignore all that there emerged about our concept of the subject–predicate distinction. But it could be less challengingly interpreted. We could see it, rather, in the guise of a suggestion as to how the subject–predicate distinction is to be extended downwards from the paradigm cases to the special case of a feature-placing sentence. In the paradigm case, there are two expressions, both of which introduce terms and one of which, as carrying a presupposition of fact, has a completeness which the other lacks. The former is the paradigm subject-expression, the latter the paradigm predicate-expression. In the feature-placing sentence there is no such antithesis between completeness and incompleteness; but there are two distinguishable elements which together yield a proposition, and if we choose to extend the distinction to this case, then the force of analogy is on the side of the present suggestion. Feature-universals can, after all, appear as subjects in propositions of a different kind which have already been admitted as subject–predicate propositions by one early analogical extension from the paradigm case (i.e. in such propositions as 'Snow is white'); but there is no type of already admitted case in which demonstrative adverbs have the role of subject-expressions.

The proposal, so interpreted, may be admitted; but, so admitted, it does not contradict the assertion that if we *confine* ourselves to the feature-placing level of statement, the subject–predicate distinction has no place.

[2] Let us now turn to consider briefly some of the problems which would confront us in an attempt to frame a language without particulars—or, at least, without any such particulars as are instances of ordinary sortal universals. The attempt to frame sentences in such a language which would correspond more or less in force to the things we normally wish to say even about basic particulars would not only call for an enormous inflation of the class of expressions used to introduce feature-concepts; it seems likely that it would also force us into some extremely tortuous constructions. For ordinary particulars there exist, in the nature of the sortal universals they exemplify, principles

for distinguishing one from another, and for reidentifying a particular as the same again. A condition of the existence of particulars in our conceptual scheme is the existence of such principles. Now if we are to frame, in our new language, statements having roughly the force of statements about particulars, we must find some surrogate, in the conceptual materials we are allowed, for these features of the conceptual materials we are not allowed. We must somehow make explicit those bases for distinguishing and reidentifying particulars, which are implicit in the use of the sortal universals which particulars exemplify. There is no reason to think that this is impossible; but there is also no reason to think that it is simple. We may expect that we should find it expedient, in attempting this task, to delimit extents of time and place, to introduce and to quantify over spatial and temporal terms. Evidently, however, there are no answers to such bare questions as: What are the limits of a volume of space? When does one period of time end and another begin? If we are to distinguish such volumes and spaces from one another, without depending upon ordinary particulars, we must have recourse to the features which occupy or occur in space and time, to give us our limits and our persistences. Of course, there ·are universals of spatial or temporal quantity, such as a foot cube or an hour; and it is possible that we might find a use for these. But if we are to identify particular instances of such universals, it seems that we must again have recourse to the features that occupy such shaped volumes of space, such stretches of time.

One problem that would face us at an early stage is that of deciding upon the exact force of a statement to the effect that some feature is somewhere at some time. This problem does not exist at the level of the feature-placing sentence itself; for, as already remarked, the demonstrative adverbs do not introduce spatial or temporal terms. But it does face us as soon as we admit the need to refer to and quantify over places and times as spatial and temporal terms. A first suggestion might be that a feature is at a place at a time if no part of that place is not occupied by that feature at that time. But it will quickly be seen that, at least for the case of feature-concepts which include the idea of a characteristic shape, a characteristic pattern for the occupation of space, this suggestion is ambiguous. What are we to mean by saying that a place is 'occupied by a feature' at a certain instant or during a certain time? Suppose 'ϕ' and 'ψ' are expressions for ordinary sortal universals, and 'it ϕs' and 'it ψs' are expressions for introducing the corresponding feature-concepts. Then the ambiguous suggestion just mentioned might mean that 'it ϕs p, t' holds for any point or area or volume, p, and for any instant or stretch of time, t, such that the spatial boundaries of p are co-extensive with a set of spatial boundaries traced out by the ϕ-feature during the whole of t. Alternatively that suggestion might mean that 'it ϕs p, t' holds for any p, t, such that the spatial boundaries of p are *either* co-extensive with *or* lie within a set of spatial boundaries traced out by the ϕ-feature during the whole of t. (E.g. suppose 'ϕ' is 'cat' and 'it ϕs' introduces the corresponding cat-feature. Suppose there is a cat which does not move throughout t. Then, on the first interpretation, 'it ϕs p, t' holds only for that p which is the whole volume of space taken up by the cat during t; on the second interpretation, it holds also for any part of that volume of space.) These possibilities do not, of course, exhaust the meanings we might give to saying that a feature is somewhere at some time; but it seems difficult to think of other interpretations which are likely even to suggest a possible means of solving our problem. Of these two interpretations, the former seems the more likely to minimize our difficulties in general, whatever limitations it may carry with it on our ability to find versions of all the things we ordinarily say. For it at least allows us, as it were, to borrow criteria of *distinctness* for places from the feature-concepts which we introduce; and thereby encourages us to hope that, in so far as we are concerned merely with distinguishing particulars at an instant or over a period during which their positions and boundaries are unchanged, we shall find ourselves not much worse off in speaking of places and features than in speaking of particulars themselves. This can be made clear with the help of an example. Suppose we want to express in our particular-free language a proposition corresponding to that which we should normally express by saying 'There are just three ϕs in this ψ now'—a statement which both introduces₁ a particular and quantifies over particulars. On the first suggested convention, we could at least get somewhere near the desired result with: 'There is a place here such that it ψs at that place now and such that it ϕs at just three places within that place now'. On the second suggested convention, we should have to say something much more complicated. We should have to say at least: 'There is a place here such that it ψs at that place now and such that there are, within that place, three places at which it ϕs now and which are such that any place at which it ϕs now and which is within that place falls within one or another of these three places and also such that no two of these three fall within any place at which it ϕs now'.

I said that these formulations would bring us somewhere near the desired result. But not, after all, very near. More is implied by saying that there are three ϕs in a certain place than that it ϕs at three distinct places in a certain place; for the concept of the ϕ-feature lacks altogether what the concept of the sortal universal, ϕ, incorporates, viz. criteria of reidentification for particular ϕs. We might succeed in temporarily overlooking this fact for an example such as the one chosen, in which no question of the identity of particular ϕs through time comes to the fore. But such questions would come to the fore soon enough when we moved outside the area of a few examples such as this one, and would bring with them problems the solution of which, in terms of the materials at our disposal, would be a matter of greater complexity than I care now to undertake. But though the detailed solution of these problems would tax one's ingenuity to no very great purpose, their general character is clear enough. We have just seen that, so long as we are concerned with distinguishing particulars at an instant or during a period over which their positions and boundaries remain unchanged, we can simplify our problem by, as it were, borrowing criteria of *distinctness* for places from the feature-concepts themselves corresponding to the sortal universals of which those particulars are instances. But no similar resource is available for conveying the idea of identity of particulars through time. If it *were* available, this could only be because the whole announced project of talking in terms of features, times and places, instead of in terms of ordinary particulars, was a fraud. If the project is not to be a fraud, then we shall find ourselves under the necessity of making explicit, in the terms at our disposal, all those considerations regarding spatio-temporal continuities and discontinuities which are implicit in the meaning of ordinary sortal universal expressions and logically relevant to the identity through time of the particulars which fall under them. This is a project which I leave to anyone whose taste for exercising ingenuity for its own sake is greater than mine.

[3] Although I shall not pursue this project, there are various points of interest associated with it, which I shall now briefly discuss. In the course of trying to meet the requirements of the projected language, we should find ourselves using forms from which we can frame identifying descriptions of times and places. We shall be able to introduce₁ spatial and temporal terms, which is something we do not do so long as we remain at the level of the merely demonstrative feature-placing sentence; for the demonstratives merely serve as pointers, though indispensable ones, pointing in the right spatio-temporal direction. The simplest possible form of example of such a description of a place, *granted the first of the alternative conventions distinguished in the previous section*, would be: 'The place here at which it ϕs now'. Such a description would apply to an area or volume, roughly indicated demonstratively, the boundaries of which were co-extensive with those occupied, throughout a time roughly indicated demonstratively, by a particular ϕ which did not, during this time, change its position or boundaries. Evidently, more complicated forms of identifying description of places could be framed; we should not be confined, for example, to identifying places by allusion to their *present* mode of occupation. There would be no reason for denying to such place- or time-identifying expressions the status of logical subject-expressions. So this language would be a subject–predicate language. But this admission can be made without prejudice to the 'completeness' theory of the subject–

predicate distinction. For the identification of a spatial or temporal term would always rest upon a fact about the occupation of space and time by a feature or features. The introduced spatial and temporal terms might even themselves be said to be particulars. But evidently they would be particulars of a very special kind. With the possible exception of certain temporal particulars, like nights and days, they would not be instances of sortal universals. One and the same place could be very differently occupied at different times; no feature could ever be named of which a given place was an instance; the fact that a certain place was at a certain time occupied in a certain way would be an accidental fact about it in just the sense in which it is not an accidental fact about Socrates that he is a man.

Other theoretical possibilities may suggest themselves. I said that the definitely identified spatial terms introduced by descriptions in our imagined language would not be instances of sortal universals. This remark must be qualified. They would certainly not be instances of sortal universals corresponding to the feature-universals of the language. But might they not be instances of what might be called universals of shape-and-size? Thus a definitely identified place might be adopted as a standard instance of a foot cube. If we are prepared in theory to admit one universal of this kind, there is no reason why we should not admit others, and no reason why we should not also admit the idea of a mathematical, or extensionless, point. Could we not then think of the world in general somewhat as we sometimes in fact think of a part of it when we have a map of that part before us? With a map before us, we sometimes think of a part of the world as made up of a definite number of extended places of standard shape and unit area, represented on the map by squares, and an indefinite number of extensionless points, each in principle identifiable by giving a map reference. So, in terms of this theoretically possible scheme, might we not think of the world in general as a system of identifiable points, and identifiable areas and volumes of standard shapes and sizes, to which general features were to be ascribed, whilst particulars in the ordinary sense did not figure in our scheme at all? Add the possibility of a corresponding introduction of instants, and of units of time, and we have a scheme the thought of which has not always been treated by philosophers as wholly non-serious. Once established, such a scheme would greatly simplify the problems of paraphrase considered in the previous section.

I mention the possibility of such a scheme for the sake of completeness. Of course we can and do operate a scheme of such spatial and temporal individuals within the wider scheme which also contains ordinary particulars. But if we are to think of its being operated without this ordinary setting, we have at least to think of it as presupposing the scheme in which we frame identifying descriptions of areas or volumes the boundaries of which are traced out by universal features. We have to think of it as merely the *extension* and *refinement* of a scheme in which places and times take the place of ordinary particulars as identifiable individuals; not as the whole, or the fundamental part, of such a scheme.

Now, by way of modulating towards a variant possibility, let us consider one curious fact about any scheme in which places and times thus take the place of ordinary particulars as identifiable individuals. Suppose there were a block of granite which maintained its position and its boundaries unchanged. Suppose an identifying description is framed in our imagined language of the corresponding place occupied by the granite-feature. So long as the situation remains stable, the difference between the language of particulars and the language of places remains, so to speak, inoperative. There is no difference between the place and its occupant. The criteria of identity for places and those for particulars yield in this case no divergent result. We might express this by saying that if we did not have to allow for the phenomenon of movement and alteration of shape and size, the two conceptual schemes would collapse into one. Given that we do have to allow for these things, the language of particulars is the simpler.

Now suppose it were suggested that instead of taking places and times as our individuals, we took place-times. Place-times are both spatially and temporally bounded. Their bounds, too, might be set in various ways. Their limits might be those of their continuous occupation by a certain feature. Thus, suppose our block of granite moved, or had a piece chopped off it. Then the individual place it had occupied would continue to exist, though differently occupied; the individual block would continue to exist, though possessing a different shape or location; but the individual place-time it had occupied would simply cease to exist. Individuals so delimited would perhaps correspond more closely to ordinary particulars than any others we have so far considered in this chapter—though the correspondence would still not be very close. They might, as I earlier suggested, be identified with the 'spatio-temporal slices' of ordinary particulars of which philosophers sometimes speak. But again we could think of space-times as delimited in different ways, as consisting, for example, of areas or volumes of standard shape and size throughout a standard unit of duration—e.g. a foot-cube hour. Individuals so delimited would be only accidentally, if ever, identical with spatio-temporal slices of ordinary particulars. As in the case of standard place-individuals, however, it is impossible to think of a scheme of such standard place-time units except as a theoretically possible extension and elaboration of another, viz. that in which spatio-temporal individuals are delimited by the spatio-temporal distribution of general features.

The considerations of the present chapter yield no reason for modifying the conclusions of the last. Two things emerge clearly. If, while still avoiding the introduction of ordinary particulars, we introduce into a feature-placing language definitely identifiable items or terms other than the general features themselves, the term-introducing expressions for these items will manifest the 'completeness' which was the theme of our previous chapter. The identification of such a term rests upon an empirical fact. It might seem that this remark should be qualified, in view of the possibility of a language in which spatial or temporal or spatio-temporal individuals were systematically orderable units of shape-and-size, or duration, or of shape-and-size-and-duration, items to which it would seem to be possible to make identifying references without empirical presuppositions. But, again, it seems impossible to conceive of such a language except as an extension of another for which the original comment holds. In general, then, even in a language in which ordinary particulars do not figure, the connexion is maintained between, on the one hand, the idea of a definitely identifiable non-general item and, on the other, the idea of the 'completeness' of the expressions which introduce such items. We noted also that the non-general items concerned, though certainly no ordinary particulars, may be counted as particulars of a kind. Under certain conditions, indeed—remote enough from those in which we actually find ourselves—the distinction between them and ordinary particulars would remain inoperative.

The second thing which emerges clearly is this. Given our actual situation, and given that we wish to say things having approximately the force of the things we actually do say, then the premium on the introduction of ordinary concrete particulars is enormous, the gains in simplicity overwhelming. But this is scarcely surprising.

8

LOGICAL SUBJECTS AND EXISTENCE

[1] So far the discussion has concentrated on particulars and their status as the paradigm logical subjects, the fundamental objects of reference. But paradigm cases are not the only cases; and we have seen already how the subject–predicate distinction allows of analogical extension. One basis of the extension, already noted,[1] is analogy between the ways in which non-relationally tied items may collect each other. Predicates of particulars collect particulars in a way which contrasts with the ways in which particulars collect their predicates. When one non-particular principle of collection collects another rather in the way in which a predicate of particulars collects a particular, then we may say that it operates, in respect of the other, as a principle of collection of like things. If the two are identifyingly introduced into a proposition and asserted to be non-relationally tied, the first appears as predicate, the second as subject. Whenever, then, you have something which can be identifyingly introduced into a proposition, and can be brought under some principle of collection of like things, then you have the possibility of that thing's appearing as an individual, as a logical subject.[2] Now nothing, I suppose, satisfies the first condition, namely that it can be identifyingly introduced into a proposition, without also satisfying the second, namely that it can be brought under some

---

[1] See Chapter 5, pp. 171–2.

[2] These conditions might indeed be described as the conditions of minimum analogy for the *possibility* of appearance as an individual. But we should note that to say this is not to say that any proposition in which something in fact figures as an individual is a proposition which brings that thing under a principle of collection of like things. To say the latter would be to restrict our notion of reference and predication more than we may wish to, or need—as we shall see in the course of the discussion in this chapter.

general principle of collection of like things. So anything whatever can appear as a logical subject, an individual. If we define 'being an individual' as 'being able to appear as an individual', then anything whatever is an individual. So we have an endless variety of categories of individual other than particulars—categories indicated by such words as 'quality', 'property', 'characteristic', 'relation', 'class', 'kind', 'sort', 'species', 'number', 'proposition', 'fact', 'type' &c. And some names for categories of particulars are also names for categories of non-particulars: as 'process', 'event', 'state', 'condition' &c.

An index of appearance in a proposition as an individual, or logical subject, is the use of a singular definite substantival expression, such as a proper name, a name of a universal, like 'wisdom', or a definite description. It is not an infallible index. It is not so even in the case of expressions which might seem to designate particulars. We must not suppose that the man-in-the-moon appears as an individual in the proposition expressed by 'The man-in-the-moon does not exist', or in that expressed by 'The man-in-the-moon does exist'. Nor, it seems, may we suppose that the man-in-the-moon appears as an individual in the proposition expressed by 'The man-in-the-moon lives on cheese'. For there is in fact no such individual so to appear.

The problems presented by these two types of case are, however, quite different problems. In the first, we have an explicit affirmation or denial of existence joined to what looks like an expression for referring to a particular. In the second, we have an ordinary predicate-expression joined to an expression which seems to refer to a particular; but there is *in fact* no such particular. In the first type of case, we cannot coherently construe the substantival expression as a referring expression; for to do so is to construe it as carrying, as a presupposition, precisely that content which the proposition as a whole asserts or denies. We are therefore required, in this case, to find a different way of construing the proposition. There are familiar alternatives at our disposal. We can construe it as referring to nothing (except, in this case, the moon) and as saying merely that there is, or that there is not, just one man-in-the-moon; or, perhaps, as referring to a concept and affirming, or denying, of it, that it is instantiated; or even, following Russell, as referring to a propositional function and saying that it is 'sometimes true' or 'never true'.[1]

But the second type of case, while similarly one in which a particular appears to be, but is not, introduced into a proposition does not require that we differentiate in *analysis*, in logical classification, between sentences of this kind and sentences, similar in form, in which reference is made to an existent particular. The form of the sentence concerned is in no way misleading. The apparent referring expression really is such. Its role is to introduce a particular, and its failure to do so is a failure of fact, the factual falsity of the presupposition it carries. Because of the falsity of this presupposition, we in some cases deny a truth-value to the proposition as a whole.[2] Or again, in other cases, we have an alternative way of looking at the matter, which once more does not involve adopting a different form of analysis for the proposition. We can see it simply as operating in a different realm of discourse, the realm of myth, fiction or fancy rather than that of fact. In these realms, within limits which we lift and impose in various ways, we can presuppose existences and allocate truth-values as we choose.

It is then the first, and not the second, type of case, the case typified by the explicitly existential proposition containing an apparent referring phrase, which provides the *interesting* exception, as far as particulars are concerned, to the general index of appearance in a proposition as an individual. What of the suggested glosses on this type of proposition? The first suggested gloss raises no problem. The grammatical appearances readily give way in favour of quantification; and the constructions of logic here have close analogues in ordinary speech. But we might be more inclined to hesitate over my descriptions of the alternative glosses, which I spoke of in terms of reference and predication, casting concepts or propositional functions for the role of subject-terms. Are we to say that *having instances* or *being 'sometimes true'* are principles of collection of like concepts, or of like pro-

[1] See *The Philosophy of Logical Atomism*, Part V; and elsewhere.
[2] For an extended treatment of these questions, see 'On Referring' (*Mind*, 1950) and a discussion in the *Philosophical Review* (1954).

positional functions? Would not this involve stretching almost
intolerably the idea of a principle of collection of like things?
This question could be answered in two formally different ways.
First, we might try to argue that the stretch could be justified.
We might readily think, for example, of *having three instances* as a
principle of collection of like concepts; and then be the more
ready to extend the notion to the number, nought, of instances
and thence to the denial of the number, nought.[1] Alternatively, we
might simply plead that there *are* principles of collection of like
concepts; that there *are* subject–predicate sentences bringing concepts under such principles; and that no incoherence or abandon-
ment of principle is involved in extending the subject–predicate
classification from these sentences to sentences similar in grammatical form, in which concepts are merely asserted or denied to
have instances. For here, as throughout, we are not concerned to
give a single statement of strict conditions for reference and predication. We are concerned, rather, to produce an account, at
once coherent and explanatory, of the ways in which these notions
may, and do, extend their application from the central cases to
others. We may readily admit that this particular extension of the
notion of a predicate carries it about as far from the paradigm
cases as the limits of tolerance will allow. In particular, we may
note that while the expression 'is instantiated', as applied to concepts, does not have just that kind of completeness which would,
in the paradigm cases, disqualify it from ranking as a predicate-
expression, neither does it have just that kind of incompleteness
which we found characteristic of predicate-expressions in the
paradigm cases. We should very shortly find ourselves in a
familiar region of paradox if we tried to claim for it this kind of
incompleteness. We cannot, then, in support of this extension of
the notion, invoke either of the characteristic marks of predicates
in the paradigm cases; and approaching so close to the limits of
tolerance in one direction, we may feel some sympathy with those
philosophers who perhaps overstepped them in the other, saying
that existential propositions were subject–predicate propositions
of which the logical subject was Reality as a whole.

[1] Cf. Frege, *Foundations of Arithmetic.*

Neither in the case of particulars nor in the case of non-particulars is the presence of the definite singular substantival expression an infallible guide to the appearance, as an individual, of the term it might seem to introduce. In some cases, though not in all, we could illustrate the point for non-particulars by examples parallel to those which we use to illustrate it for particulars. But we may also recall an example of a different type, for which there can be no parallel in the case of particulars, an example discussed in an earlier chapter: [1] viz., 'Socrates is characterized by wisdom', or 'Wisdom is a characteristic of Socrates'. Here we have two definite singular substantival expressions, viz. 'Socrates' and 'wisdom'; we have no option but to count 'Socrates' as a subject-expression; but we have no *need* to count 'wisdom' as a subject-expression, since an alternative description of the sentence is available. To insist, in spite of this, that wisdom here appears as a logical subject would be to claim, roughly, that being wise is one thing and being characterized by wisdom is another. It would be to claim that there are two principles of collection of particulars where there is in fact only one.

The grammatical guide, then, to appearance in a proposition as an individual, or logical subject, is not an infallible guide. But it is a good guide. As far as our reasoning goes, it can be accepted, with such easily understood reservations as I have indicated.

[2] It must be admitted, however, that, precisely on this account, such reasoning is liable to meet with resistance from empirically or nominalistically minded philosophers. They are reluctant to admit non-particulars as individuals, as logical subjects. Why, in general, this should be so, is a question I shall consider in sections [3] and [4] of this chapter. There is another question which we may consider first. Those who experience the resistance I speak of are inclined to feel that they have, so far, proved their point, if they are able to paraphrase a sentence in which a non-particular is referred to, by means of another sentence in which the non-particular appears, if at all, only in the form of a grammatical predicate. Characteristically, this reductionist programme aims at

[1] See pp. 174–6 above.

replacing sentences involving reference to non-particulars by sentences involving quantification over particulars. But the strength and success of the reductionist pressure in this direction are not constant for all types of non-particular. In some cases a proposed reduction seems very natural and satisfyingly explanatory; in others less so; in yet others, strained, artificial or even ridiculous; and there are other cases in which no such reduction seems even remotely possible. Thus the paraphrase of, say, 'Anger impairs the judgment' into 'People are generally less capable of arriving at sound judgments when they are angry than when they are not' seems natural and satisfying. But the suggestion that, for instance, sentences about words or sentences should be paraphrased into sentences about 'inscriptions', is apt, except in the bosom of the really fanatical nominalist, to produce nothing but nausea. In brief, some kinds of non-particulars seem better entrenched as individuals than others. Qualities (e.g. bravery), relations (e.g. fatherhood), states (e.g. anger), processes or activities (e.g. swimming), even species (e.g. man) seem relatively poorly entrenched. Sentence-types and word-types seem well-entrenched. So do numbers. So do various other kinds of things to which the general title of 'types', often, though rather waveringly, confined to words and sentences, may well be extended. I have in mind, for example: works of art, such as musical and literary compositions, and even, in a certain sense, paintings and works of sculpture;[1] makes of thing, e.g. makes of motor-car, such as the 1957 Cadillac, of which there are many particular instances but which is itself a non-particular; and more generally other things of which the instances are made or produced to a certain design, and which, or some of which, bear what one is strongly inclined to call a proper name, e.g. flags such as the Union Jack. Non-particulars of a very different kind which I

---

[1] The mention of paintings and works of sculpture may seem absurd. Are they not particulars? But this is a superficial point. The things the dealers buy and sell are particulars. But it is only because of the empirical deficiencies of reproductive techniques that we identify these with the works of art. Were it not for these deficiencies, the original of a painting would have only the interest which belongs to the original manuscript of a poem. Different people could look at exactly the same painting in different places at the same time, just as different people can listen to exactly the same quartet at different times in the same place.

should also regard as fairly well-entrenched as individuals are propositions. But I do not aim, or claim, to give a list of well-
entrenched non-particulars which is in any way systematic or
complete.

The question I want to raise is: Why are some non-particulars
better entrenched than others as individuals? First we may note
that there are two distinct, though not mutually exclusive, ways
in which a non-particular may be well-entrenched. It may be well-
entrenched because the difficulties of reductionist paraphrase are
relatively great; or it may be well-entrenched because the zeal for
reductionist paraphrase is relatively small. We may speak of
logical and psychological entrenchment. They certainly do not
always go together. The point may be illustrated by considering
the interesting case of noun-clauses headed by the conjunction,
'that'. Sometimes we regard, and perhaps speak of, what they
introduce, as facts; at other times we do not commit ourselves in
this way. Philosophers, seeking a general word for items that may
be so introduced, a word that does not commit us in the way in
which the word 'fact' does commit us, have used the expression
'proposition'. Of course, facts and propositions alike may be introduced, not only by being specified in a 'that'-clause, but in
other ways as well. There is no reason to suppose that facts are
better entrenched, logically, than propositions. But there is every
reason to suppose that facts are better entrenched psychologically than propositions. A very slight familiarity with the
philosophical writing of the age is enough to remove doubt on
this point.

The case of facts is rather a special one, and I shall not now dwell
on it. We shall return to it when we consider the general question
of the reasons for reductionist pressure on non-particulars. Let us
consider other cases of psychologically well-entrenched non-
particulars, viz. those to which I extended the title of 'types'. It
would be satisfactory, from the point of view of the theory of the
previous chapters, if the items concerned should satisfy more than
the minimum conditions of analogy with particulars. The analogy,
in the case of such things as musical compositions, motor-car
types, flag types, etc. is in fact peculiarly rich. Indeed one might

say that an appropriate model for non-particulars of these kinds is that of a *model particular*—a kind of prototype, or ideal example, itself particular, which serves as a rule or standard for the production of others. The Platonic model for non-particulars in general— an ideal form of which the instances are more or less exact or imperfect copies—is, in these cases, an appropriate model, though it becomes absurdly inappropriate if generalized to cover non-particulars at large. The non-particulars here in question are all such that their instances are artefacts. But the concepts concerned are not just rather broadly functional, like those of other artefacts such as tables and beds. Rather, to produce an instance, one must conform more or less closely to more or less exact specifications. Fully to describe a non-particular of this kind is to *specify* a particular, with a high degree of precision and internal elaboration.

Of course, not all well-entrenched non-particulars exhibit this kind of relationship to particulars. Numbers do not. Nor do propositions. But there are other ways in which things can exhibit analogies with particulars besides being themselves, as it were, models of particulars. Particulars have their place in the spatio-temporal system, or, if they have no place of their own there, are identified by reference to other particulars which do have such a place. But non-particulars, too, may be related and ordered among themselves; they may form systems; and the structure of such a system may acquire a kind of autonomy, so that further members are essentially identified by their position in the system. That these non-empirical relationships are often conceived on analogy with spatial or temporal relationships is sufficiently attested by the vocabulary in which we describe them. But this detail of analogy is comparatively unimportant except as a symptom. What is important is the possibility of such systems of relationships. The more we exploit these possibilities, the better entrenched, logically, become the non-particulars concerned, the more logically secure the realm of individuals which we bring into being.

Those non-particular items which are most commonly called 'types' in philosophy, viz. words, sentences, &c., are well entrenched in both the ways I have alluded to. The type-word can be thought of, on the one hand, as an *exemplar* for its own physical tokens (particulars), and, on the other, as a unit of meaning, a rule-governed member of a language-system.

[3] I have argued in an earlier chapter that particulars are the paradigm logical subjects, that an expression which makes, or purports to make, an identifying reference to a particular, is the paradigm of a logical subject-expression. If this is so, the fact may seem of itself sufficient to explain the nominalistic zeal for reductionist paraphrase of sentences in which reference is apparently made to non-particulars. An insufficiently reflective sense of the pre-eminent position of particulars among logical subjects, and, perhaps also, of basic particulars among particulars, may generate the idea that particulars, and perhaps even basic particulars, are the only true logical subjects. It may lead us to think that if we admit, without reservations, the right of non-particulars to the status of logical subjects, we thereby invest them with a character they do not really possess and delude ourselves with myths. No doubt some philosophers have deluded themselves with myths, have invested non-particulars with a character they do not really possess. There is Platonistic zeal as well as nominalistic zeal. But zeal of either kind is out of place. If we fully understand the analogies which underlie the structure of our language, we shall not be made, in either way, their zealous dupes.

There are, however, further features of this dialectical situation which need explaining. A mediating idea which is never absent from arguments of the kind I have just referred to is the idea of *existence*. The question, whether we should acquiesce in non-particulars enjoying the status of logical subjects or not, is said to be the same as the question, whether we are committed to acknowledging their *existence* or not, to acknowledging that there are such *entities*. What, one may wonder, is the connexion here? One may get an answer of a sort by blindly following current logic. As far as that goes, whenever something of the form 'Fx' is asserted, then the corresponding statement of the explicitly existential form, '$(\exists x)Fx$', can be inferred. Subject-expressions can, and predicate-expressions cannot, be replaced by variables of existential quantification. And since '$(\exists x)Fx$' is to be read 'There exists something which F', it follows that a thing which can be referred to by a logical subject-expression is the sort of thing which we can say exists; and conversely.

Now this answer may very well seem, at least at first, oddly arbitrary. It invites two questions which are to some extent at war with each other: (1) Why should it always be subject-expressions which give place to the apparatus of quantification, and never predicate-expressions? (2) Granted that (1) can be satisfactorily answered, why should we construe the resulting quantified sentence in the recommended way? i.e. why should we construe it as making a claim to existence on behalf of something which may be referred to in a subject–predicate sentence rather than on behalf of something which may be predicated in such a sentence? These questions may be filled out as follows. (1) We are invited to think of an existential statement as one which is entailed by any member of a range of propositions with varying subjects and a constant predicate and which itself contains that same predicate. But we can easily form the idea of a range of propositions with varying predicates and a constant subject. Can we not equally well form the idea of a proposition entailed by any member of *this* range and itself containing that same subject? What is the reason for the onesidedness of the logician's picture? (2) Granted that the first question can be satisfactorily answered, another arises. We read '$(\exists x)Fx$' as 'There exists something which F'. But what compels this reading? Why should we not, making such amendments as may be grammatically necessary, read it as 'F' exists', where 'F'' is a singular substantival expression designating the property predicated in the original proposition?

Let us approach the first question by recalling the paradigm of a subject–predicate statement. In the simple case, it is one in which a particular term and a universal term are both identifyingly introduced, the former appearing as subject, the latter as predicate. If we consider the existentially quantified statement in relation to this simple case, it is easy to understand the onesidedness of the logician's picture. Taking 'Socrates' as our subject-expression, and 'is wise' as our predicate-expression, and following Russell's model for the treatment of existentially quantified statements, we may put our first question as follows: Why, on the basis of 'Socrates is wise' do we have

(1) '(. . . is wise) is sometimes true'

but not

(2) '(Socrates . . .) is sometimes true'?

Now the subject- and predicate-expressions of our simple statement equally identify the terms they introduce. But, as was shown in Chapter 6, the conditions of their doing so are different. The expression 'is wise', in introducing its term, carries no empirical presupposition; it identifies its term for us whether or not we know or think that anyone is wise. Consequently (1) represents a genuine part of the empirical information conveyed by the statement as a whole. 'There is someone who is wise' makes a genuine empirical statement which follows from the statement, 'Socrates is wise'. But a condition of the referring expression, viz. 'Socrates', performing *its* role is that a presupposed empirical fact, or facts, should be known to its user or hearer. Consequently there is no way of construing (2) which allows to 'Socrates' the role of a referring expression. We might construe (2) as stating, in effect, that Socrates exists, that the presuppositions of a certain referring use of 'Socrates' are satisfied; but we cannot in that case also take 'Socrates' as having that referring use in (2). If, on the other hand, we try to construe 'Socrates' as already having this use in (2), then there is no statement which we can construe (2) as making; all that it tries to say is already presupposed by the referring use of 'Socrates'. At least for the range of subject–predicate statements we are considering, therefore, it must be the case that the blank inside the parentheses in the derived Russellian form is always such as a referring expression could fill, and never such as a predicate-expression could fill. In the transition from the Russellian form to the explicitly existential (quantified) form, it is these blanks which are replaced by the variables of existential quantification.

We have, then, an answer to our first question. The one-sided-ness of the logician's picture is intelligible enough. If, following Russell, we are to explain existence-statements in terms of the idea of the truth of a subject–predicate statement; and if we are to take, as the model of a subject–predicate statement, that in which a universal is predicated of a particular; then it is clear that it must be referring expressions and not predicate-expressions which give place to the apparatus of existential claim. This apparatus cannot be intelligibly joined to referring expressions which can occur in the model type of subject–predicate statement. Nor is this rule confined to the fundamental type of subject–predicate statement. Once granted the category-criterion for the subject–predicate distinction, *together with all the analogical extensions of that criterion*, it holds throughout the entire resulting range of subject–predicate statements. To put the point crudely. That an already identified item, of whatever type, has *some* (unspecified) property or other, i.e. falls under *some* (unspecified) principle or other of collection of like things, is never news; that something or other unspecified has an already identified property, i.e. falls under an already identified principle of collection of things, is always news. The former can never be regarded as part of what is asserted by a proposition in which an identified thing and an identified principle of collection of suchlike things are assertively tied; but the latter is always part of what is asserted by such a proposition.[1]

But this answer to the first question only makes the second question more pressing. For why should we think that the force of (1) above, i.e. of

'(. . . is wise) is sometimes true'

is better rendered by 'There exists someone who is wise' than by 'Wisdom exists'? Or, to put it differently, why, when I say that Socrates is wise, am I to be regarded as committed to the view that there is such a thing as a wise man, but not to the view that there is such a thing as wisdom? Admittedly, having said that

---

[1] Here, then, we have the explanation, and justification, of the doctrine considered, and shelved, in Part II, Chapter 5, pp. 156–7. But now we see that the justification lies in the fundamental character of the subject–predicate distinction, and its analogical extensions. The doctrine cannot be used to explain, but is explained by, the nature of the distinction.

Socrates is wise, I cannot consistently go on to say that there are, or exist, no wise men; but nor can I consistently go on to say that there is, or exists, no such thing as wisdom.

The connexion, then—or rather the exclusiveness of the connexion—between being the sort of thing which appears as a logical subject, and being the sort of thing on behalf of which existence is claimed, is still not made out. We have to consider what further reason we can find for insisting on the exclusiveness of this connexion. Here again we must turn to the fundamental form of subject–predicate proposition, and the contrast between the conditions under which its referring and predicative elements introduce their terms. We find a somewhat curious result. So long as we confine our attention to what may reasonably be said to *follow from* such a proposition, in the way of existence-claims, there seems no reason for preferring the empirical claim that there exists some instance of the predicated term to the empirical claim that the predicated term exists. For these are just alternative formulations of the same claim. But if we turn from the question of what is entailed by the statement as a whole to the question of what is presupposed by the use of its term-introducing parts, the situation is altered. The subject-expression, introducing a particular, carries a presupposition of definite empirical fact; the predicate-expression, introducing a universal, does not. Here is an asymmetry regarding *presupposed* existence-claims which may be the ground of the preference for one mode of statement of the *entailed* existence-claim over the other. But how can this asymmetry be a *good* ground for this preference? What have the presuppositions of the parts of the statement to do with the mode of expression of the entailments of the statement as a whole? Now we might think it a good ground just because we were already determined to wed the notion of existence to empirical fact—the ultimate stuff with which we have to deal—and hence to those items, viz. particulars, the designations of which necessarily present or presuppose empirical facts. I do not say that this determination is unnatural; only that we must note it. Once noted, it explains both the association between existence and logical subjects—for are not particulars the paradigm logical subjects?—and at the same time the drive to eliminate non-particulars from the sphere of logical subjects. The philosopher who succumbs to these drives is not, however, in a very comfortable position. His unexpressed motto is Locke's: 'All things that exist being only particular'. It is for this reason that, so long as he thinks only of the fundamental type of subject–predicate proposition, he feels able to assert that the sorts of things said to exist are just things of the sort which appear as logical subjects in subject–predicate propositions. But this association, once made, fights against his motives for making it. For no drive to eliminate all non-particular subjects ever approaches success.

[4] There is, however, another and less metaphysically charged way of looking at the logician's reconstruction, by means of quantifiers, of the concept of existence, and hence at the association between existence and logical subjects. The crucial point is the requirement that the apparatus of explicit existential claim is to occupy the same place in sentences as logical subject-expressions may coherently occupy. This requirement can be seen as the result of a highly respectable wish to work with a *formal* and *univocal* concept of existence. Here again, it is best to begin with the case of *particular* terms. As we have already seen,[1] when an expression which looks as if it might be used to make an identifying reference to a particular (or, for that matter, to a plurality of particulars) is followed in a sentence by the word 'exists' (or 'exist'), we cannot coherently take the first expression as functioning in a particular-referring way, i.e. as making an identifying reference to a particular (or to certain particulars). To attempt to do so would make the sentence unconstruable. We must rather take it as asserting the existence-presupposition of the use of the expression in question in a particular-referring way. Fortunately there are idioms available which allow us to escape from the misleading suggestions of the form described; and these are the idioms which are reconstructed in logic by the device of existential quantification. The expression which looks as if it might be used in a particular-referring way is replaced by a predicate-expression

[1] pp. 227-8.

corresponding to it in sense, and the word 'exists' appears merely as part of the apparatus of quantification. Thus we allow that particulars can be said to exist without committing ourselves to the incoherent attempt to construe existence as a predicate of particulars.

Now this manoeuvre results in the word 'exists' appearing only as part of an expression which could, as a whole, be replaced by a logical subject-expression. Here the possibilities of generalization begin to appear. Admittedly, in the cases just mentioned, the logical subject-expression would have to be the designation of a particular. But the general structure of the sentence can be characterized without any such limitation. In this structure we have the makings of a completely general, formal and univocal concept of existence. Every subject–predicate statement entails the statement in which the subject-expression is replaced by the apparatus of existential claim, i.e. by 'There exists something which . . .'. Conversely, for every true statement of the latter kind, at least one true statement could in principle be framed in which a term-identifying subject-expression replaces the apparatus of existential claim. The resulting conception has many merits. It is explicable quite formally in terms of the ideas of a logical subject and predicate. It is in no way restrictive as regards the categories of things which can be said to exist; for, as I remarked at the beginning of this chapter, there is nothing of which we can speak which cannot appear as a logical subject. By the same token, this conception corresponds satisfactorily with the ordinary employment of such expressions as 'There is (are) something (things) which . . .'. 'There exists (exist) a so-and-so (so-and-so's) which . . .' &c. For these are expressions which we are prepared to use, and do use, in respect of items of any and every kind or category. But, of course, in so far as we have these motives, and see these merits,[1] in the adoption of this conception of existence, we shall have no inclination to join in the reductionist drive to narrow the field of logical subjects. The root of the conception is still, no doubt, to be found in the characteristics of the fundamental kind of subject–predicate proposition in which the logical

[1] I do not say there are not other merits. The formal logician will find many others.

subject is a particular. But its flower is a purely formal idea, detached from categorial commitment or preference, and schematized in formal logic itself.

Once this conception is established, we can, without prejudice to its univocality, admit the possibility of another formulation of every such existentially quantified statement, and, with it, the possibility of another use of the word 'exists', a use which is equally univocal throughout the range of its applications. We can, that is to say, reconstrue every such quantified proposition as a subject–predicate proposition in which the subject is a property or concept and in which the predicate declares, or denies, its instantiation. (This applies as much to quantified propositions in which a unique particular is declared or denied to exist as to any others; for such a proposition may be construed as one asserting or denying that a certain complex property, or concept, is uniquely instantiated). Such constructions as these also have their parallels in ordinary speech, as when one says, for example, that saintliness *exists*, or even that *there is such a thing as* saintliness, and means by this the same as we mean by saying that there exist, or that there are, saintly people. Because both types of construction are found, and because the word 'exists' and the phrases 'there is' and 'there are' may occur in both of them, there is, perhaps, some possibility of confusion. But this double use of these expressions gives rise to no difficulties in practice, and there is no reason why it should trouble us in theory, if we are clearly aware of it. One could even, in one breath, affirm existence in one of these uses and deny it in the other, without any very great obscurity: e.g. if one said, meaning perhaps to speak of saintliness, '*There is a condition* to which even the best of us never attain, a condition *which does not really exist*'. These uses could reasonably be distinguished as the non-predicative and the predicative uses respectively. It is, of course, the former which is reconstructed in the logical apparatus of quantification. The non-predicative use has application in connexion with any type of thing whatever, the predicative use only in connexion with concepts or properties. But each use remains univocal throughout the range of its applications.

My purpose in these last two sections has not been to add to theory on the subject of existence, nor to go into any detail; but to rearrange some familiar thoughts with a particular explanatory purpose. A full treatment of the subject would call for much qualification of what I have said and, in particular, for a further extension of the idea of using 'exist' predicatively.

[5] There are certain subsidiary matters which I shall not treat of in detail, but which I wish to mention before concluding.

(1) *Statements of Identity.* It might seem that propositions of this class raise difficulties of classification on my principles. In such statements we have two definitely identifying expressions: what is referred to by one is asserted to be identical with what is referred to by the other. If we are to treat such a statement as a subject–predicate statement, it seems that each referring expression has a title to be counted as a subject-expression. So far the case is parallel to that of an ordinary relational statement. But in an ordinary relational statement the phrase formed by taking the universal-introducing expression in conjunction with one of the referring expressions will normally have the kind of incompleteness which qualifies it to rank as a predicate-expression; or at least will be analogous to a phrase of this kind.[1] At this point the parallel breaks down. We cannot say that a phrase of the form, 'N is identical with', or 'is identical with N', has this kind of incompleteness. It cannot be the case both that 'N' has a reference and that nothing is identical with N. So 'is identical with N' has the same kind of completeness as 'N'. So no part of the sentence qualifies to rank as a predicate-expression.

Of course we may say that identity statements are a distinct class of statements, not to be assimilated to subject–predicate statements. Yet we might sometimes find it convenient to classify 'is identical with N' as a predicate-expression, as the grammatical criterion invites us to. It is not hard to see a justification for doing

[1] Not all predicate-phrases in ordinary relational statements will have the kind of incompleteness in question. It cannot, perhaps, be the case both that 'N' refers to a person and that nobody begot N. So 'begot N' has the same kind of completeness as 'N'. But *begetting* is a genuine universal, collecting pairs of terms on a resemblance principle. So 'begot N' has this degree of analogy to e.g. 'struck N'.

so, not hard, that is to say, to point to steps which make the transition, the extension, an easy one. We may note, to begin with, that if 'ϕ' is a standard predicate-expression, it is an easy enough extension to count 'uniquely ϕ' or 'is alone in ϕ-ing' as a predicate-expression; since, even though we thereby drop the idea of a principle of collection of like things, we do not thereby drop the idea of incompleteness; for perhaps nothing uniquely ϕ. Now I have many times emphasized that particular-introducing expressions carry a presupposition of empirical fact, in the shape of propositions, known to users of the expression, which suffice to identify the particular in question. Sometimes the relation between the empirical presupposition and the introducing expression may be particularly close. Let us suppose that an expression of the form 'The man who ϕ' is used in the presence of a hearer who antecedently knows only one relevant individuating fact, (viz. that there is just one man who ϕ), and who is not, as far as he knows, in a position to assert any other propositions about the particular so identified. Let us now suppose that what the hearer is told is that 'N is identical with the man who ϕ', where 'N' is the name of a particular familiar to the hearer. Then the force of this proposition for the hearer differs not at all from that of the admittedly subject–predicate statement, 'N uniquely ϕ'. What makes the chosen form of words, the form of an identity statement, appropriate, is simply the speaker's knowledge of the hearer's knowledge that *someone* uniquely ϕ. To insist on a rigid classification which excluded such an identity statement as this from the class of subject–predicate statements would seem artificial. But once this case is admitted, it is not easy to see reason for not extending the classification to cover other cases of identity-statements about particulars; for the differences between other cases and this case are differences of degree. Once the case is admitted for identity statements about particulars, then, in spite of differences, analogy may carry us on to admit it for identity statements about non-particulars as well. It should be noted that, in thus extending a classification, we by no means blur or deny a distinction: we can still distinguish between statements which are statements of identity and statements which are not.

(2) *Plural subject-expressions*. I have conducted the argument throughout in terms of singular subject-expressions. This is partly in deference to the best-known current systems of formal logic, which make no provision for anything else. It is a familiar fact, however, that there are powerful logical analogies between those singular substantival expressions which qualify as subject-expressions, and certain plural substantival expressions. These analogies are certainly adequate to justify some extension of the notions we have been concerned with into the realm of grammatically plural sentences, with which, indeed, they were traditionally most closely associated. But this is a question which I have treated of elsewhere [1] and shall not argue here.

(3) *Reference, Predication and Propositions*. It might be felt to be a defect of my treatment in Chapter 5 that the notion of predication is confined exclusively to propositions, things which are true or false. It is admitted that reference occurs in non-propositional types of construction, such as commands and undertakings, which are certainly not true or false. And is there not a sense in which the total *content* of a command may be the same as that of a proposition? These points at least suggest that there is room for a generalized notion of predication, a notion of predication in general as something of which propositional predication is merely a species. If we admit this generalized notion of predication, it may appear as a weakness, or at least a provincialism, in my account that it begins by selecting the presence of a merely propositional verb-form as one of the criteria of a predicate-expression. Such an account, it might be felt, at least falls short of full generality, and runs the risk of mislocating the problem altogether. This objection brings us to the threshold of many questions of great interest which I shall not discuss. As an objection, however, it is easily answered. Let us admit the idea of this more general notion of predication. Let us admit, for example, that a command and a proposition may have the same content and that, when they do, the same elements of reference and predication, in this general sense, occur in both. What name shall we give to the upshot of the reference and predica-

[1] See *Introduction to Logical Theory*, Ch. 6.

tion here, to the unified thing which results? Let us call it a thought. We may not say that thoughts have a truth-value, for only propositions have that, and the thought is something which may be common to, say, a proposition, a command, an undertaking. But just as it is the nature of a proposition to be true or not, so it is in the nature of a command to be obeyed or not, and in the nature of an undertaking to be honoured or not. So perhaps we may say that the thought has a fulfilment-value: a positive fulfilment-value if the proposition or command or undertaking in which it is embodied is true or obeyed or honoured, a negative fulfilment-value if the proposition, command or undertaking is not true, obeyed or honoured. Now we must first remark that the propositional indications which I took as a mark of a predicate-expression, because they indicate the *propositional* linkage of the terms of the thought, are necessarily also indications of something more general. They indicate that we are presented with a certain mode of expression of a unified thing, a thought; and thereby they indicate the more general fact that we are presented with a unified thing, a thought, and not with a list. The propositional symbolism, because it symbolizes a specific mode of coupling, also symbolizes, in a specific mode, coupling in general. Next we must ask how exactly we are to understand the distinction between reference and predication in the generalized sense we have provisionally granted to the latter word. If the distinction is to be understood solely in terms of the category criterion of Chapter 5, as explained and underpinned by the completeness–incompleteness antithesis of Chapter 6, then the generalization of the notion of predication makes no important difference to our account. It merely renders the first part of Chapter 5 somewhat superfluous, except, perhaps, as a possible way of introducing the topic. If, on the other hand, there is to be any further mark or criterion of distinction between reference and generalized predication, then we must inquire what this further criterion is; and it is difficult to see what other thing it could be than a difference in the location of the coupling symbolism, i.e. of the symbolism that shows that what we are presented with is a unified thought and not a list. But if this is the answer, then, since there is no single universal coupling symbolism for thoughts in general,[1] there can be no objection to carrying on the discussion in terms of the coupling symbolism of that mode of presentation of thoughts which is, philosophically speaking, the most significant and pervasive, viz. the propositional mode. This mode of predication may stand as the representative, and the most important case, of predication in general. If this is provincialism, then I do not mind being provincial.

CONCLUSION

Now to bring things summarily together. At the beginning of this book, I was concerned to bring out the central position held among particulars by material bodies. They appeared as the basic particulars from the point of view of identification. Later I added to them, as in a different though related way basic, the category of persons. The admission of this category as primitive and underived appeared as a necessary condition of our membership of a non-solipsistic world. Given, then, that our scheme of things includes the scheme of a common spatio-temporal world of particulars, it appears that a central place among particulars must be accorded to material bodies and to persons. These must be the primary particulars. In the latter part of the book I was concerned with the more general task of trying to explain the central position held by particulars among individuals in the broadest, logical sense of this word. I found that particulars held a central position among logical subjects because the particular was the paradigm of a logical subject. Taking these two results together, we obtain, perhaps, a rational account of the central position of material bodies and persons among individuals, i.e. among things

---

[1] In a great many sentences or clauses or phrases which present a thought, whatever indicates that we are presented with a thought and not a list also gives at least some indication of the mode of presentation (imperative, propositional etc.) of the thought. This is not always so, however, and we can perhaps imagine a language in which it is not so at all. Philosophers have sometimes used referring expressions followed by participial phrases (e.g. 'John being about to get married') to attempt to give form to this possibility. Other devices might suggest themselves: e.g. what is *in fact* the general form of a propositional clause (e.g. 'that John is about to get married') might be regarded simply as the general form for the presentation of a thought, to be preceded by an operator to indicate the mode in which it is presented.

in general. I noticed also, and in part explained, the close connexion between the idea of an individual in the logical sense, and the idea of existence, of what exists; so perhaps may even be said to have found some reason in the idea that persons and material bodies are what primarily exist. There seems no doubt that these things of which I have tried to give a rational account are, in a sense, beliefs, and stubbornly held ones, of many people at a primitive level of reflection, and of some philosophers at a more sophisticated level of reflection; though many other philosophers, at a perhaps still more sophisticated level, have rejected, or seemed to reject, them. It is difficult to see how such beliefs could be argued for except by showing their consonance with the conceptual scheme which we operate, by showing how they reflect the structure of that scheme. So if metaphysics is the finding of reasons, good, bad or indifferent, for what we believe on instinct, then this has been metaphysics.

INDEX

INDEX

'about', 143–6
actions, 89, 111–12, 176
adverbial demonstratives, *see* demonstratives
agency, 83–4, 88
angels, 125n.
Aristotle, 9, 11, 164, 170n.
art, works of, 231
artefacts, 233
ascribing, 139–40, *see also* predication
   states of consciousness, 89 ff.
assertion, 143–6, 149–51
assertive style, 149 ff.
   ties, *see* 'ties'
attributive ties, *see* 'ties'
auditory experience, world, 65 ff., 87–9

basic particulars, *see* particulars
behaviourism, 109–10
Berkeley, 9
bodies, material, 39–40, 44, 46, 52, 53–8, 59–63, 246–7
   personal, 58, 89 ff., 133
Bradley, 167

Cartesianism, *see* Descartes
calendars, 25
categories, 39, 46, 56–7, 59, 154, 161, 166, 172
'category criterion', 167–79, 180, 188, 245

category-preference, 59
characterizing tie, *see* 'ties'
   universal, *see* universals
'collection' of terms, 167–71, 226
   principles of, 167–70, 174, 226–7, 228–30, 243
'completeness', 152–3, 161, 187–90, 192–3, 195, 210–12, 214–17, 224–5, 229, 242–3, 245
'complete notion' (Lebniz), 120 ff.
commands, 149, 244–6
concepts, 126–31, 227–9, 241
'concepts' (Frege), 142, 152
conditional clauses, 149–50
conditions, 46 ff.
consciousness, individual, 102–3, 114–16, 121, 124–6, 131–4
   non-solipsistic, 69, 72–3, 81–5, 88
   solipsistic, 69
   states of, 61, 89 ff., 134
continuity of existence, 34, 37, 56, 71 ff.
   of observation, 32–6, 208
   of sound, 69 ff.
   spatio-temporal, 37, 170–1, 207, 221
Cook Wilson, 144, 168
counting, 168

days, 48
demonstrative identification, *see* identification

251

Index

Index